THE BRONTËS' SECRET

Haworth Parsonage as it is today

THE BRONTËS' SECRET

Charlotte Maurat

Translated from the French by
MARGARET MELDRUM

CONSTABLE LONDON

Published in 1969
by Constable and Co Ltd
10 Orange Street London WC2

SBN 09 456720 4

Printed in Great Britain by
The Anchor Press Ltd, Tiptree, Essex

This book originally appeared in the
Esprit Vivant series edited by Armand Pierhal

'Objectivity and detachment are prime aesthetic virtues.
A biographer, like a novelist, should expose his subject,
not impose his opinion. . . .
Nothing can replace the personal impression which one gains from
direct contact with a man's letters or journal. Writers who
comment on them have already distorted them.'

ANDRÉ MAUROIS *Aspects of Biography*

CONTENTS

Acknowledgments *page* 13

Preface 15

1 – The Reverend Patrick Brontë. Miss Maria Branwell. Their marriage. The Brontë family. Haworth. Death of Mrs Brontë. Matrimonial problems 21

2 – Miss Elizabeth Branwell. Mr Brontë. His children. The parsonage and the children's life 31

3 – Cowan Bridge. Death of Maria and Elizabeth. Return to Haworth. Tabby. Miss Branwell and Mr Brontë educate the three little girls 41

4 – First part of the 'Plays' or *Juvenilia*. The kingdom of Glasstown 50

5 – Charlotte's departure for Roe Head. Accounts by Ellen Nussey and Mary Taylor 57

6 – Return to Haworth. Charlotte teaches her sisters. The origin of Thornfield Hall in *Jane Eyre*. Ellen Nussey's account of her first visit to Haworth. Emily and Anne separate from Branwell. The influence of romanticism. The evolution of the manuscripts 62

7 – Second part of the *Juvenilia*. The kingdom of Angria. Percy, Earl of Northangerland and his wife Lady Zenobia Ellrington. The Duke of Zamorna. The Duchess of Zamorna. *Mina Laury* 72

8 – Charlotte Brontë deals with love. The double life. Branwell. Charlotte leaves again for Roe Head 78

9 – Christmas 1836. Branwell's failure at the Royal Academy. His literary ambition revives. Charlotte writes to the poet Southey. Branwell writes to Wordsworth. Dewsbury Moor. Mary Taylor's evidence. Charlotte's sensibility and her scruples. Christmas 1837. Branwell the portrait painter 86

10 – Charlotte returns to Haworth ill. Her first proposal. Henry Nussey. Charlotte becomes governess with the Sidgwicks at Stonegappe 97

11 – Return to Haworth. A second proposal. The holiday with Ellen. The three sisters are together again. Branwell goes as tutor to Broughton-in-Furness. He writes to Hartley Coleridge. Charlotte writes to Wordsworth. Miss Celia Amelia. Branwell leaves for Sowerby Bridge 104

12 – Charlotte goes to the Whites at Upperwood, Rawdon. Plan to start a little school. Preparations for the stay in Belgium. Charlotte returns to Haworth 112

13 – Brussels. Madame Heger's boarding-school. M. Heger and his new pupils. Charlotte and Emily accept Mme Heger's proposal. Death of Miss Branwell. Departure for Haworth. Miss Branwell's will. M. Heger's letter to Mr Brontë 117

14 – Charlotte's second stay in Brussels. Mme Heger's attitude towards Charlotte changes. Charlotte's isolation grows. Her confession in Ste Gudule. Her feelings about Mme Heger 126

15 – Charlotte returns to Haworth. The boarding-school. Four letters from Charlotte to M Heger. Failure of the boarding-school plan. Mary Taylor leaves for New Zealand 135

16 – Concerning Charlotte's letters and her confession. Branwell and Mrs Robinson. Charlotte discovers Emily's poems. 148

17 – The kingdom of Gondal. Emily's tragic genius 156

18 – A plan to publish the three sisters' poems. Mr Brontë and his new curate. In search of a publisher for *The Professor, Wuthering Heights* and *Agnes Grey*. Mr Brontë in Manchester. Charlotte begins to write *Jane Eyre*. The winter of 1846–7 162

19 – *Jane Eyre*. Charlotte reveals her secret to her father. Her fame. Charlotte seeks comfort. *Jane Eyre* and Thackeray 174

20 – *Wuthering Heights* and *Agnes Grey*. Branwell and *Wuthering Heights*. The identity of Currer, Ellis and Acton Bell is revealed. Charlotte and Anne go to London 183

21 – Return to Haworth. Death of Branwell. Illness and death of Emily 190

22 – *The Quarterly Review*. Illness and death of Anne 197

23 – *Shirley*. Charlotte plans to go to London 204

24 – Charlotte's first visit alone to London (1849). Charlotte calls on Harriet Martineau. Back in Haworth. Ellen Nussey. Winter again. Charlotte's fame in her own village. Charlotte and Mr Lewes. Sir James Kay-Shuttleworth 211

25 – Charlotte's second stay in London (1850). Dinner with Thackeray. Charlotte's journey to Scotland. Visit to the lakes. Her meeting with Mrs Gaskell. The article by Sydney Dobell. Visit to Miss Martineau 221

26 – *Villette*. Charlotte and Mr James Taylor. Charlotte and Mr George Smith. Charlotte's third visit to London (1851). Return to Haworth via Manchester. Charlotte falls ill. Visit to Scarborough. Charlotte returns to her writing 228

27 – The Reverend Arthur Bell Nicholls. His proposal to Charlotte. Mr Brontë and Mr Nicholls. Charlotte's last visit to London (1853). The huge success of *Villette*. Miss Martineau's opposition. The Bishop of Ripon's visit. Charlotte returns to Mrs Gaskell in Manchester. Mr Nicholls leaves. Charlotte decides to marry Mr Nicholls. The marriage. Mrs Nicholls. *Emma*. Charlotte's illness and death 236

Appendices

1 – A comparison of extracts from *Paradise Lost, Book 1* and *A Romantic Tale* 253

2 – *Mina Laury* 254

3 – A summary of *Gondal's Queen* 258

4 – Mr Brontë's opposition to Charlotte's marriage 264

Index 265

ILLUSTRATIONS

Haworth Parsonage as it is today *frontispiece*
(Photo by Bob Collins)

Facsimile of opening page of *The Secret* *page* 73

The 'Gun Group' by Branwell Brontë, *c.*1833, showing Emily, Charlotte, Branwell, Anne *facing page* 64
(Courtesy Brontë Society)

The Reverend Patrick Brontë 65
(Photo by Walter Scott)

Charlotte Brontë, painting by J. H. Thompson 80
(Courtesy Brontë Society)

Emily Brontë, 1833, painting by Branwell Brontë 80
(Courtesy National Portrait Gallery)

Branwell Brontë bas-relief, by John Leyland 81
(Photo by Walter Scott)

Anne Brontë, 1834, water-colour by Charlotte Brontë 81
(Courtesy Brontë Society)

Miss Elizabeth Branwell, *c.*1835, presumed portrait, artist unknown 128
(Courtesy Brontë Society)

Ellen Nussey, drawing by Charlotte Brontë 129
(Courtesy Brontë Society)

The moors near Haworth 144
(Photo by Bob Collins)

The Reverend Arthur Bell Nicholls 145
(Courtesy Brontë Society)

ACKNOWLEDGMENTS

I wish to express my affection and gratitude to Miss Margaret Meldrum, M.A., of Sunderland College of Education, for her invaluable co-operation in finding material which was difficult for me to obtain.

And I would like to thank Mrs Joanna Hutton, the zealous curator of the Brontë Parsonage Museum, Haworth, for her very kind welcome.

My thanks also go to Miss Frances Catherine Branwell of Penzance, Maria Branwell's great niece five times removed. She was kind enough to show me a very fine engraving which she has of Charlotte Brontë from the Richmond pastel, and portraits of the father and mother of Maria Branwell, as well as of Maria herself and her sister. She also showed me her family tree.

C.M.

The publishers would like to thank: Messrs Longmans and the British Council for permission to include an extract from *The Brontë Sisters* by Phyllis Bentley; Oxford University Press and Columbia University Press for permission to quote from *The Brontës' Web of Childhood* by Fannie Elizabeth Ratchford; Mr Bob Collins for his photographs of the Haworth district; the Director of the National Portrait Gallery, and the Brontë Society for illustrations.

PREFACE

Charlotte Brontë died on 31 March 1855, aged thirty-nine. On 6 June of the following year, her friend and life-long correspondent, Miss Ellen Nussey, was filled with indignation on reading an article in *Sharpe's Magazine* entitled: 'A Few Words about *Jane Eyre*'. She at once informed Charlotte's husband, the Reverend Arthur Bell Nicholls. 'The writer of the article deserves the contempt of silence', she wrote, 'but there will be readers and believers. Shall such be left to imbibe a tissue of malignant falsehoods or shall an attempt be made to do justice to one who so highly deserved justice?' Why not ask Mrs Gaskell who was very well qualified, she added, to make the reply and undertake the just defence of Charlotte? Mr Nicholls rather shrank from publicity but, when other articles equally full of errors appeared, he told Ellen Nussey that the Reverend Mr Brontë, Charlotte's father, had decided that her suggestions be adopted without delay. He had himself asked Mrs Gaskell, and she had agreed to write a life of his daughter.

Mrs Gaskell, the well known novelist, had first met Charlotte Brontë in 1850 at the home of mutual friends, Sir James and Lady Kay-Shuttleworth, who lived in the Lake District. They had at once become firm friends.

Ellen put at Mrs Gaskell's disposal hundreds of her friend's letters which she still possessed, for she had destroyed very few of them. These naturally contained Charlotte Brontë's life story.

Mrs Gaskell was worthy of this good fortune which few biographers can congratulate themselves on having had. She began her research at once, and travelled with her husband to Haworth where she spent a fortnight at the Black Bull, near the parsonage. Next she made the acquaintance of Miss Wooler, the headmistress of the boarding-school where Charlotte had been a pupil and later a teacher. In London she met Mr Smith, publisher of *Jane Eyre*, *Shirley* and *Villette*. Finally she went to Brussels where Charlotte had stayed on several occasions.

The Life of Charlotte Brontë by Mrs Gaskell appeared in two volumes in the spring of 1857, two years after Charlotte's death, and already, on 14 May of the same year, Charles Kingsley wrote to her: 'You have had a delicate and great work to do, and you have done it admirably. Be sure that the book will do good.'

However, it was harshly criticised. Mrs Gaskell, in spite of her loyalty and her scruples, had not been careful enough in checking the accuracy of her information about Charlotte's family: her father and brother. She believed too easily what she was told in Haworth and elsewhere, and came to her conclusions too naïvely and too hastily, without sifting the reports that flowed in, some of which should have been suspect. But, with these reservations, what is important for us is that Mrs Gaskell speaks of Charlotte Brontë whose memory she revered 'with a rightness which no biographer and no critic of the Brontës has ever so securely attained', as May Sinclair[1] was to write in her preface to the 1908 edition of *The Life of Charlotte Brontë*. Miss Sinclair's opinion of the well-known biography is also worth quoting here: 'The first chapter of the *Life* is like the opening of a great novel, the sombre and elaborate setting of a tragedy. Before ever you meet with any of the Brontës . . . you are brought face to face with these tablets in Haworth Church, recording the dead Brontës with a funereal five-fold reiteration[2] of HERE LIE THE REMAINS. Never afterwards do you lose sight of those tablets in the church, of those tomb-stones in the churchyard, of that grey house overlooking them. . . .

'*The Life of Charlotte Brontë* can only be written as Mrs Gaskell wrote it, prefaced by memorial inscriptions. Mrs Gaskell was only presenting things in their true proportions. . . .

'And it is impossible to put the book down . . . it contains the finest, tenderest portrait of a woman that a woman ever drew.'

Since Mrs Gaskell's *Life of Charlotte Brontë* and especially during the last thirty or forty years, there have been numerous romanticised lives of the Brontës, not to mention plays and films. The Brontës have become the object of a veritable cult, not only in England but throughout the world. In too many cases the

1. May Sinclair (1865–1946), militant suffragette and author of *The Three Brontës* (1912), a biography remarkable for the subtlety of its psychological analysis and its brilliant style.
2. The five inscriptions are for Mrs Brontë, Maria, Elizabeth, Branwell and Emily. Anne was buried in Scarborough, and an inscription was added on a special plaque for Charlotte, the last survivor of the six Brontë children.

real picture has become masked, sometimes unintentionally, sometimes deliberately. And one has to keep coming back to Mrs Gaskell's biography in order to be sure of re-establishing the truth about Charlotte Brontë and, by using undisputed facts, bring to life her unusual, fascinating and very attractive personality.

For the same reasons it is essential to consult Mr Clement Shorter, literary critic and admirer of the Brontës, who in 1896 published *Charlotte Brontë and her Circle* and in 1908 a massive work with the comprehensive title *The Brontës' Life and Letters, being an attempt to present a full and final record of the lives of the three sisters, Charlotte, Emily and Anne Brontë from the biographies of Mrs Gaskell and others, and from numerous hitherto unpublished manuscripts and letters.*

On 17 February 1855, shortly before she died, Charlotte had made a will in favour of her husband. 'In case I die without issue I give and bequeath to my husband all my property. . . .' As Charlotte died without giving birth to her child, Mr Nicholls was her sole heir. After the death of his father-in-law, Mr Brontë, in 1861, Mr Nicholls returned to Banagher in Ireland and gave up the Church to become a farmer. Nine years after the death of Charlotte, he married his cousin Mary Bell. He died in 1906 at the age of 88.

In 1894, twenty-nine years after the death of Mrs Gaskell, Mr Clement Shorter paid a visit to Mr Nicholls and on behalf of Mr Thomas Wise[3] bought from him the majority of the letters and papers in his possession. So he had in his hands numerous little manuscripts which the Brontës had written as children, in writing so small that it was illegible without the use of a magnifying glass. There were also bundles of letters. He could not have hoped for such rich spoils! The letters were published by Shorter in his book, *Charlotte Brontë and her Circle*, which was so successful that from all sorts of places he was sent other documents and more letters. He assembled these for a second book, *The Brontës' Life and Letters etc*. However, Mr Shorter paid no attention to the

3. Mr Thomas J. Wise (1859–1932), editor and bibliophile, who was also a dealer in manuscripts. In 1894, he bought all the Brontë manuscripts then in the possession of Mr Nicholls. He founded the Ashley Library, a manuscript collection which the British Museum bought after his death.

B

little manuscripts. Only one of the stories found favour in his eyes, *An Adventure in Ireland*, which he published.

Mrs Gaskell had conscientiously examined some of them, which Mr Nicholls, urged by Sir James Kay-Shuttleworth, had given her when she was writing the biography. But, having with great difficulty read a few passages which she quoted in *The Life of Charlotte Brontë*, she thought that was sufficient. Could she continue this forbidding task, which seemed interminable? She had to complete the tribute to her friend without delay and without further complication. So the little manuscripts, or *Juvenilia*, retained the secret of the Brontës' childhood and adolescence, and of Charlotte's in particular.

Mrs Gaskell's work is undoubtedly an essential one, a masterpiece of its kind, but it is nonetheless incomplete. Neither she nor Mr Clement Shorter had realised what a treasure they had at their disposal. They overlooked documents which revealed much more about Charlotte's nature and genius than the letters on which they based their work. After that, no other biographer of the Brontës was ever able to get to know the whole of the little manuscripts. In fact, Mr Thomas Wise, after choosing a few to keep, sold the rest by auction. He even divided some into two parts and had them bound separately. The collectors seized everything, even single pages, and the *Juvenilia* were scattered over England and America. Fortunately Mr Henry H. Bonnell of Philadelphia succeeded in collecting a fairly large number, which he bequeathed to the Haworth Museum.

Much later certain English editors became interested in these little manuscripts. Thomas Wise and J. H. Symington published *Miscellaneous and Unpublished Writings of Charlotte and Patrick Branwell Brontë*.[4] Finally an American, Miss Fannie Elizabeth Ratchford, Librarian at the University of Texas, set about deciphering the scattered texts which she was able to collect: about a hundred little manuscripts, their length almost equalling the whole of the published work of the three sisters. 'These manuscripts', she was to write in the preface to *The Brontës' Web of Childhood* (1941), 'are a closely connected series of stories, poems, novels, histories, and dramas having a common setting and common characters, written through the sixteen years between

4. The Shakespeare Head Brontë (Oxford, 1936–8).

1829–1845, a period comprehending approximately one-third of Charlotte's life and one-half of Branwell's. . . . They are the epic cycle of an imaginary world in which the four young Brontës lived, moved, and had their being. . . . They are the frank, unembarrassed, unselfconscious diary of a Charlotte the world has never known, who built for herself a refuge in the "silent, unseen land of thought" where her romantic spirit found escape from the discipline and restraints of ordinary life, a refuge shared by no one but her brother and sisters. Even more, they are the laboratory in which developed all the elements that in their several combinations make up *The Professor, Jane Eyre, Shirley,* and *Villette*. . . .

'These little books hold in their tiny script the most remarkable romance in literature and the most accurate record of the evolution of genius extant in any language.'

In the course of the present study it will be easy to judge what Mrs Gaskell did not have at her disposal for a knowledge of Charlotte Brontë in all her aspects. What shocked her, in spite of herself, in her friend's novels and what she attributed to the influence of Branwell, would have had a completely natural explanation had she read the *Juvenilia*.

There is nothing extant of the *prose* stories of Emily and Anne in the *Juvenilia*. Large extracts of those by Branwell[5] were published by Daphne du Maurier.

The essential passages of Charlotte's will be found here. Through a reading of these pages which remained secret for so long, along with the letters and the evidence of those who knew her, Charlotte Brontë will appear as she really was.

C.M.

Note to the reader

To avoid interrupting the reading by reference to too many footnotes, the numerous quotations from Mrs Gaskell's *Life of Charlotte Brontë* will simply be followed by the letter (G).

To make the text less unwieldy, I have also decided to give certain passages from Charlotte's *Juvenilia* in an appendix which might be of interest to those readers who are anxious to deepen their acquaintance with her work and personality.

5. *The Infernal World of Branwell Brontë* (1960).

For the same reason, this appendix includes a summary of *Gondal's Queen* (1955), a verse novel by Emily Jane Brontë, reconstituted by Miss Ratchford with the help of the Gondal poems, along with extracts from these poems.

I

The Reverend Patrick Brontë – Miss Maria Branwell – Their marriage – The Brontë family – Haworth – Death of Mrs Brontë – Matrimonial problems

The Reverend Patrick Brontë was born on St Patrick's Day, 17 March 1777 at Drumballyroney in one of the valleys of County Down, Emdale, in the north-east of Ireland. He was the eldest of the ten children of Hugh Brunty, a Protestant, who had recently come to the district, and of Eleanor McClory, a woman of remarkable beauty, a Catholic who had turned Protestant on her marriage. Hugh Brunty brought up his large family by farming the few acres he rented. His gift was well known: in the evenings by the glow of the bakehouse he told strange stories like the bards of old, able to hold his listeners spellbound or terrified. It was from him that his son Patrick and even more his granddaughters, Charlotte and Emily, were to inherit their gift of story-telling.

Attracted to study from his childhood, Patrick succeeded in educating himself while working at various trades. At the age of twelve he was apprenticed to a blacksmith but soon left this ill-paid work to become a weaver. Tall, strong, handsome and striking in appearance, he was aware, poor as he was, of a powerful ambition growing within him, an ambition which was to carry him on to make a success of life.

A schoolmaster at sixteen in one village and later in another, he then became tutor in the household of his vicar, Mr Tighe, an enthusiastic follower of John Wesley, who was to shape his destiny. Mr Tighe encouraged Patrick's studying, gave him lessons and kept holding out the bright prospect of Cambridge, its university, and the laurels he might win there as a result of patient and persistent hard work. By pinching and scraping Patrick put by the necessary funds and in September 1802 left his family and Ireland and entered St John's College as a scholarship student. He was twenty-five and he had seven pounds in his pocket.

On 1 October Patrick Brunty was matriculated by mistake in the name of Patrick Branty. Two days later Patrick, who had noticed the error without daring to ask to have it put right there and then, went to the registrar of the college and had the name Branty removed and replaced by that of Bronte. Why did Patrick Brunty change his name to Bronte, Bronté and then Brontë? Mr Clement Shorter thinks that it might well be the result of the admiration he had for Admiral Nelson, the idol of England, who had just been created Duke of Bronte by King George. His brothers and sisters, who remained in Ireland and with whom he corresponded all his life, enthusiastically adopted the new name, sanctified by such nation-wide fame.

In 1806, after four years of study, Patrick Bronte was awarded his B.A. degree and took orders in the Church of England.

On 10 August in the same year he was appointed curate to the little parish of Wethersfield in Essex. As he was not to take up his appointment until the beginning of October, he yielded to the desire to return to Ireland. It was for the last time. His father died in 1808 and his mother, to whom he continued to send regularly part of what he saved, died in 1822.

Patrick remained for three years at Wethersfield. There, when he asked for the hand of Mary Burder, his landlady's niece, he was rejected by the family for reasons no one has been able to specify.

His destiny awaited him elsewhere, in Yorkshire, that northern county which was to be his to the end of his long life.

At Cambridge Patrick had succeeded in attracting the attention of prominent Methodists, in particular of his fellow-student and friend, Henry Martyn, the famous Cornish missionary who was to die of fever in Anatolia in 1812 at the age of thirty-one. It was Henry Martyn who wrote to Wilberforce recommending Patrick as one who showed great promise, in order to get him the financial help which he could not do without. Like many enthusiastic young clergymen of the period, Patrick was anxious to be called to Yorkshire, the centre of the religious revival which had resulted from the fervent preaching of Charles and John Wesley. Patrick had been privileged to see the latter before, in Ireland.

To begin with, he was appointed to Wellington in Shropshire. He remained there only eleven months, long enough to make the acquaintance of the Reverend William Morgan who became his best friend and later his cousin by marriage. At last, in December 1809, his dream came true: he was appointed curate in Yorkshire, first at Dewsbury, then at Hartshead, where he revealed himself to be a writer and a poet: in 1811 he published *Cottage Poems*. After his marriage there appeared in 1813 *The Rural Minstrel*, a collection of descriptive poems; in 1815 and 1818 two novels, *The Cottage in the Wood* and *The Maid of Killarney*; and subsequently pamphlets and sermons. After the death of his wife he published no more books.

At the beginning of April 1811 the Reverend William Morgan was appointed curate in Bradford, and so joined him in this region of their choice.

At Hartshead in 1812 Patrick met Miss Maria Branwell, niece of Mr Fennell, a Methodist preacher who later became a clergyman in the Church of England and whose daughter was engaged to Mr Morgan.[1]

Miss Maria Branwell was born in Penzance. She was one of the eleven children – three sons and eight daughters – of Thomas Branwell, a merchant and a member of the Town Council, and Anne Carne, both of whom belonged to a distinguished group which enjoyed meeting to savour the pleasures of conversation. Disciples of Wesley, their piety was sincere, earnest and mystical.

Miss Maria Branwell had lost her parents several years before leaving Penzance to stay with her uncle Mr Fennell, in whose house she met the Reverend Patrick Brontë.

This Irishman of thirty-five, with the good looks of a noble line, bright fair hair and expressive light blue eyes, brimming over with life and enthusiasm, was a poet, a good talker with a gift for unexpected, sometimes caustic repartee, whose inherent melancholy was concealed beneath an open gaiety; he was exactly the person to win the heart of the charming creature who seemed to have suddenly materialised there to admire him. She did not have to prevent herself from falling in love with him for he was soon captivated by this rather delicate-looking girl, who was very small, gentle, unassuming and modest; who, without being pretty, looked elegant and refined and whose qualities of

1. Many Methodist preachers were in fact laymen, like Mr Fennell. If Mr Brontë retained all through his life a certain sympathy for Methodism as it originally was, neither he nor Mr William Morgan, no more than Mr Fennell approved of the excesses of certain disciples of Wesley whose daring innovations contained such an element of defiance that a break with the Church of England became inevitable.

heart and mind bound him to her for ever. He urged her to become his wife. She was nearly thirty.

During the few months before their marriage, which took place on 29 December 1812 in the church at Guiseley,[2] Miss Maria Branwell wrote her fiancé letters which he kept piously, and thirty-eight years later, on 16 February 1850, Charlotte Brontë wrote to her friend Ellen Nussey: 'A few days since, a little incident happened which curiously touched me. Papa put into my hands a little packet of letters and papers, telling me that they were mamma's, and that I might read them. I did read them, in a frame of mind I cannot describe. The papers were yellow with time, all having been written before I was born: it was strange now to peruse, for the first time, the records of a mind whence my own sprang; and most strange, and at once sad and sweet, to find that mind of a truly fine, pure, and elevated order. They were written to Papa before they were married. There is a rectitude, a refinement, a constancy, a modesty, a sense, a gentleness about them indescribable. I wish she had lived, and that I had known her.'

Charlotte, the eldest of the surviving children, was the only one in a position to recall a few vague memories of her mother. She could describe her playing with Branwell on her knee.

Many passages from the letters which moved her so much reveal profound affinities between mother and daughter. Charlotte might have written these lines:

'3rd October 1812. . . . I trust in your hours of retirement you will not forget to pray for me. . . . I assure you I need every assistance to help me forward; I feel that my heart is more ready to attach itself to earth than heaven. I sometimes think there never was a mind so dull and inactive as mine is with regard to spiritual things . . .'

'5th December 1812. . . . Real love is ever apt to suspect that it

2. The marriages of Patrick Brontë to Maria Branwell and of William Morgan to Jane Fennell were celebrated together. As Mr Fennell was not yet in the Church of England and had to give away his daughter and his niece, William Morgan performed the marriage ceremony of Patrick and Maria, and immediately afterwards Patrick Brontë performed that of William and Jane. In Penzance, on the same day and at the same time, Maria's sister, Charlotte Branwell, married her cousin, Joseph Branwell.

meets not with an equal return; you must not wonder then that my fears are sometimes excited. . . . I am certain no one ever loved you with an affection more pure, constant, tender, and ardent than that which I feel. Surely this is not saying too much; it is the truth, and I trust you are worthy to know it. I long to improve in every religious and moral quality, that I may be a help, and if possible an ornament to you. . . .'

These letters also show unexpected traits of character. Miss Branwell addresses her betrothed one day as 'My dear saucy Pat', so revealing to us a new aspect of Mr Brontë at this period.

In a letter of 21 October 1812, she confesses her attachment to her dear town of Penzance:

'. . . Unless my love for you were very great how could I so contentedly give up my home and all my friends – a home I loved so much that I have often thought nothing could bribe me to renounce it for any great length of time together, and friends with whom I have been so long accustomed to share all the vicissitudes of joy and sorrow. Yet these have lost their weight, and though I cannot always think of them without a sigh, yet the anticipation of sharing with you the pleasures and pains, the cares and anxieties of life, of contributing to your comfort and becoming the companion of your pilgrimage is more delightful to me than any other prospect which this world can possibly present. . . .'

Accompanying the letters there was a little manuscript, *The Advantages of Poverty in Religious Concerns*. It was not published until a century later. It is the expression of a deeply religious soul. The style is fluent, noble and elegant.

To her sisters and her nieces, whose favourite aunt she was, Maria Branwell left an enduring memory. The whole of her family admired her keen piety which was unassuming and broad-minded, her modesty and the intellectual gifts she had inherited from her father.

Maria Branwell was born at 25 Chapel Street, Penzance. It is one of three cottages which look alike, fronting on to the street, with the back overlooking a garden with fine, tall trees. Inside the house, the right-hand side has been altered but the left, with the doorway, the staircase leading to the first floor, the dining-room and the kitchen, has remained as it was in the time of Charlotte Brontë's mother. In what was the kitchen, now a dining-room, there is a peculiar stove set into the wall, rising in several tiers and faced with patterned tiles, in front of which the family used to gather on winter evenings.

Maria Branwell, now Mrs Brontë, settled with her husband in Hartshead, and it was there that she gave birth to Maria in 1813 and Elizabeth in 1815. They then moved to Thornton, near Bradford, where Charlotte was born on 21 April 1816, Branwell Patrick in 1817, Emily in 1818 and Anne in 1820.

All the Brontë children inherited from their father and mother the gift of poetry, a love of literature, a passion for writing, the ambition to be an author.

It is unlikely that anything written by the parents would have been saved from oblivion had it not been for their remarkable children. Their fame lies in having had children of genius.

Miss Elizabeth Firth, who lived at Kipping House in Thornton, and whose father became a friend of Mr Brontë, writes in note form – only too briefly – in her diary: '1st July, 1816. Mr Brontë drank tea here. . . . 17th. We drank tea at Mr Brontë's. 18th. The ladies assisted me in altering a gown. . . . 28th. I took leave of Miss Branwell.[3] She kissed me and was very affected. She left Thornton that evening. . . .'

'26th June 1817. Went to see Mrs Brontë. Branwell Patrick was born early in the morning. . . .'

'7th January 1818. Mr Brontë to supper. 8th. Mr Brontë spent the evening here. . . . 22nd. I drank tea with Mrs Brontë. . . . 12th February 1819. Expected Mr Brontë to tea, but Mrs Brontë was poorly. . . .'

'4th October 1819. The little Brontës called. . . . 28th. Mr and Mrs Brontë to tea. . . . 17th January 1820. Anne Brontë born. The other children spent the day here. . . . 25th February. Mr Brontë was licensed to Haworth. . . .'[4] Haworth, to which Charles and John Wesley had so often come, invited by the vicar, Mr Grimshaw, a very strong Methodist.

These facts may seem unimportant but, however trivial, they nevertheless do convey an impression of Mr Brontë going out and about in the parish, accepting invitations from his friends

3. Miss Elizabeth Branwell.
4. *The Brontës' Life and Letters,* edited by Clement K. Shorter (London, 1908), Vol. II, pp. 413–16.

with pleasure and liking to entertain them in return, whereas Mrs Brontë was often kept at home by her children and by their closely spaced births. Mr Brontë bore no resemblance then to the austere, lonely man he was to become at Haworth.

The portrait of the Brontë children cannot come to life in a meaningful way unless it is set in relief against a particular landscape which became inseparable from their essential selves. This was Haworth, with its heathery moors gashed by stone quarries, its bare rocky soil brown and gloomy or magnificently purple according to the season, with its few paths disappearing among the ravines hidden by bracken and its low dry-stone walls dividing the barren earth, with its isolated houses, evil-looking and secretive, suddenly coming into view beyond a fold in the ground; with hill after hill, the kingdoms of the wild, formidable rain and wind.

It must be remembered that Haworth lies in the West Riding of Yorkshire. The hill on whose slope the village is built forms part of the Pennine Chain, 'the rocky spine of England, which runs due north and south for one hundred and fifty miles from the Scottish border. Poor farming land, but amply provided with sheep and streams, the West Riding had for some five hundred years been the seat of a woollen cloth manufacture, which was in process of mechanising itself precisely at the time when Patrick Brontë entered Yorkshire. Some of the more skilled cloth workers resisted the introduction of machinery which threatened as they thought to deprive them of employment; forming themselves into bands known as Luddites, they attacked the inventors and owners of the new machines and the mills where they were housed. . . .

'Haworth was therefore in a state of transition during the early part of the Brontës' lives. Surrounded by wild tracts of moorland and innumerable steep interlocking hills, the people of Haworth communicated with the outer world only by walking, by a carrier's cart or by a hired gig; but the railway came to Keighley . . . . four miles away . . . in the 1840s. Up in the folds of the hills, at the end of rough stony pack-horse tracks, still lived farmers and hand-loom weavers of fiercely independent character, who had never had any master save themselves; but down in the valley three large mechanised mills were at work, busily creating on the one hand a class of wage-earning operatives, on the other the new industrial middle class, rising to wealth on the wings of steam and aspiring to gentility with the characteristic ostentation of the *nouveau riche*. . . .'[5]

The people of the West Riding were rough, descended from the Anglo-Saxons and the Danes, with a harsh provincial accent and strong emotions, proud, free, and brutally frank; strong-willed to the point of obstinacy and with a keen eye to profit, they were keen on dog-fighting and on cock-fights, which were always followed by long drinking bouts. They were not a very effusive race, did not rely on others nor make friends easily but they were capable of love that outlasted death, capable also of hatred, violent and implacable enough to be perpetuated for generations.

I have walked over these hills and moors and felt their spell. They have been described so often that a more subjective description of the village of Haworth seems appropriate here. John Stores Smith, a writer contemporary with Charlotte Brontë and who had the same publishers, Smith & Elder, visited the author of *Jane Eyre*, then in the first flush of her popularity, in September 1850. He later described the interview he had and the journey of discovery he undertook to become acquainted with Haworth. '. . . Inquiring my way in the town of Keighley, I was told that the village of Haworth lay some three miles off, on the road to Bradford and Halifax; accordingly I set my face southward, with a brisk foot and a light heart. After walking a good half-hour, I perceived the long line of a single street which, leaving the main road abruptly, climbed steeply to the western hills for about a mile and then terminated sharply and at once with the grey-green tower of a church. . . . I made inquiries and then found that this village-street was the Haworth I was in search of. . . . What Haworth may be now I do not know. . . . But in 1850 it was the most dead-alive, melancholy-looking place it has ever been my lot to see. No sign of life, or trade, or traffic, was perceptible. The very houses seemed miserable, and if stones could look positively heartless they did. . . . By the time I had reached the end of its steep hill, my body was wearied, and my high spirits had all given

5. *The Brontë Sisters,* Phyllis Bentley (Longmans, London, 1954), pp. 11–12.

way to an oppressive numbness of soul . . . now I could read the secret of Patrick Brontë's life, some details of which had even reached me. . . . But when I had traversed the damp and depressing churchyard – a flagged congregation of the dead, which seemed to combine all the dismal ugliness of a city graveyard with the savage isolation of the wilds – and stood in front of the parsonage, all the inner mysteries of *Wuthering Heights* and *Wildfell Hall* . . . were clear to me . . . a little garden was before the parsonage and you stepped straight off the gravestones into it. . . .'[6]

It was in this unpretentious two-storeyed house, built of grey stone and roofed with heavy slates to resist the squalls of wind, that the Reverend Patrick Brontë came to live with his wife and six children in February 1820.

'There are those still alive who remember seven heavily-laden carts lumbering slowly up the long stone street, bearing the "new parson's" household goods to his future abode.' (G)

At this time Mrs Brontë, with her kind lovable nature, was already beginning to suffer from bad health, but only a hard grim-looking village, an angry sky and threatening tombstones were there to welcome her in her exhausted condition. She made her way with her family towards her new home by the old church which was so soon to be her last resting place. She died of cancer the following year on 15 September 1821 after enduring, uncomplainingly, eight months of atrocious pain. His wife's anguish, in her despair at the thought of leaving her children, and with her faith wavering, shook Mr Brontë deeply. He supported her in her final struggle against 'the great enemy, envying her life of holiness. . . . Still in general she had peace and joy in believing; and died, if not triumphantly, at least calmly. . . and when my dear wife was dead and buried, and gone, and when I missed her at every corner, her memory was hourly revived by the innocent, yet distressing prattle, of my children,' he wrote to one of his former vicars.[7] He had tended her selflessly and with much thoughtfulness, sending for various doctors at very great expense;

6. Clement K. Shorter, op. cit., vol. II, pp. 439–40.
7. Quoted by John Lock and Canon W. T. Dixon in *A Man of Sorrow* (Nelson, London, 1965), p. 232.

but their skill was unavailing. He sat up with her, and his servant, Nancy Garrs, with her artlessness, has given the highest commendation of him as a husband.

'One day,' she relates, 'he entered the kitchen, apparently in great excitement. "Nancy," said he, "is it true what I have heard that you are going to marry a Pat?" "Yes, sir, I believe it is, and if he prove but a tenth part as kind a husband to me as you have been to Mrs Brontë, I shall think myself very happy in having made a Pat my choice." '[8]

Left alone, how was he to bring up six children, the eldest of whom was eight and the youngest twenty months? Mr C. C. Moore Smith, the grandson of Mrs Franks (Miss Firth of Thornton), was to write in *The Bookman* of October 1904: '. . . At this time, according to a family tradition, Mr Brontë wooed Miss Firth to be his second wife. . . . Mr Brontë did not succeed in his suit, perhaps because the lady's heart was already engaged elsewhere.'[9]

Mr Brontë, grief stricken and in a perplexing situation, turned his thoughts to almost fifteen years before and remembered Mary Burder of Wethersfield. After writing to her mother in April 1823 to remind her of him, he wrote Mary a very self-conscious and tactless letter. He expressed his pleasure in knowing that she was 'still single', recalled the past – which must have been rather a tricky thing to do – and concluded, 'I would like to see a dearly Beloved Friend, kind as I *once* saw her, and as *much* disposed to promote my happiness.' Then he asked if she and her mother would agree to receive him 'like an old friend' at Finchingfield Park.

The kindness which Mr Brontë attributed to Mary Burder had gone and, with her pride perhaps incurably wounded, she must have nursed an ineradicable bitterness. In her reply to Mr Brontë's letter she reminded him opportunely but not without some malice that God would provide for his needs and those of his children, and firmly refused to see him.

The following year, 1824, she was to marry a Non-conformist minister of Wethersfield.

8. Clement K. Shorter, op. cit., vol. I, p. 60.
9. Ibid., vol. II, pp. 410–11.

2

Miss Elizabeth Branwell – Mr Brontë – His children – The parsonage and the children's life

At this point Mr Brontë with some courage gave up the idea of remarrying. To look after his children and his house he sought the help of an elder sister of his wife, Miss Elizabeth Branwell, who had visited them in Thornton and who had later come to Haworth in May 1821 to nurse her sister in her illness.

In the face of so much trouble and for the sake of Maria's memory, Elizabeth did not hesitate to give up Penzance, in spite of all her ties there – family, friends, a comfortable way of life – for this desolate northern village, whose cold she never grew accustomed to, and where she was to die twenty years later without seeing Cornwall again. She was small like her sister; she always wore silk dresses, old-fashioned in style, huge bonnets which showed a fringe of false auburn curls, and wooden pattens to protect her from the cold and damp of the parsonage stone floors.

Reserved and rigid in her principles, she was kind and, although careful of her money, she was always ready to help her nieces financially. Her father had left her and his other daughters an annual income of fifty pounds. It was thanks to her that Charlotte and Emily were able to go to Brussels to continue their education and that the book of *Poems* by the three sisters, *Wuthering Heights* by Emily and *Agnes Grey* by Anne were published. She was cultured and sure in her judgements; she read the newspapers to her brother-in-law and discussed them with him. An ardent Methodist, her actions were all inspired by her piety. She wanted to make her nieces true Christians, but her religion had affinities with that of Mr Brocklehurst, the parson in *Jane Eyre*: it was a religion of fear which bore down heavily on the young mind of Anne in particular. The eager, generous hearts of the three sisters needed a religion of love and compassion and a God whose mercy was as great as his glory. And so they gradually freed themselves from the Calvinistic doctrines of election and eternal damnation. Miss Branwell was also anxious that the five little girls should grow up to be well educated, well bred and refined; she wanted them to be good housekeepers, able to sew, iron, cook and make bread – the special task of Emily when their servant Tabby be-became old and frail – wax and polish the furniture which always shone like a mirror. Charlotte, Emily and Anne were to owe to her their marvellous attention to detail, their rejection of all familiarity and their deep reserve. The feeling she was to arouse in them was affectionate and grateful respect rather than spontaneous tenderness. The emptiness left in their hearts by the death of their mother was never to be filled and the unconsoled sadness that was its result was to become one of the most valuable and creative elements in their genius.

Gradually as the years passed Miss Branwell spent more and more time in her room and eventually had all her meals there.

As for Mr Brontë, he had a stomach complaint and, compelled to follow a diet, often ate alone in his study at two o'clock.[1] He did not try to make new friends but stoically sought isolation in his grief. His strong will always dominated his passionate nature, without succeeding in taming it. According to certain accounts, which Mrs Gaskell was too ready to listen to, this carefully controlled impetuosity revealed itself now and again even when his wife was alive in a strange and even quaint manner, freeing him from the restraint he imposed on himself.

'Mrs Brontë's nurse told me,' says Mrs Gaskell, 'that one day when the children had been out on the moor, and rain had come on, she thought their feet would be wet, and accordingly she rummaged out some coloured boots which had been given to them by a friend, the Mr Morgan, who married "cousin Jane", she believes. The little pairs she ranged round the kitchen fire to warm; but when the children came back, the boots were nowhere to be found, only a very strong odour of burnt leather was perceived. Mr Brontë had come in and seen them; they were too gay and too luxurious for his children, and would foster a love of dress; *so he put them on the fire*. He spared nothing that offended his antique simplicity.

'Long before this, someone had given Mrs Brontë a silk gown; either the make, the colour, or the material was not according to his notions of consistent propriety, and Mrs Brontë in conse-

1. It was then the custom to have the midday meal at two o'clock.

quence never wore it. But for all this she kept it treasured up in her drawers, which were generally locked. One day, however, while in the kitchen, she remembered that she had left the key in her drawer, and hearing Mr Brontë upstairs, she augured some ill to her dress, and running up in haste, she found it cut to shreds. . . . He did not speak when he was annoyed or displeased, but worked off his volcano wrath by firing pistols out of the back door in rapid succession. . . . Now and then his anger took a different form, but still was speechless. Once he got the hearth rug, and stuffing it up the grate, deliberately set it on fire, remained in the room in spite of the stench, until it had smouldered and shrivelled away into uselessness. Another time he took some chairs, and sawed away at the backs till they were reduced to the condition of stools. . . .'

In July 1857, Mr William Dearden[2] who had known Mr Brontë for many years, read the recently published *Life of Charlotte Brontë*, and wrote a defence of Mr Brontë in *The Halifax Examiner*. In his opinion, almost all that Mrs Gaskell had said in the biography was 'a tissue of falsehoods'. Mr Brontë was very annoyed at this excessive zeal and his correspondence with Mrs Gaskell, polite, friendly and slightly malicious, clears up the issue, proving that he was not offended by the way in which she had depicted him. But, if he allowed her complete freedom to interpret the facts, he nevertheless did want these facts to be exact: '. . . I do not deny', he wrote to her on 30 July 1957, 'that I am somewhat eccentrick . . . only don't set me on in my fury to burning hearth-rugs, sawing the backs of chairs, and tearing my wife's silk gowns. . . . And my opinion, and the reading World's opinion of the *Memoir*, is . . . that it ought to stand, and will stand, in the first rank of Biographies till the end of time. Some slips there have been, but they may be remedied. It is dangerous to give credence hastily to informants – some may tell the truth, while others, from various motives, may greedily invent and propagate falsehoods. . . . I am not in the least offended at your telling me that I have faults – I have many – and, being a Daughter of Eve, I doubt not that you have some.'

At the beginning of September 1857 the third edition of the biography appeared with the necessary corrections. In his letter

2. Clement K. Shorter, op. cit., vol. I, pp. 55–61.

of 9 September, Mr Brontë, to whom Mrs Gaskell had immediately sent a copy, expressed his complete satisfaction and his desire that these corrections should always be included.

Later, Mr Clement Shorter was to confirm what Mr Brontë wrote to Mrs Gaskell. 'It has been explained already in more than one quarter that this was not the real Patrick Brontë, and that much of the unfavourable gossip was due to the chatter of a dismissed servant, retailed to Mrs Gaskell on one of her missions of inquiry in the neighbourhood. The stories of the burnt shoes and the mutilated dress have been relegated to the realm of myth. . . .'

Although he was a clergyman, Mr Brontë had the heart of a soldier and a love of combat. During the Luddite riots he had taken sides with fearless courage, now for the owners, now for the workers, according to the justice of their cause, guided in his choice by nothing except his conscience. But, thinking that he would be risking his life if he took long walks alone without being armed, he had got into the habit of always having a loaded pistol on him, a habit which he continued.

When he thought he was right, nothing could change his mind. In a letter of 28 April 1831, to Miss Firth, then Mrs Franks, he said of himself:

'I am in all respects *now*, what I *was* when I lived in Thornton in regard to all political considerations. A warmer or truer friend to church and state does not breathe the vital air. . . . It is with me merely an affair of conscience and judgment, and sooner than violate the dictates of either of these, I would run the hazard of poverty, imprisonment, and death. . . .'

However, he lived on good terms with those who did not share his opinions for, in spite of his strong attachment to Church and State, he had a great respect for the liberty of others. Without being a mystic he was upheld in the trials of his difficult life by his deep faith. It was again to Mrs Franks that he wrote on 6 July 1835:

'. . . Amidst all the chances, changes, and trials of this mortal life, we have still the glorious conviction on our minds that we may have our hope immovably anchored in heaven, by the throne of God, in whom there is no variableness, neither shadow of turning. . . .'

He bore ill fortune, solitude and sometimes poverty with moving dignity and in spite of his proud reserve there was never any change in his kindness, his devotion to duty and his great courtesy.

As Mrs Gaskell wrote: 'One day I asked an inhabitant of a district close to Haworth, what sort of a clergyman they had at the church which he attended: "A rare good one," said he: "he minds his own business, and never troubles himself with ours." ' (G)

In the midst of this somewhat recalcitrant flock, Mr Brontë was a respected shepherd, discreet but attentive, never hesitating to go to the help of his people near or distant; and in the leisure left over from the duties of his parish his concern was for his children of whom he was very fond. He soon discovered their exceptional natures, their aptitudes and gifts. He took an interest in them and taught them intelligently, but in an unusual way, as is shown by what he wrote to Mrs Gaskell on 30 July 1855, in connection with the biography of Charlotte.

'When my children were very young, when, as far as I can remember, the oldest was about ten years of age and the youngest about four, thinking that they knew more than I had yet discovered, in order to make them speak with less timidity, I deemed that if they were put under a sort of cover I might gain my end; and happening to have a mask in the house, I told them all to stand and speak boldly from under cover of the mask.

'I began with the youngest [Anne, afterwards Acton Bell], and asked what a child like her most wanted; she answered, "Age and experience". . . . I then asked Charlotte what was the best book in the world; she answered *The Bible*. And what was the next best; she answered, *The Book of Nature*.'

Passionately fond of reading, these children had no access to books meant for their age. *The Bible*, the book *par excellence*, *Paradise Lost* by Milton, Bunyan's *Pilgrim's Progress* were the living sources always available that continually nourished their souls, their minds, their imagination. They also read *Gulliver's Travels* by the Irish writer, Swift: 'This book I had again and again perused with delight. I considered it a narrative of facts. . . . Lilliput and Brobdingnag being, in my creed, solid parts of the earth's surface,' says Jane Eyre[3] of her childhood.

Shakespeare was their god; they knew whole scenes by heart

3. *Jane Eyre,* Charlotte Brontë (Collins edition), p. 18.

and later, in her novels, Charlotte was often to quote him, thus enhancing her narrative as if under the influence of sudden inspiration.

Of Walter Scott they read the *Tales of a Grandfather* very early. Charlotte was to draw on *Ivanhoe* when she wrote *The Green Dwarf* in 1833.

There is no doubt that they were thrilled by MacPherson's *Ballads of Ossian.* These primitive songs of the old Celtic bard had a deep effect on Emily in particular. Shortly before reading *Ossian* 'in the same year 1829', writes Miss Ratchford in *The Brontës' Web of Childhood*, 'Charlotte read Branwell's recently acquired copy of *Childe Harold*, and though but dimly understanding the hero's character, she immediately grafted his salient qualities upon Arthur Wellesley, Marquis of Douro . . . thus creating a personality that dominated her imagination for the rest of her life.'[4] They were interested in ancient history and loved the Greek tragedians. In 1830 Charlotte, aged fourteen, wrote in *Albion and Marina*: 'Albion the Marquis of Tagus was a devoted worshipper of the divine works that the Greek tragedians have left for all succeeding ages to marvel at, particularly those of Sophocles the Majestic. . . .'

In a long and curious poem, 'The Violet', written on 10 November 1830, Charlotte refers to Homer: 'The bard that swept the lyre . . . whose aged eyes shot heavenly fire', to Sophocles, to the 'tender' Euripides, to the 'terrible' Aeschylus, to Tasso, 'that sang Jerusalem', to Virgil, 'Mantua's glorious swain'.

The Greek sites are known to her:

> Athens and Sparta are no more
> Unswept by swans Eurotas laves
> As yet its laurel shaded shore.
>
> Parnassus now uplifts her head
> Forsaken of the holy nine
> They from her heights for aye have fled.[5]

It was perhaps the reading of mythology, which was constantly

4. The Marquis of Douro, one of the principal heroes of Charlotte's tales, who subsequently became Duke of Zamorna, was the son of the Duke of Wellington.

5. The MS in the British Museum has hardly any punctuation.

evoked by these tragedians, and the even more fascinating reading of *The Arabian Nights* that gave the Brontë children their fondness for strange, sonorous and magical names.

As they grew older they discovered Dr Johnson, Richardson whose *Pamela* had provided copious material for Tabby's tales[6], Fielding, Goldsmith, Sheridan and so on.

They read a wide variety of religious publications, some of which came from their mother's family: 'some mad Methodist magazines, full of miracles and apparitions, and preternatural warnings, ominous dreams, and frenzied fanaticism; the equally mad Letters of Mrs Elizabeth Rowe from the Dead to the Living.'[7] They devoured *Blackwood's Magazine*, which exerted an outstanding influence on them.

'Mr Brontë at times would relate strange stories, which had been told him by some of the oldest inhabitants of the parish, of the extraordinary lives and doings of people who had resided in far-off, out-of-the-way places, but in contiguity with Haworth . . . stories which made one shiver and shrink from hearing.'[8]

He often delighted in speaking to them of his own country, a distant Ireland peopled by witches, elves and airy sprites with scented wings. Every day he gathered them together to read the Bible, presenting and commenting on the oracles of God, a God who did not confuse the good with the wicked. The ardour of his faith exalted their fervent souls.

He undertook the education of his son who seemed to him the most gifted of them all and reminded him of his own childhood. He first taught him Latin and Greek, his former ambition transferring itself to this very precocious boy, full of promise, almost too intelligent, extremely impressionable, this Patrick whom they also called Branwell, no doubt in memory of his mother.

Mr Brontë considered that it was his duty to give his daughters the opportunity of education, a priceless benefit. But neither he nor Miss Branwell, in spite of their efforts, was adequate for the task of educating all these children. So when he learned that at Cowan Bridge in Westmorland one of his colleagues, the Reverend Carus Wilson, had just opened a boarding-school supported

6. 2. Cf. chap. 3, p. 45.
7. See *Shirley* (Collins edition), p. 353.
8. E. Nussey, cf. chap. 5, p. 60.

by rich families for the daughters of poor clergymen, he saw in it the means of solving the difficult problem. He was to take the two eldest, Maria and Elizabeth, there in July 1824, Charlotte in August and Emily in November of the same year.

So, after the death of their mother in 1821, and until the four girls left for Cowan Bridge in 1824, Maria, Elizabeth, Charlotte, Patrick Branwell, Emily and Anne lived at home with their father and aunt in a cheerless and gloomy atmosphere.

Between the parsonage and the church there was only the churchyard. It was the last house in the village, the nearest to the moor. There were two windows on each side of the front door, to which a flight of three steps led up, and five windows upstairs. To the right of the hall – stone-flagged and spacious – was Mr Brontë's study, on the left the square dining-room where the children took their meals. It will often figure in Charlotte's life later in the book.

Behind the study was the kitchen with a huge store-room opposite. Right at the back of the hall, in line with the front door, an attractive archway led to the stone staircase with its elegant banister of heavy wood, and every evening when he went to bed Mr Brontë stopped to wind a grandfather clock that stood half way up the stairs.

His bedroom, which he shared with Branwell, was over his study and his wife's over the dining-room. Miss Branwell later used it and Charlotte was to die in it. The little room in the middle, without a fireplace, was used as the children's study before it was Emily's bedroom. Next came the children's bedroom over the kitchen and the servants' bedroom above the store-room.

Grave, silent, apparently docile and calm, but in a permanent state of inner excitement, these children lived for each other, bound by close ties. The eldest, Maria, who looked serious and thoughtful, aware of her responsibilities and of the great task Mamma had entrusted to her, had no childhood. Her extraordinary precocity was all the more striking because she was tiny and very slight, and her memory allowed her to repeat without a mistake all the news she had just read in the newspaper. A fervent Tory, she was keenly interested in politics and her father enjoyed talking to her of the events of the day as freely as if she had been an adult.

'I used to think them [the Brontë children] spiritless,' the woman who nursed Mrs Brontë told Mrs Gaskell. 'In part I set it down to a fancy Mr Brontë had of not letting them have flesh-meat to eat . . . he thought that children should be brought up simply and hardly: so they had nothing but potatoes for their dinner; but they never seemed to wish for anything else; they were good little creatures. Emily was the prettiest.'

This kind of diet did not continue permanently, however, for in a diary fragment dated Monday 24 November 1834 and signed: Emily and Anne,[9] we read: 'It is past twelve o'clock . . . we are going to have for Dinner Boiled Beef Turnips, potatoes and Applepudding. . . .'

Ellen Nussey, who had frequently stayed at the parsonage from 1833 onwards, told Mr Clement Shorter that the very simple menu included only one kind of meat, always followed by milk pudding of various kinds. They never had pastry at the Brontës'. But there is more evidence. Mr Brontë himself answers this accusation in his letter to Mrs Gaskell on 30 July 1857: 'I think that I have already stated . . . that I never forbade my wife or children, or servants, the use of animal food.' Charlotte preferred a vegetarian diet. It was only when she was a pupil at Roe Head that she gradually got used to eating meat. In a letter of 24 July 1855 to Mrs Gaskell, Mr Brontë brings his children to life before our eyes: 'The servants often said that they had never seen such a clever child [as Charlotte], and that they were obliged to be on their guard as to what they said and did before her. . . . When mere children, as soon as they could read and write, Charlotte and her brother and sisters used to invent and act little plays of their own, in which the Duke of Wellington, my daughter Charlotte's hero, was sure to come off conqueror; when a dispute would not unfrequently [*sic.*] arise amongst them regarding the comparative merits of him, Buonaparte, Hannibal and Caesar. When the argument got warm, and rose to its height, as their mother was then dead, I had sometimes to come in as arbitrator, and settle the dispute to the best of my judgment. Generally, in the management of these concerns, I frequently thought that I discovered signs of rising talent, which I had seldom or never before seen in in any of their age. . . .'

The spartan régime which suited Mr Brontë and which he

9. cf. p. 50.

imposed in part on his children with the laudable intention of training them in abstinence and endurance was possibly not suitable for them. Delicate, with a need to develop and gain equilibrium, they lived on their nervous energy but wore themselves out prematurely and the two eldest, Maria and Elizabeth, were easy victims of the deadly Cowan Bridge school.

Their only relaxation, their supreme delight, was to go wandering on the moor whose wild beauty cast its spell on them, carried them away. In one bound, out by the kitchen door, they were all at once on its rough carpet of heather, sometimes bright with flowers, at others brown and dried. Drawn to the hills which concealed from them a whole world they did not know, they went, all six, the older ones taking care of the younger, heading for adventure, already in quest of escape.

3

Cowan Bridge – Death of Maria and Elizabeth – Return to Haworth – Tabby – Miss Branwell and Mr Brontë educate the three little girls

Three years of this spartan régime passed, and then they went to school at Cowan Bridge. To learn the details of the disastrous time they spent there one need only re-read *Jane Eyre*. Helen Burns at Lowood is none other than Maria Brontë at Cowan Bridge.

'Lowood' had been identified almost immediately after the publication of *Jane Eyre* in 1847. So, when the Reverend William Carus Wilson, the Brocklehurst of *Jane Eyre*, saw that Mrs Gaskell in *The Life of Charlotte Brontë* took literally and defended with unusual vehemence all that Charlotte had written on the subject, he became furious and with the help of his friends threatened Mrs Gaskell with legal proceedings.

Mr Carus Wilson, a rich and influential man, after being the promoter of the Cowan Bridge school, had become its treasurer and administrative officer.

'He was an energetic and evangelical clergyman, [he] may have been as well-meaning as his friends asserted, but a study of his writings reveals a temperament which was in no way exaggerated as presented by Charlotte Brontë in her picture of Brocklehurst in *Jane Eyre* . . .' writes Mr Clement Shorter; an opinion which is reinforced by that of the Reverend Angus M. Mackay in *The Brontës at Cowan Bridge:*

'He wrote many books for the young, which show very clearly what manner of man he was. *Youthful Memoirs*, published in 1828, is full of deathbed scenes of little children, all of whom speak an unnatural language, are precocious in prayer, and have a most unchildlike love of death. . . .

'A local children's magazine called *The Children's Friend* (1826–1828), of which Mr Wilson was the author rather than the editor, abounds in stories of sudden death and damnation. . . . A glance through these little volumes proves that the portrait in *Jane Eyre* is exact. The very expressions put into the mouth of the "black marble clergyman" may be found repeatedly in *Youthful Memoirs*.

'It has been questioned whether the whipping scene in *Jane Eyre* represented a fact. . . . Mr Wilson frequently insists on the necessity of corporal punishment. I quote one of his anecdotes because it seems to refer to some girl at Cowan Bridge: "A poor little girl who had been taken into a school was whipped. She asked: 'If they love us, why do they whip us?' A little girl of six replied, 'It is because they love us, and to make us remember what a sad thing sin is. . . .' "

'No one, I am sure, could read Mr Carus Wilson's *Thoughts Suggested to the Superintendent* without being astonished at the accuracy with which Charlotte Brontë has represented in *Jane Eyre* his aims and religious ideas. . . .

'Let me repeat, these extracts – which might be increased indefinitely – are not given for the purpose of reopening the question of Mr Carus Wilson's character. . . . My purpose is only to show how marvellously accurate was the insight into character and the memory for words and incidents of Charlotte Brontë when she was a little girl of eight. . . . We see here one of the constituents of the genius which produced *Villette* and *Shirley*.'

After Charlotte's death in 1855, her husband, the Reverend Arthur Bell Nicholls, left alone in the parsonage with Mr Brontë, was forced to abandon his dignified silence to answer the attacks of the son of the Reverend Carus Wilson. In the first of his admirable letters, of 23 May 1857, he wrote to the editor of the *Halifax Guardian*: 'To the day of her death "Currer Bell" [Charlotte Brontë] maintained that the picture drawn in *Jane Eyre* was on the whole a true picture of Cowan Bridge School, as she knew it by experience. . . .'

In his second letter of 6 June 1857, he sent an extract from a letter written to him by a former pupil of Cowan Bridge: 'On first reading *Jane Eyre* several years ago I recognised immediately the picture there drawn, and was far from considering it any way exaggerated; in fact, I thought at the time, and still think the matter rather understated than otherwise. I suffered so severely from the treatment that I was never in the schoolroom during the last three months I was there. . . . I attribute my illness to the unhealthy situation of the school, the long walks to church in bad weather . . . and the scanty and ill-prepared food. . . .'

One can easily imagine what were the consequences of this for the little Brontës. At Haworth, even if the food was simple, at least meticulous cleanliness reigned in the kitchen. In fact these children often suffered from hunger at Cowan Bridge.

No doubt, Maria and Elizabeth had never completely recovered from the whooping cough that they had had before going to Cowan Bridge. Maria's health got worse daily. One of her fellow-pupils was to tell Mrs Gaskell later: 'One morning, after she had become so seriously unwell as to have had a blister applied to her side (the sore from which was not perfectly healed), when the getting-up bell was heard, poor Maria moaned out that she was so ill, so very ill, she wished she might stop in bed; and some of the girls urged her to do so, and said they would explain it all to Miss Temple, the superintendent. But Miss Scatcherd was close at hand, and her anger would have to be faced before Miss Temple's kind thoughtfulness could interfere; so the sick child began to dress, shivering with cold, as, without leaving her bed, she slowly put on her black worsted stockings over her thin white legs (my informant spoke as if she saw it yet, and her whole face flashed out undying indignation). Just then Miss Scatcherd issued from her room, and, without asking for a word of explanation from the sick and frightened girl, she took her by the arm, on the side to which the blister had been applied, and by one vigorous movement whirled her out into the middle of the floor, abusing her all the time for dirty and untidy habits. . . . Maria hardly spoke, except to beg some of the more indignant girls to be calm; but, in slow, trembling movements, with many a pause, she went downstairs at last – and was punished for being late.'

'Her [Charlotte Brontë's] heart, to the latest day on which we met,' continues Mrs Gaskell, 'still beat with unavailing indignation at the worrying and the cruelty to which her gentle, patient, dying sister had been subjected by this woman. Not a word of that part of *Jane Eyre* but is a literal repetition of scenes between the pupil and the teacher. . . . In this spring [of 1825] Maria became so rapidly worse that Mr Brontë was sent for. He had not previously been aware of her illness, and the condition in which he found her was a terrible shock to him. He took her home by the Leeds coach. . . . She died a few days after her arrival at home. . . . Elizabeth was sent home in charge of a confidential servant of the establishment; and she, too, died in the early summer of that year. Charlotte was thus suddenly called into the responsibilities of eldest sister in a motherless family. She remembered how anxiously her dear sister Maria had striven, in her grave, earnest way, to be a tender helper and counsellor to them all, and the duties that now fell upon her seemed almost like a legacy from the gentle little sufferer so lately dead.' (G)

Those painful events in Charlotte Brontë's life were permanently branded on her sensibility. From her cruel suffering came a fiery intensity and such an accuracy of expression which blasted those she could not help considering as the cause of these disasters.

That same spring of 1825, before Maria and Elizabeth died, an epidemic of fever (which takes up quite a long section of *Jane Eyre*) had been raging at Cowan Bridge. The little Brontës escaped it and it was of consumption that the two eldest died.

It is astonishing that in spite of these dreadful warnings Charlotte and Emily returned to Cowan Bridge after the summer holidays. However, their father decided that it was safer to bring them home before the winter, and this time for good. It was not too soon. Charlotte and Emily may have come back alive from that 'prison that holds youth captive' – to use a phrase of Montaigne – but their health was permanently impaired.

No doubt they were delighted to be home again with their father and aunt, their brother and little sister Anne. But Maria and Elizabeth were no longer there. The memory of their dying sisters was never to be forgotten. All of them, in their different ways, suffered from having lost them, as only children can suffer, without being able to work out their anguish. And so they felt closer than ever and safer now that they were together once more.

'A kind of adoration [for Maria and Elizabeth] dwelt in Charlotte's feelings which, as she conversed, almost imparted itself to her listener.'[1]

God tempers the wind to the shorn lamb.

It was at this point that a new person, a widow of fifty-three, Tabitha Aykroyd, came to the parsonage as a maid. A typical Yorkshire woman remarkable for her good sense, perception and frankness, Tabby had a heart of gold under her native roughness. In her short, sometimes blunt way, she was to shower her unstinted tenderness and devotion on these motherless children,

1. 'Reminiscences of Charlotte Brontë', Ellen Nussey (reprinted from *Scribner's Magazine*, May 1871).

and they as a result were to be given new heart and be transformed. For thirty years she was to love, tend and protect them as if they had been her own children.

'Tabby had lived in Haworth in the days when the pack horses went through once a week, with their tinkling bells and gay worsted adornment, carrying the produce of the country from Keighley over the hills to Colne and Burnley. What is more, she had known the "bottom" or valley, in those primitive days when the fairies frequented the margin of the "beck" on moonlight nights, and had known folk who had seen them. But that was when there were no mills in the valleys; and when all the wool-spinning was done by hand in the farm houses around.' (G)

Tabby loved to tell stories and there was no end to the supply of them. Charlotte Brontë brings her to life in *Jane Eyre* in the guise of the nurse Bessie: 'She fed our eager attention with passages of love and adventures taken from old fairy tales and older ballads; or, (as at a later period I discovered) from the pages of *Pamela*[2] and *Henry*, *Earl of Moreland*.'

Her picturesque way of speaking set off her stories and gave them an air of truth all the more convincing because she believed them herself. Some stories of the past left the children trembling. Their setting was the lonely, rough-looking dwellings lost in the hills, ghost-haunted, encircled by will o' the wisps – creatures that would lure you into bogs and marshes – dwellings threatened by evil fates, instruments of terrifying and dramatic vengeance.

Once more, however, the serious problem of his daughters' education faced Mr Brontë. It was then that their aunt, Miss Branwell, with courage and self-denial transformed her bedroom into a school room and herself into a teacher, and transmitted in a regular way to her three nieces all the knowledge she had.

Their father did the rest by talking to them and discussing politics or any event or piece of news likely to interest them and develop their powers of observation and judgement, and in addition by encouraging their taste and their need for reading.

'We take the *Leeds Intelligencer*, Tory, and the *Leeds Mercury*, Whig . . . we also read *John Bull*; it is a high Tory, very violent. Mr Driver lends us it, as likewise *Blackwood's Magazine*, the most able periodical there is', writes Charlotte, aged thirteen.

2. Cf. p. 37.

At the time of the Catholic Emancipation Act, politics absorbed them to the extent of making them break off for a time the stories they had begun to write.

'Parliament was opened, and the great Catholic question was brought forward, and the Duke's measures were disclosed, and all the slander, violence, party spirit and confusion. Oh, those six months, from the time of the King's speech to the end! Nobody could write, think, or speak on any subject but the Catholic question, and the Duke of Wellington, and Mr Peel. I remember the day when the *Intelligence Extraordinary* came with Mr Peel's speech in it, containing the terms on which the Catholics were to be let in! With what eagerness Papa tore off the cover, and how we all gathered round him, and with what breathless anxiety we listened, as one by one they were disclosed, and explained, and argued upon so ably, and so well. . . .'

They were ardent defenders of the Anglican Church, and like their father opposed to the emancipation of the Catholics.

Their thirst for knowledge extended to all aspects of culture. Mrs Gaskell found a list of the painters whose work Charlotte, not yet thirteen years old, wanted to know: 'Guido Reni, Julio Romano, Titian, Raphael, Michael Angelo, Corregio, Annibal Carracci, Leonardo da Vinci, Fra Bartolomeo, Carlo Cignani, Vandyke, Rubens, Bartolomeo Ranmerghi.

'There is a paper remaining which contains minute studies of and criticisms upon, the engravings in *Friendship's Offering* for 1829, showing how she [Charlotte] had early formed these habits of close observation, and patient analysis of cause and effect which served so well in after life as handmaids to her genius.' (G)

In spite of the strictness of a timetable which was practically never set aside by any unexpected event, the children were not without free time. How were they to use it? They had no relatives nearby, except their uncle and aunt Fennell, whom they did not see often; Ireland, beyond the sea, was not real to them, and Penzance was at the world's end.

They had no friends into whose home they could come and go at will and, since the death of their mother, visitors to the parsonage were few.

Branwell went from time to time to play with the village boys, those who came to the Sunday School and whom his father considered well-mannered, but even that could not keep him interested for long.

Charlotte, Emily and Anne, reserved, shy, but always ready to do a service, never went to the village except to comfort and help someone. But the moors, mysterious, lonely and always welcoming, drew them and thrilled them. 'They clung to the purple moors behind and around their dwelling – to the hollow vale into which the pebbly bridle path leading from their gate descended, and which wound between fern-banks first, and then amongst a few of the wildest little pasture fields that ever bordered a wilderness of heath, or gave substance to a flock of grey moorland sheep, with their little mossy-faced lambs – they clung to the scene, I say with a perfect enthusiasm of attachment,' says Jane Eyre. 'I could comprehend the feeling and share both its strength and truth. I saw the fascination of the locality. I felt the consecration of its loneliness; my eye feasted on the outline of swell and sweep – on the wild colouring communicated to ridge and dell by moss, by heatherbell, by flower-sprinkled turf, by brilliant bracken and mellow granite crag . . . [these] wound round my faculties the same spell that entranced theirs.'[3]

Like the lapwing and the heath, Emily especially belonged to the moors, from which she could not stay away for long without the risk that she would perish from the separation.

Without relatives, without friends, without companions of their own age, the three tender-hearted sisters became devoted to the animals that they persisted in protecting in spite of Miss Branwell who would allow only one dog at the parsonage. Later there was Keeper, Emily's mastiff which she tamed herself with a virile energy. 'He was so completely under her control, she could quite easily make him spring and roar like a lion.'[4] Flossy, the black and white long-haired spaniel, with its silky coat, belonged to Anne, and Tom, the tabby cat, was everyone's favourite.

A watercolour by Emily which still exists shows her mastiff: 'Keeper, from life, 24th April, 1838. Emily Jane Brontë.' A second watercolour, which is in the Bonnell Collection, is a painting of Hero, Emily's falcon, and is signed: 'E. J. Brontë.

3. *Jane Eyre* (Collins), p. 428–9.
4. *Reminiscences of Charlotte Brontë*, Ellen Nussey.

27th October, 1841.' A third watercolour 'Flossy running in the wind after a bird' is signed: 'Charlotte'.

The uneventful life led by these children and their isolation encouraged a taste for day-dreaming to which their vivid imagination irresistibly led them. With the help of Shakespeare, they began again to compose little plays which they acted, as they had done before Cowan Bridge.

Branwell, happy at having his sisters again, for he had missed them very much – especially Charlotte, who was a year older than himself – was the enthusiastic leader of the little band. At eight he was quite a good-looking boy. Small and short-sighted like Charlotte, he had eyes that sparkled with intelligence behind his glasses, a high forehead, rather a prominent aquiline nose, and hair that was auburn, if not red. His sudden but short-lived enthusiasm would make him grow wild with joy and laugh, and then suddenly weep. His father must have worried about him. He was an attractive and gay little scamp, very spoilt by his aunt and sisters, and once his lessons were over, he had no master but his imagination. Here he ran a mortal risk to which he eventually succumbed.

It was in the little study on the first floor that they developed their new 'games' or 'plays' as they called them, and began to write them down. They were devoted to this strange pastime which allowed their imagination complete freedom.

It is certainly not rare to meet children who live in a happy world in which everything happens to suit them; but it is unusual to see four children share the possession of this marvellous world and collaborate to write its extraordinary story.

Mrs Gaskell has reproduced the catalogue drawn up by Charlotte, aged thirteen, of all that she had written between April 1829 and August 1830: in all, twenty-two little manuscripts. These manuscripts, wads of paper a few centimetres long and wide, sewn together with extreme care, or little notebooks like those used by laundries, were covered with microscopic writing and contained thousands of words. Some of them have finely-decorated title pages.

For nearly a century they jealously kept their authors' secret, for only they could read them. It has already been said that Fannie Ratchford, the librarian of the University of Texas, eventually deciphered all that could be saved after they had unfortunately been dispersed. In this way was revealed a fantastic world, highlighted against the back-cloth of dull, gloomy Haworth. Then the mystery surrounding Charlotte, Emily and Anne gradually disappeared. None of them had, as if by magic, written a masterly first novel. Having hardly stopped writing since they could hold a pen, they were able when the moment of maturity was reached to dip at will into the varied mines of the marvellous kingdoms in which for more than sixteen years they had lived an intensely absorbing and intoxicating life: 'That bright darling dream', as Charlotte often said, when thinking of her secret life.

4

First part of the 'Plays' or Juvenilia – *The kingdom of Glasstown*

The first part of the *Juvenilia* runs from 1825, the date of the children's return from Cowan Bridge, to 1831, when Charlotte left for Roe Head.

All four children, we have seen, contributed to them, but especially Charlotte and Branwell. Charlotte, dreaming only of metamorphosis, wrote with frenzy, never wearying. The output of Branwell, inexhaustibly prolific, was no less arresting. Emily and Anne, although they cannot have lacked enthusiasm and invention, have left little of their contribution during this period. Did they decide before they died to destroy what they had written, or did Charlotte suppress it after she lost her sisters? No doubt we shall never know.

Apart from her poems, *Wuthering Heights* and a few fragments dated between 1833 and 1841, the only things left by Emily were two letters of no great interest addressed to her sister's friend, Ellen Nussey, and a journal fragment written on the parsonage kitchen table on 24 November 1834 and signed also by Anne.

Many years later, the Reverend Arthur Bell Nicholls, Charlotte's husband, back in his native Ireland, found by chance a tiny box with four sheets of paper wadded very tightly in it. Two were written by Emily, the two others by Anne.

One of Emily's is decorated with a charming drawing which shows her sitting in the little study writing on her knee, with her dog Keeper and her cat beside her.

The first of Emily's two notes begins in a curious way with these words: 'A PAPER to be opened when Anne is 25 years old, or on my next birthday after if all be well. Emily Jane Brontë 30th July 1841.'[1]

Anne writes on the same day: 'This is Emily's birthday. She has now completed her 23rd year.'[2]

Emily's second note is dated 30th July 1845, her twenty-

1. C. Shorter, op. cit., vol. I, p. 216.
2. Ibid.

seventh birthday. '. . . This morning Anne and I opened the letters we wrote four years since, on my twenty-third birthday. This paper we intend, if all be well, to open on my thirtieth, three years hence, in 1848.' Then she speaks of what has happened since 1841.[3]

'If all be well', she wrote. Alas! It was in 1848 that Branwell and Emily died within a few months of one another.

Anne's second note is dated 31 July 1845: 'Yesterday was Emily's birthday. . . .'

But for these notes, carefully shut away in their little box, proving, as we shall see, the existence of a world which belonged only to Emily and Anne, the world of Gondal, Fannie Ratchford would no doubt have been unable to reconstruct the verse-novel, *Gondal's Queen*.[4]

Charlotte and Branwell in their different ways tell how their 'plays' began. A particular passage of *The History of the Year*, written by Charlotte in 1829, has often been quoted and I shall quote it in my turn, as it is essential:

'Here is the order of our plays:

'*Young Men*, June 1826;

'*Our Fellows*, July 1827;

'*Islanders*, December 1827.

'These are our three great plays, that are not secret. . . . All our plays are very strange ones. . . . I will sketch out the origin of our plays more explicitly if I can. . . . The *Young Men*'s Play took its rise from some wooden soldiers Branwell had; *Our Fellows* from Aesop's Fables; and *The Islanders* from several events that happened. . . .

'First, *Young Men*. Papa bought Branwell some wooden soldiers at Leeds; when Papa came home it was night, and we were in bed; so next morning Branwell came to our door with a box of soldiers. Emily and I jumped out of bed and I snatched up one and exclaimed: "This is the Duke of Wellington. This shall be the Duke!" When I had said this Emily likewise took one up and said it should be hers. When Anne came down, she said one should be hers. Mine was the prettiest of the whole and the tallest

3. C. Shorter, op. cit., vol. I, p. 304.

4. *Gondal's Queen* (Nelson, London, 1955). See also Appendix 3 (p. 258) for a summary and extracts.

and the most perfect in every part. Emily's was a grave looking fellow, and we called him "Gravey". Anne's was a queer little thing, much like herself, and we called him "Waiting-boy". Branwell chose his and called him "Buonaparte".'

A few pages here and there in Charlotte's and Branwell's manuscripts fortunately make a reference to the collaboration of Emily in the play of *Young Men*, from which sprang incidentally her future kingdom of Gondal. Charlotte goes on to reveal the new name given to Emily's soldier, that of the famous Arctic explorer, Sir William Edward Parry. Emily's kingdom, Parrysland, was to the kingdom of Charlotte and Branwell – Wellingtonsland – what Scotland is to England.

In her introduction to *Gondal's Queen* by Emily, Miss Ratchford adds, 'The only direct description we have of Parrysland comes from Charlotte in person of Lord Charles Wellesley.'

In the October 1830 number of the little review edited by the Brontë children for several months, *The Young Men's Magazine*, Charlotte in fact describes her visit to Parry's palace. With a certain disdain she underlines the simplicity, austerity and poverty of Parrysland, which was in strong contrast to the riches, the brilliant society and the princely luxury of Wellingtonsland.

In another 'play', *Our Fellows*, each child owned an island inhabited by giants.

'It was in December, 1827,' writes Charlotte, 'that the play of *The Islanders* occurred to us.

'One night, about the time when the cold sleet and stormy fogs of November are succeeded by snowstorms, and high piercing night-winds of confirmed winter we were all sitting round the warm blazing kitchen fire, having just concluded a quarrel with Tabby concerning the propriety of lighting a candle, from which she came off victorious, no candle having been produced. A long pause succeeded, which was at last broken by Branwell saying, in a lazy manner, "I don't know what to do." This was echoed by Emily and Anne. Tabby: "Wha ya may go t'bed."

'Branwell: I'd rather do anything than that.

'Charlotte: Why are you so glum tonight, Tabby? Oh! suppose we had each an island of our own.

'Branwell: If we had I would choose the Island of Man.

'Charlotte: And I would choose the Isle of Wight.

'Emily: The Isle of Arran for me.

'Anne: And mine should be Guernsey.

'We then chose who should be chief men in our islands. Branwell chose John Bull, Astley Cooper, and Leigh Hunt. Emily, Walter Scott, Mr Lockhart, Johnny Lockhart; Anne, Michael Sadler, Lord Bentinck, Sir Henry Halford. I chose the Duke of Wellington and two sons, Christopher North and Co. and Mr Abernethy. Here our conversation was interrupted by the, to us, dismal sound of the clock striking seven, and we were summoned off to bed. The next day we added many others to our list of men, till we got almost all the chief men of the kingdom. After this, for a long time, nothing worth noticing occurred. In June, 1828, we erected a school on a fictitious island, which was to contain 1,000 children. . . .

'In the great Hall of the Fountain, behind one of its statues a door, hidden by a curtain of white silk, discovered a small apartment at the far end of which was a very large iron door. This door, in its turn, opened on a long dark passage terminating in a flight of steps leading to a subterranean dungeon. . . .

'This dungeon leads to darkly vaulted cells appropriated to the private and particular use of naughty children, so far down in the earth that the loudest shrieks could go unheard by inhabitants of the upper world. In them, as well as in the dungeons, cruelest torturing might have gone on without fear of detection if it had not been that Charlotte kept the key of the dungeon and Emily the key of the cells and of the huge iron entrance. . . .

'Only young nobles were admitted to this magnificent school.'

And here is what Miss Ratchford says in *The Brontës' Web of Childhood*: 'The chief governor was the Duke of Wellington, and his sons, the Marquis of Douro and Lord Charles Wellesley, were guards keeping the children in order and taking them out to walk. . . . When the school children rose in bloody rebellion and besieged their governors in the palace, Little King and Queens, Branwell and his sisters, hastened in balloons to their relief, restoring order, bringing the dead to life, and healing the wounded by means of fairy remedies.

'The play of *The Islanders* ran for almost another year when the Brontës, becoming tired of it, as of their former inventions, sent the young nobles to their homes and left the Island of Dreams to irresponsible fairies.'

The four volumes which make up this 'play' were finished on

10 July 1830. These stories were not without interest, but they were often incomprehensible. 'They may have had some allegorical or political reference, invisible to our eyes, but very clear to the bright little minds for whom they were intended. Politics were evidently their grand interest; the Duke of Wellington their demi-god.' (G)

Gradually these different 'plays' dissolved and were transformed to become the great African adventure. The wooden soldiers into which the little Brontës breathed life, endowing them with their own personalities, became sailors, pirates, adventurers, builders of cities, dukes, kings, emperors. The Young Men or The Twelve, set sail in the *Invincible* and after many adventures at sea, finally landed on the west coast of Africa, in Guinea:

'We moored our battered ship in a small harbour,' writes Charlotte in 1829 in *A Romantic Tale*, 'and advanced up into the country. To our great surprise we found it cultivated. . . . Far off to the east the long black line of gloomy forests skirted the horizon; to the north the Gibble Kumrion Mountains of the Moon seemed a misty girdle to the plain of Dahomey; to the south the ocean guarded the coasts of Africa; before us to the west lay the desert.'

It was not for nothing that Charlotte, her brother and sisters had had in their hands a *Treatise of General Geography* by the Reverend J. Goldsmith. Its coloured maps and pretty illustrations had fascinated them.

The Young Men came out victorious from a fight with the natives (the Ashanti) whose chief they took prisoner. 'He was quite black; very tall; he had a fierce countenance and the finest eyes I ever saw.' As soon as peace was concluded, the Twelve, with the help of the four Great Genii: Tallii, Brannii, Emmii and Annii (Charlotte, Branwell, Emily and Anne) founded the Confederation of Glasstown, consisting of twelve provinces, with one of the Twelve at the head of each, and they began to build their city. Soon there rose in Glasstown[5] sumptuous buildings of gigantic proportions – the Palace of Justice, the Grand Tower of

5. The name is taken from a book of travels in Africa, and to the children's imagination represented a port with waters as smooth as glass, like a mirror reflecting the magic buildings. Cf. F. E. Ratchford, *The Brontës' Web of Childhood*, p. 16.

all the Nations (another Babel), the Fortifications, the Grand Hostelry that could take twenty thousand guests.

Thanks to magic and supernatural powers, it was all completed in a few months. Then years passed. Four of the principal leaders, after exploring certain neighbouring regions, became masters of them. The twelve provinces were replaced by four kingdoms which were no doubt to the Confederation what England, Scotland, Ireland and Wales are to the United Kingdom. When these kingdoms were firmly established, the Duke of Wellington, who had defeated Napoleon, and freed Europe, was elected King of the new Confederation.

In *A Romantic Tale* Charlotte, describing the palace of the protecting genii of Glasstown, and then the genie of the storm, certainly was inspired by *Paradise Lost* of Milton.[6] This story is an Arabian Nights' tale, a fairy tale written by a child of thirteen, but a child who had already fed her imagination on rich reading.

The 'play' *The Characters of Great Men of the Present Age* (1829) takes us into Glasstown to introduce its principal inhabitants to us. Here are the two sons of the Duke of Wellington, the Marquis of Douro and Lord Charles Wellesley, whose name Charlotte borrows to sign several of her pieces of writing, notably *The Spell*; Young Soult, the poet; Alexander Rogue, the notorious traitor; Captain Bud, the politician; Doctor Hume Badry, the father of Marian.

Young Soult and Captain Bud are incarnations of Branwell, the poet and politician, and here is what Charlotte, in a teasing but very perceptive way, writes about the poet Soult: 'His poems exhibit a fine imagination, but his versification is not good. The ideas and the language are beautiful, but they are not arranged so as to run along smoothly.' As for Captain Bud, 'this great politician . . . some of his apostrophes are high and almost sublime but others are ridiculous and bombastic'.

Branwell's poetry, clumsy and lacking in strength and rhythm, inspired Charlotte to a satire which she wrote in 1830: *The Poetaster*. Branwell's monotonous and inflated prose was no better than his poetry. His writing is without the charm which he radiated himself; the vitality and talent which characterise the stories that they wrote in partnership are due to Charlotte.

6. See Appendix I.

Branwell declared the wars as if out of pleasure, presided at all the military manœuvres, directed the politics, the Parliamentary debates, the literature and the arts. Charlotte invented the people, analysed their characters, gave life to the action. Glasstown was a complete world, with its publishers, bookshops and writers, its historians, poets and painters, its newspapers, its magazines illustrated by charming drawings and watercolours, its theatres and its actors.

One is astounded at such superabundance of invention, such a variety of stories. What surprising energy, what tireless patience, what incredible imagination these little manuscripts reveal.

Albion and Marina, Charlotte's first love story, was composed in a few hours in October 1830. On a moonlight night Albion, separated from his fiancée, Marina, for four years, hears her sweet voice call him. On just such a night Jane Eyre was also to hear a mysterious voice call, 'Jane! Jane! Jane!'. It was the voice of Mr Rochester.

5

Charlotte's departure for Roe Head – Accounts by Ellen Nussey and Mary Taylor

During the five years spent at home, Charlotte had constantly read and re-read; continuing to enrich her excellent memory which retained the finest lines of her favourite poets perfectly. And she had amassed a large number of her own manuscripts.

Her aunt had turned her and her sisters into skilled and meticulous housekeepers but her studies, which were completely haphazard, could not go on indefinitely at the parsonage.

Now Charlotte, influenced from her early childhood by her father, had been aware of the extreme importance of education which, she thought, would give her the means of reaching her secret goal. This goal became clearer and clearer: she wanted to be a writer. In the meantime she would be a teacher, the only occupation suitable for a vicar's daughter. Wasn't it necessary to reduce her father's very heavy burdens as soon as possible?

In January 1831, she left the parsonage for Roe Head, Mirfield, twenty miles or so from Haworth. She went to Miss Wooler who, with the help of her three sisters, ran a little boarding-school for seven to ten pupils.

The attractive and spacious old house which welcomed her was pleasantly situated amidst meadows at the edge of the beautiful Kirklees woods. A calm, smiling landscape, very different from Haworth. 'Here the park of Kirklees, full of sunny glades, speckled with black shadows of immemorial yew trees . . . [with] the mouldering stone in the depth of the wood, under which Robin Hood is said to lie. . . .' (G)

This separation from Branwell and her sisters took place just when their 'plays' were growing in interest and absorbing them more than ever. Charlotte was nearly fifteen.

At Roe Head she became friendly with two other boarders, Ellen Nussey and Mary Taylor. Ellen Nussey, to whom Charlotte wrote regularly all her life, kept over four hundred of her letters. Mary Taylor, alas, destroyed almost all of those sent to her. These letters revealed the part of herself which Charlotte Brontë, who was so reserved, put into them from day to day, without suspecting that they would come down to us, her distant admirers. There is no more beautiful, no more moving portrait of her. Thanks to Ellen Nussey's account, *Reminiscences of Charlotte Brontë*, which appeared in an American magazine in 1871, six years after Mrs Gaskell's death, and a letter from Mary Taylor written from New Zealand to Mrs Gaskell on 18 January 1856, a year after Charlotte's death, valuable information is available about this first period at Roe Head.

Ellen Nussey's account runs as follows:

'Arriving at school . . . I was led into the schoolroom and quietly left to make my observations. I had come to the conclusion that it was very nice and comfortable for a schoolroom, though I had little knowledge of schoolrooms in general, when, turning to the window to observe the look-out, I became aware for the first time that I was not alone; there was a silent, weeping, dark little figure in the large bay-window; she must, I thought, have risen from the floor. . . . I was touched and troubled at once to see her so sad and so tearful . . . she did not shrink however when spoken to, but in very few words confessed she was "homesick". After a little of such comfort as could be offered, it was suggested to her that there was a possibility of her too having to comfort the speaker by-and-by for the same cause. A faint quivering smile then lighted her face; the teardrops fell; we silently took each other's hands, and at once we felt that genuine sympathy which always consoles, even though it be unexpressed. We did not talk or stir till we heard the approaching footsteps of other pupils coming in from their play. . . .

'At lessons she was quickly up to the needful standard, and ready for the daily routine and arrangement of studies, and as quickly did she outstrip her companions, rising from the bottom of the classes to the top, a position which, when she had once gained, she never had to regain. She was first in everything but play, yet never was a word heard of envy or jealousy from her companions, everyone felt she had won her laurels by an amount of diligence and hard labour of which they were incapable. She never exulted in her successes or seemed conscious of them; her mind was so wholly set on attaining knowledge that she apparently forgot all else.

'Charlotte's appearance did not strike me at first as it did others.

I saw her grief, not herself particularly till afterwards. She never appeared to me the unattractive little person others designated her, but certainly she was at this time anything but *pretty*; even her good points were lost. Her naturally beautiful hair of soft silky brown [was] then dry and frizzy-looking, screwed up in tight little curls, showing features that were all the plainer from her exceeding thinness and want of complexion. . . . A dark rusty green stuff dress of old-fashioned make detracted still more from her appearance; but let her wear what she might or do what she would, she had ever the demeanour of a born gentlewoman; vulgarity was an element that never won the slightest affinity with her nature. . . .

'She had taught herself a little French before she came to school; this little knowledge of the language was very useful to her when afterwards she was engaged in translation or dictation. She soon began to make a good figure in French lessons. Music she wished to acquire, for which she had both ear and taste, but her near-sightedness caused her to stoop so dreadfully in order to see her notes, she was dissuaded from persevering in the acquirement, especially as she had at this time an invincible objection to wearing glasses. . . .

'Her appetite was of the smallest; for years she had not tasted animal food; she had the greatest dislike of it; she always had something specially provided for her at our midday repast. Towards the close of the first half-year she was induced to take, by little and little, meat gravy with vegetable, and in the second half-year she commenced taking a very small portion of animal food daily. She then grew a little bit plumper, looked younger and more animated, though she was never what is called lively at this period.

'She always seemed to feel that a deep responsibility rested upon her; that she was an object of expense to those at home, and that she must use every moment to attain the purpose for which she was sent to school i.e. to fit herself for governess life. . . . When her companions were merry round the fire, or otherwise enjoying themselves during the twilight, which was always a precious time of relaxation, she would be kneeling close to the window busy with her studies, and this would last so long that she was accused of seeing in the dark; yet, though she did not play, as girls style play, she was ever ready to help with suggestions in those plays which required taste or arrangement....'

Miss Nussey goes on to record a few facts which give an idea of the scope of Charlotte's imagination at that time and of her poetic gifts. A few pupils grouped round one of the boarders who was convalescing after a recent illness were telling stories. Charlotte then began to tell a story about the adventures of a sleep walker. Such a weird and terrifying story that her hearers were trembling with fear. She realised this and stopped, distressed and apparently filled with remorse. She never again made up for the benefit of her fellow-pupils any stories that might frighten them. She was none the less passionately fond of magic, ghosts and secrets.

It was at Roe Head that 'she made acquaintance with the scenes and prominent characters of the Luddite period; her father materially helped to fix her impressions, for he had held more than one curacy in the very neighbourhood which she describes in *Shirley*....

'I must not forget to state that no girl in the school was equal to Charlotte in Sunday lessons. Her acquaintance with Holy Writ surpassed others in this as in everything else. She was very familiar with all the sublimest passages, especially those in Isaiah, in which she took great delight.'

Mary Taylor wrote to Mrs Gaskell on 18 January 1856: 'I first saw her coming out of a covered cart, in very old-fashioned clothes, and looking very cold and miserable.... She looked a little old woman, so short-sighted that she always seemed to be seeking something, and moving her head from side to side to catch a sight of it. She was very shy and nervous, and spoke with a strong Irish accent.... We thought her very ignorant, for she had never learnt grammar at all, and very little geography.

'She would confound us by knowing things that were out of our range altogether. She was acquainted with most of the short pieces of poetry that we had to learn by heart; would tell us the authors, the poems they were taken from, and sometimes repeat a page or two, and tell us the plot. She had a habit of writing in italics (printing characters) and said she had learnt it by writing in their magazine.... No one wrote in it and no one read it but herself, her brother, and two sisters. She promised to show me some of these magazines but retracted it afterwards, and would never be persuaded to do so. . . . She always showed physical feebleness in everything. . . . It was about this time I told her she was very ugly. Some years afterwards, I told her I thought I had been very impertinent. She replied, "You did me a great deal of good, Polly, so don't repent of it."

'She used to draw much better, and more quickly, than anything we had seen before, and knew much about celebrated pictures and painters. Whenever an opportunity offered of examining a picture or cut of any kind, she went over it piecemeal, with her eyes close to the paper, looking so long that we used to ask her "what she saw in it". She could always see plenty and explained it very well. . . . She worshipped the Duke of Wellington, but said that Sir Robert Peel was not to be trusted; . . . she said she had taken interest in politics ever since she was five years old. . . .

'This habit of "making up" interests for themselves, that most children get who have none in actual life, was very strong in her. The whole family used to "make out" histories, and invent characters and events. I told her sometimes they were like growing potatoes in a cellar. She said, sadly, "Yes, I know we are." . . .'

'She always said there was enough of hard practicality and *useful* knowledge forced on us by necessity, and that the thing most needed was to soften and refine our minds. She picked up every scrap of information concerning painting, sculpture, poetry, music, etc. as if it were gold.'

Although Charlotte had written to her family each week, always addressing her brother, 'It is to you I find the most to say', Mr Clement Shorter has found only two letters dating from this first stay at Roe Head.[1]

So eighteen months of very hard work went by. During that time Charlotte never got the black ribbon worn by pupils who had done badly in something, but from the first term, she won the silver medal and kept it right to the end. When she left, Miss Wooler made her a present of it; it can be seen in the parsonage at Haworth.

1. One very short letter was addressed to Mrs Franks (Miss Elizabeth Firth), the other to Branwell after the unexpected visit he had paid to her.

6

Return to Haworth – Charlotte teaches her sisters – The origin of Thornfield Hall in Jane Eyre *– Ellen Nussey's account of her first visit to Haworth – Emily and Anne separate from Branwell – The influence of romanticism – The evolution of the manuscripts*

Charlotte came home transformed. Her second contact with the real world outside had been beneficial. Appreciated and admired by Miss Wooler, liked by her fellow-pupils, two of whom had become her friends, she had known the pleasure of mutual understanding. Henceforth nothing in life was to be more important.

If Charlotte's heart had opened, her mind had been enriched. She was no longer ignorant of the rules of the English language: grammar had become familiar knowledge to her and the apprentice writer experienced a feeling of security because of it. She had also made great strides in French; from this period there exists a translation into English verse of the first book of *La Henriade* of Voltaire. And lastly, being fond of drawing, she was able to bring home about twenty sketches and copies of engravings which were meticulous in their detail.

Then she enjoyed the satisfaction of sharing what she had learned with her sisters now that they were together again, deepening and extending her own knowledge in this way.

On 31 May 1831, during the holidays following her going to Roe Head, Charlotte had written Ellen Nussey a first letter, the stilted tone of which was soon to disappear. In the second, of 13 January 1832, she said to her without reserve: 'The receipt of your letter gave me an agreeable surprise for, notwithstanding your faithful promises, you must excuse me if I say that I had little confidence in their fulfilment . . .'

On 21 July 1832, Charlotte answered Ellen again: 'You ask me to give you a description of the manner in which I have passed every day since I left school; this is soon done, as an account of one day is an account of all. In the mornings from nine o'clock to half past twelve, I instruct my sisters and draw, then we walk till dinner, after dinner I sew till tea time, and after tea I either read, write, do a little fancy work, or draw as I please. Thus in one delightful, though somewhat monotonous course, my life is passed. I have only been out to tea twice since I came home. We are expecting company this afternoon, and on Tuesday next we shall have all the female teachers of the Sunday school to tea. . . .'

Invited by Ellen and her mother, Charlotte went in a gig to the Rydings, not far from Roe Head, to spend a fortnight. Branwell accompanied her on the journey, and, when he left her, said he 'was leaving her in paradise'.

The Rydings and the manor house of Norton Conyers, near Ripon, are both sources of Charlotte Brontë's description of Thornfield Hall, the mysterious and tragic house in which Jane Eyre found her destiny. It is certain that many important details of Norton Conyers, a beautiful fourteenth-century house with which a real tradition of a mad woman is associated, are to be found in Thornfield Hall.

Charlotte Brontë went to Norton Conyers in 1839 when she was governess with the Sidgwicks. However, the Rydings, in Birstall, where the Nussey family then lived, was less vast, but much better known to Charlotte, and also served as a model for Mr Rochester's manor house, for there we find the Rydings battlements and its grounds with clumps of trees in which there were crows nesting.

In the course of this visit the two friends resolved to write to one another in French so as to improve their command of it and, once back at the parsonage, Charlotte writes thus to Ellen:

'18 octobre 1832 . . . J'arrivait [*sic.*] à Haworth en parfaite sauveté sans le moindre accident ou malheur. Mes petites soeurs couraient hors de la maison pour me rencontrer aussitôt que la voiture se fit voir, et elles m'embrassaient avec autant d'empressement et de plaisir comme si j'avais été absente pour plus d'un an. Mon Papa, ma Tante, et le Monsieur dont mon frère avait parlé furent tous assemblés dans le salon, et en peu de temps je m'y rendis aussi. . . . J'ai donné à mes soeurs les pommes que vous leur envoyiez avec tant de bonté; elles disent qu'elles sont sûr que Mademoiselle Nussey est très aimable et bonne: l'une et l'autre sont extrèmement impatientes de vous voir: j'espère que dans peu de mois elles auront ce plaisir. . . .'

['I arrived in Haworth quite safely without the slightest accident or mishap. My little sisters ran out of the house to meet me as soon as the carriage appeared and they kissed me with as much eagerness and pleasure as if I had been absent for more than a year. Papa and Aunt and the gentleman of whom my brother spoke were all together in the sitting room and I soon joined them. . . . I gave my sisters the apples you so kindly sent them: they say that they are sure Miss Nussey is very nice and kind; both are extremely impatient to see you; I hope that they will have that pleasure in a few months. . . .']

This pleasure was postponed until the summer of 1833. In fact how could they invite Ellen to come during the winter to these bare heights buffeted by the fierce wind, to Haworth buried beneath the snow or held fast in frost? Even spring, whose smile might herald marvels beneath other skies, was often to be feared here. The moors were a spongy waste, gloomy and desolate, not for walking on, for one could not venture there safely. Wisdom, in the person of Miss Branwell, decreed that they must wait until the middle of the summer which would deck the bleak, cold house with its reassuring graces and revive the marvellous beauty of the moors.

The two friends, who had agreed to write once a month, beguiled the slowly passing time by an exchange of news. But Ellen never had enough self-confidence to dare to write in French.

At last the long awaited moment came. Ellen was then sixteen, Charlotte seventeen, Emily fifteen and Anne thirteen and a half. Here is Ellen's account:

'Charlotte was waiting at the parsonage gateway having caught the sound of the approaching gig. . . .

'Even at this time [he was fifty-six] Mr Brontë struck me as looking very venerable, with his snow-white hair. His aristocratic courtesy showed in his bearing and his way of speaking. . . . His white cravat was not then so remarkable as it grew to be afterwards. He was in the habit of covering this cravat himself. We never saw the operation. . . . he cut up yards and yards of white lute-string [silk] in covering his cravat; and like Dr Joseph Woolffe [the renowned and learned traveller] who "went into a clean shirt every day for a week, without taking one off", so Mr Brontë's cravat went into new silk and new size without taking any off, till at length nearly half his head was enveloped in cravat. . . .

'Miss Branwell their aunt, was a small, antiquated little lady.

'The Gun Group' by Branwell Brontë, *c.* 1833 showing (l. to r.) Emily, Charlotte, Branwell, Anne

The Reverend Patrick Brontë

She wore caps large enough for half a dozen of the present fashion, and a front of light auburn curls over her forehead. She always dressed in silk. She had a horror of the climate so far north.... She talked a great deal of her younger days; the gaieties of her native town, Penzance in Cornwall; the soft, mild climate etc.... She took snuff out of a very pretty gold snuffbox, which she sometimes presented to you with a little laugh, as if she enjoyed the slight shock and astonishment visible in your countenance.... She was very lively and intelligent....

'"Tabby", the faithful, trustworthy old servant, was very quaint in appearance – very active, and, in these days, the general servant or factotum. We were all "childer" and "bairns" in her estimation. She still kept to her duty of walking out with the "childer" if they went any distance from home, unless Branwell was sent by his father as a protector....

'Emily Brontë had by this time acquired a lithesome, graceful figure. She was the tallest person in the house, except her father. Her hair, which was naturally as beautiful as Charlotte's, was in the same unbecoming tight curl and frizz, and there was the same want of complexion. She had very beautiful eyes – kind, kindling, liquid eyes; but she did not often look at you: she was too reserved. Their colour might be said to be dark grey, at other times dark blue, they varied so. She talked very little. She and Anne were like twins – inseparable companions, and in the very closest sympathy, which never had any interruption.

'Anne, dear, gentle Anne – was quite different in appearance from the others. She was her aunt's favourite. Her hair was a very pretty light brown, and fell on her neck in graceful curls. She had lovely violet-blue eyes, fine pencilled eyebrows, and clear, almost transparent, complexion. She still pursued her studies, and especially her sewing, under the surveillance of her aunt. Emily had now begun to have the disposal of her own time.

'Branwell studied regularly with his father, and used to paint in oils, which was regarded as study for what might be eventually his profession. All the household entertained the idea of his becoming an artist and hoped he would be a distinguished one.

'In fine and suitable weather delightful rambles were made over the moors, and down into glens and ravines that here and there broke the monotony of the moorland.... Emily, Anne and

Branwell used to ford the streams, and sometimes placed stepping-stones for the other two. . . . Emily especially had a gleesome delight in these nooks of beauty – her reserve for the time vanished. One long ramble made in these early days was far away over the moors to a spot familiar to Emily and Anne, which they called "The Meeting of the Waters". It was a small oasis of emerald green turf, broken here and there by small clear springs; a few large stones served as resting places; seated here, we were hidden from all the world, nothing appearing in view but miles and miles of heather, a glorious blue sky, and brightening sun. A fresh breeze wafted on us its exhilarating influence. . . . Emily, half reclining on a slab of stone, played like a young child with the tadpoles in the water, making them swim about, and then fell to moralising on the strong and the weak, the brave and the cowardly, as she chased them with her hand. . . .

'Mr Brontë's horror of fire forbade curtains to the windows. . . . There was not much carpet anywhere except in the sitting room, and on the study floor . . . the walls were not papered, but stained in a pretty dove-coloured tint; hair-seated chairs and mahogany tables, bookshelves in the study. . . . A little later on there was the addition of a piano. Emily, after some application, played with precision and brilliancy. Anne played also. . . . She sang a little; her voice was weak, but very sweet in tone.

'Mr Brontë's health caused him to retire early. He assembled his household for family worship at eight o'clock; at nine he locked and barred the front door, always giving, as he passed the sitting room door, a kindly admonition to the "children" not to be late. . . .

'Every morning was heard the firing of a pistol from Mr Brontë's room window; it was the discharging of the loading which was made every night.'

After Ellen's return to the Rydings, Charlotte wrote to her on 11 September 1833:

'Were I to tell you of the impression you have made on everyone here, you would accuse me of flattery. Papa and Aunt are continually adducing you as an example for me to shape my actions and behaviour by. Emily and Anne say they never saw anyone they liked so well as Miss Nussey! and Tabby talks a great deal more nonsense about you than I choose to report.'

To have been able to gain Tabby's approval says much for the character of Ellen, whose attractive portrait Charlotte was to trace in her letters. Tabby, a typical native of Haworth, certainly possessed the proud and subtle qualities of her race, if she also had its less serious faults. She opened her heart wide only on memorable occasions. Her direct, quick judgement, rarely at fault, made her approval very valuable.

At the beginning of 1834, Ellen went to London for the first time, to the great alarm of Charlotte who, no doubt as a result of her reading, imagined that a visit to the great capital 'that Babylon, that Nineveh, that ancient Rome' could have nothing but disastrous consequences. She must have got that opinion from reading Sheridan, and recalling Charles Surface in *The School for Scandal*, that certainly endearing libertine who, nevertheless, and with what casual, easy grace, sells the portraits of his ancestors to pay his debts. London 'was the Vanity Fair of the *Pilgrim's Progress* to her'. (G) Accordingly she was astonished when she received a letter from Ellen, still unchanged, a simple constant soul, whom nothing had upset.

She wrote to Ellen on 4 July 1834: 'I *must* thank you for your very handsome present. The bonnet is pretty, neat, and simple, as like the giver as possible; it brought Ellen Nussey with her fair, quiet face, brown eyes, and dark hair full to my remembrance. . . . I am not grown a bit . . . you ask me to recommend some books for your perusal. I will do so in as few words as I can. If you like poetry, let it be first-rate: Milton, Shakespeare, Thomson, Goldsmith, Pope (if you will, though I don't admire him), Scott, Byron, Campbell, Wordsworth, and Southey. Now don't be startled at the names of Shakespeare and Byron. Both these were great men, and their works are like themselves. You will know how to choose the good, and to avoid the evil; the finest passages are always the purest, the bad are invariably revolting; you will never wish to read them over twice. Omit the comedies of Shakespeare and the "Don Juan", perhaps the "Cain" of Byron, though the latter is a magnificent poem, and read the rest fearlessly; that must indeed be a depraved mind which can gather evil from *Henry VIII*, from *Richard III*, from *Macbeth*, and *Hamlet*, and *Julius Caesar*. Scott's sweet, wild, romantic poetry can do you no harm. . . . For history, read Hume, Rollin, and the *Universal History*, if you *can*: I never did. For fiction, read Scott alone; all novels after his are worthless. For biography, read Johnson's *Lives of the Poets*, Boswell's *Life of Johnson*, Southey's *Life of Nelson*, Lockhart's *Life of Burns*, Moore's *Life of Sheridan*, Moore's *Life of Byron*. . . . For natural history read Bewick. . . .'

That is a wonderful list of authors and masterpieces from Mr Brontë's library; it was of high quality although of modest size, and he welcomed new works. What would have become of him without his books? For this man, living the life of an ascetic, they were a necessary luxury. So he understood his children's love of books; they were unfailing friends. With what broadmindedness he allowed them to browse through the shelves in his study – the place of honour of the finely bound volumes – and those in the bedrooms, to which were relegated the shabby, worn books – those which had been eagerly and even impatiently sought after, and which had passed back and forth from hand to hand. How often, after much hesitation, he must have renounced the pleasure of buying a new book in order to have an old disintegrating volume rebound.

To enrich and vary his children's reading Mr Brontë allowed them to take books from the Keighley library, where they would often go, returning delighted and absorbed, turning over the pages of the new book as they walked, quite unconcerned about the four long miles to be covered and the steep village street to be climbed.

The children also borrowed books from the rich collection of their friends, the Heatons of Ponden Hall. Fortunately Miss Branwell, a wise mentor, kept watch so that only when all the household work was properly done did Charlotte, Emily and Anne have leisure to go to Keighley or to resume the reading that was always left off with regret, the story, the chronicle or the poems that they were in the middle of writing.

According to a poem of Charlotte's, *The Trumpet has sounded* (1831), it seems quite clear that the four Grand Genii – Charlotte, Emily, Branwell and Anne – meeting in a solemn council before Charlotte's departure for Roe Head, had really considered the destruction of their creation, Glasstown.

Branwell, unable to bring himself to this, had continued to write with increased ardour. Except during holiday time, Charlotte could only collaborate in these new chronicles of Glasstown at long intervals, and only by a few suggestions in her letters, always addressed to her brother. Away from home, cast out of her imaginary world and into the real one, Charlotte seemed dispossessed and as if lost. So she attached great importance to the rare moments of solitude in which, without any constraint, she could return to 'that darling dream'.

Taking advantage of Charlotte's departure in 1831, Emily refused to remain under Branwell's power, leaving him to struggle on alone until their sister's return. She was quite capable of creating her own kingdom, working alone with Anne.

Thus it was that, deserting the burning African heat of the Niger mouth where everything did not happen as she would have liked, Emily's imagination, scouring the seas as far as the northern mists, discovered in the North Pacific the island of Gondal. This island, divided into four kingdoms, Gondal, Angora, Exina and Alcona, had as its federal capital Regina, famous for its cathedral and its public buildings.

In addition, the royal families of Gondal ruled over an island recently discovered by Gondal sailors, the island of Gaaldine situated partly in the tropics, in the South Pacific, and itself divided into kingdoms and provinces with resounding names, like the kingdom of Almedore.

In spite of Branwell's protests in a Glasstown newspaper, Emily and Anne became passionately attached to their islands and never gave them up. Charlotte, when she came back from Roe Head, plunged again into the 'plays' and along with Branwell founded the new kingdom of Angria.

In successive waves, Romanticism had invaded the parsonage. Walter Scott was the bard of Scotland. Renewing the sources of poetry, he had held his eager new disciples spellbound since they were very young. After reading *Kenilworth*, Charlotte wrote to Ellen who had also just read it:

'I am glad that you like *Kenilworth* . . . in my opinion one of the most interesting works that ever emanated from the great Sir Walter's pen. . . . Varney is certainly the personification of consummate villainy, and in the delineating his dark and profoundly artful mind, Scott exhibits a wonderful knowledge of human nature. . . .'

She had read *Marmion*. Jane Eyre was to say later: 'After sitting nearly an hour on the hearth listening to the muffled fury of the tempest, I lit a candle, took down *Marmion* and beginning,

'Day set on Norham's castled steep
And Tweed's fair river wide and deep,
And Cheviot's mountains lone;
The massive towers, the donjon keep,
The flanking walls that round them sweep
In yellow lustre shone.

'I soon forgot storm in music.'[1]

Byron, that volcanic imagination from which poetry flowed out like lava, in his turn overwhelmed the Brontës. Had he not written to Annabella Milbanke who, to her misfortune, was to marry him, 'Poetry is the lava of the imagination whose eruption prevents an earthquake?'[2]

Byron, with his powerful personality, continually simmering, continually offended, disillusioned, cynical, perpetually in conflict with society and himself, was at once Childe Harold, Manfred, Don Juan. His extravagantly adventurous youth, his disconcerting mysteriousness, the spell of this creature of doom exerted an irresistible attraction.

Conrad the corsair, Lara, Manfred embody the byronic hero, and it was this 'hero', without any doubt, that Charlotte Brontë was in love with. How unusual and how powerful were the stirrings of this burning imagination, this vibrant sensibility. Everything that Charlotte wrote between her thirteenth and her twenty-second year was deeply marked by the grip of this romanticism and her heroes are 'byronic' heroes animated by her individual genius.

The first manuscripts of the little Brontës would have nothing particularly remarkable about them were it not for their choice of heroes, who were the heroes of the time. Very quickly, nevertheless, a personality emerges, in spite of the childish naïveté and the confusion that resulted from random reading which they could not always assimilate completely. When they lost their bearings in this way, their imagination went to the length of inventing monsters. Jane Eyre says clearly what went on in her childish head

1. *Jane Eyre* (Collins edition), p. 462.
2. 10 November 1813.

after a certain kind of reading: 'Of these death-white realms I formed an idea of my own: shadowy, like all the half-comprehended notions that float dim through children's brains, but strangely impressive.'[3]

Like wizards throwing into their cauldrons the most varied and unusual ingredients to concoct their spells the Brontë children, putting together the most dissimilar elements, the simplest with the most unexpected, transmuted them at once as if in a white-hot crucible.

An Adventure in Ireland, 28 April 1829, like other tales of the same year, already gives us a glimpse of Charlotte's powers of observation, her poetic temperament and her descriptive ability.

Mr Thomas J. Wise,[4] who had *Ernest Alembert* (written in 1830) printed privately in 1895, says of this fairy tale: 'This tale reveals creative ability not yet matched by the power of expression.'

In the course of her vast reading over the years, Charlotte eventually discovered the secret subtleties of grammar of which she had been taught the essentials at Roe Head, and greater subtleties of style, the strange process by which genius works in its search for a characteristic mode of expression.

It was at this point that she and Branwell stopped recounting strange fairylike adventures – where life was as children liked it to be: hovering between the beautiful and the terrible – and began to celebrate love and the passionate feelings it creates: jealousy and ambition in a world in which violence, illegitimacy, even incest are not excluded (at this time a man who married a dead wife's sister was considered incestuous). The echoes of the vague, insidious rumours, mostly hostile, that had been spread about Byron and his half-sister Augusta must have resounded in the minds of these wide-awake adolescents. All this created in them a disturbance like a 'dark deposit in a turbid well'.[5]

3. *Jane Eyre* (Collins edition), pp. 2–3.
4. Cf. Preface, p. 17.
5. *Jane Eyre* (Collins edition), p. 10.

7

Second part of the Juvenilia – *The Kingdom of Angria – Percy, Earl of Northangerland and his wife Lady Zenobia Ellrington – The Duke of Zamorna – The Duchess of Zamorna* – Mina Laury

The first of the stories in the second part of the *Juvenilia, The Bridal*, was written in August 1832, soon after Charlotte's return from Roe Head. In it she tries to depict jealousy, and Lady Zenobia Ellrington, the passionate heroine of this fantastic tale, foreshadows Bertha Mason, the mysterious mad woman in *Jane Eyre*, shut away in Thornfield Hall. *The Bridal* has a vehemence and a certain maturity but, to finish it off, Charlotte turns once again to magic, an easy way of putting everything right. Industrial disturbances, very like the Luddite riots, come into this story.

Then followed *The Foundling*, a long tale written in 1833. The description of Glasstown, then in all its splendour, is lively and poetic here. *Arthuriana* (1833) contains various tales with the Marquis of Douro as their hero, told by his younger brother, Lord Charles Wellesley. *The Secret* was also written in 1833. Mrs Gaskell later reproduced the facsimile of a page in *The Life of Charlotte Brontë*. In December of that same year Charlotte also wrote *Richard Lionheart and Blondel*. She was trying to recapture the spirit of the old minstrels, and was really inspired. 'The poem . . . shows so strikingly the influence of the great Walter Scott – his influence as a ballad maker and his influence also as the author of *Ivanhoe* and *The Talisman*', writes Mr Clement Shorter in his introduction to the poem published in a limited edition.

High Life in Verdopolis which Miss Ratchford describes as a 'delightful byronic orgy' was closely followed by *The Spell* (1834), directly inspired by the complex, mysterious personality of Byron. If the action moves too slowly, no doubt because of the letter-form of some of the chapters (in imitation of Richardson's *Pamela*),[1] Charlotte's narrative skill becomes obvious here. She holds her reader in suspense until the end in spite of a very involved thread of intrigue and the multiplicity of the heroes'

1. Cf. p. 37.

THE - SECRET
CHAPTER THE 1st

Facsimile of opening page of *The Secret*

Christian names and titles. In *My Angria and the Angrians* (1834) in which one can trace a similar evolution, the Duke of Wellington gives his son, the former Marquis of Douro, a letter addressed to his Grace the Right Honourable Arthur, Augustus, Adrian, Duke of Zamorna, King of Angria, who replies to any one of these Christian names or titles according to the author's whim.

Since she lived apart from society and so did not have to submit to any of its constraints, Charlotte let her quick pen run on unchecked, and her freedom of expression is one of the essential elements of her originality.

In *The Spell* the style anticipates that of *Jane Eyre*; it has become simple and clear, varied, colourful and passionate, and the sentences unfold with a pleasing and compelling rhythm.

A Peep into a Picture Book (1834) is amusing, ingenious and graphic. General Thornton, who is having an afternoon nap, is really Mr Brontë. Lord Charles Wellesley, his young pupil, the narrator, does not dare stir for fear of wakening him and doesn't know what to do to pass the time. He notices a portrait album at the other end of the room. Holding his breath he goes over to it with noiseless tread, looks at the portraits one after the other and at the same time describes them.

But the general eventually wakes up and scolds Charles for having touched the portraits with inky fingers: 'Get me the Cook's guide; you shall learn a page of receipts for this business before ever you taste a morsel of supper.'

This kind of punishment was current at the time and unconsciously Charlotte betrays her identity: we are back in Haworth parsonage.

A Leaf from an Unopened Volume (17 January 1835), writes Miss Ratchford in the course of her study, 'illustrates her unbounded literary curiosity. The most melodramatic and unpleasant of all her writing, it is a confused medley of intrigue, licentiousness, and fraternal hate, with illegitimate or disowned children, dwarfs, and Negroes playing leading parts.'

The Scrapbook, finished on 16 March 1835, is the last act of the 'play', the *Young Men*.

Finally, in the course of the summer of 1836, Charlotte wrote a long untitled poem which Miss Ratchford considers the best production of the Angrian cycle.

By 1838 Charlotte, aged twenty-two, was in full possession of her magnificent talent for writing and this is revealed in *Mina Laury*. And in 1839 she was deep in the love stories of Caroline Vernon and her brother-in-law. It was at that point that she left home to become a governess with the Sidgwicks.

A long, though incomplete, list of the *Juvenilia* manuscripts is given in Appendix V to the second volume of *The Brontës' Life and Letters*, by Mr Clement Shorter. One must read *Legends of Angria* (1937) by Miss Ratchford to have 'a panoramic view of Charlotte Brontë's early work', as Miss Ratchford herself says in the preface to this book.

The little manuscripts of earlier days had gradually been replaced by bigger ones but the minute writing remains difficult to decipher. The handwriting of the Brontë children was very similar. This has caused much confusion, making people attribute to one the tales or poems of another.

These *Juvenilia*, at last brought to light, form an undeniable part of the literary output of the three sisters. Charlotte, Emily and even Anne drew upon them freely, sometimes going far back into the past; this is shown, as in many other examples, by this very simple passage from *An Adventure in Ireland*, by Charlotte (1829), which appears again in *Jane Eyre* when Mrs Fairfax welcomes the governess on her arrival at Thornfield Hall.

'When we arrived at the castle I was shown into a large parlour, in which was an old lady sitting in an armchair by the fireside, knitting. On the rug lay a very pretty tortoiseshell cat.' (*An Adventure in Ireland*.)

'A snug, small room; a round table by a cheerful fire, an armchair, highbacked and old fashioned, wherein sat the neatest imaginable little elderly lady . . . she was occupied in knitting; a large cat sat demurely at her feet.' (*Jane Eyre*.)[2]

When Charlotte and Branwell, in close collaboration and with wild enthusiasm, established the new kingdom of Angria, many persons in the 'play', *The Characters of Great Men*, belonging to the first part of the *Juvenilia*, changed their names. The Marquis of Douro becomes Duke of Zamorna; Alexander Rogue becomes Earl of Northangerland, that Alexander Rogue whom Branwell had imagined as a pirate, and Charlotte a soldier, the perfidious

2. Collins edition, p. 111.

Colonel Percy, banished from Glasstown for treason. Glasstown itself is renamed Verreopolis and later Verdopolis.

Thanks to the title of his new wife, Lady Zenobia Ellrington, Alexander Rogue, back from exile, introduces into Verdopolis society his daughter, Mary Percy, whom he had by a former marriage (Zenobia is his third wife). The Duke of Zamorna, already married to Marian Hume, frees himself in order to marry Mary Percy, and makes his father-in-law Earl of Northangerland. Marian Hume dies of despair.

The Earl of Northangerland, who adored his daughter, hated his two sons: Edward Percy, the manufacturer, and Captain William Percy, the scholar. These two brothers were always irreconcilable adversaries and reappear in *The Professor*. The Duke of Zamorna, who defeats the African chief, Quashia, saves the Confederation of Verdopolis from invasion and as a reward for his victories calls on Parliament to cede to him the territory of Angria situated to the east. With the help of his crafty father-in-law, the Earl of Northangerland, he obtains it and becomes king of Angria.

In Angria, as formerly in Glasstown, Branwell was kept busy with the political struggles in parliament, and on the battle field, whereas Charlotte wound and unwound the intrigues of the action which always revolved round the two protagonists, the Duke of Zamorna, her favourite hero, and the Earl of Northangerland, the hero whom Branwell dreamed of being and whose satanic personality he undertook to bring to life.

Zamorna and Northangerland hate one another and are always in opposition, but they can never do without one another. Northangerland, the evil genius, eventually starts a revolution that brings with it the fall and exile of Zamorna who, with the changing rhythm of events, later wins back his kingdom.

Here are the couple, Percy (Earl of Northangerland) and Zenobia from *A Peep into a Picture Book*:

'O Percy! Percy! In my opinion this head embodies the most vivid ideas we can conceive of Lucifer, the rebellious archangel; there is such a total absence of human feeling and sympathy; such a cold frozen pride; such a fathomless power of intellect; such passionless yet perfect beauty. . . . I turn the leaves and behold – his countess. Hem! Hem! I am not on very good terms with this celebrated lady, as all the world knows; yet, *non obstante*, truth compels me to confess that she is a very fine woman, a superb daughter of Verdopolis. . . . What eyes! What raven hair! What an imposing contour of form and countenance! She is perfectly grand in her velvet robes, dark plume and crown-like turban. The Lady of Ellrington House, the wife of Northangerland, the prima donna of the Angrian Court, the most learned woman of her age, the modern Cleopatra, the Verdopolitan de Staël; in a word, Zenobia Percy! Who would think that that grand form of feminine majesty could launch out into the unbridled excesses of passion in which her ladyship not infrequently indulges?'

Is that not already the likeness of Lady Ingram in *Jane Eyre*, or of her daughter, the imposing, beautiful Blanche?

'[The Duke of Zamorna] paused just opposite to where I sat and thus I was enabled to take a full and leisurely view of him. He seemed to be in the full bloom of youth; his figure was toweringly, overbearingly lofty, moulded in statue-like perfection and invested with something which I cannot describe – something superb, impetuous, resistless, something, in short, no single word can altogether express. His hair was intensely black, curled luxuriantly, but the forehead underneath, instead of having the swarthy tinge proper to such Italian locks, looked white and smooth as ivory. His eyebrows were black and broad, but his long eyelashes and large clear eyes were deep sepia brown.'[3]

Mary Percy, Duchess of Zamorna, Queen of Angria, 'had very small and feminine features, handsome eyes, a neck of delicate curve, and fair graceful little snowy aristocratic hands, and sandalled feet to match'.[4]

In *Mina Laury*, a charming, rather disconcerting work that Charlotte Brontë seems to have enjoyed writing,[5] the heroine is the daughter of a villager. Tall, beautiful and distinguished looking, she might have been an earl's daughter.

All these great ladies of the court of Angria are just a transposition of Charlotte's friends into her secret world. Ellen Nussey, pretty Mary Taylor, Miss Wooler and her sisters were far from suspecting that they had undergone any such metamorphosis.

3. *My Angria and the Angrians,* cf. p. 74.
4. Ibid.
5. See Appendix 2.

8

Charlotte Brontë deals with love – The double life – Branwell – Charlotte leaves again for Roe Head

Mina Laury anticipates Jane Eyre as the Duke of Zamorna foreshadows Mr Rochester. Many passages in *The Spell* and *Mina Laury* are found again in *Jane Eyre*. The Duchesses of Zamorna and Mina Laury are noble, disinterested women, as Jane Eyre will be. The genuine, absorbing passion which Mina Laury feels for the Duke of Zamorna, but which she holds in check, is already the passion which will rouse and exalt Jane Eyre.

In eighteenth-century England, when gaming and drinking were considered good form, love was often confused with licentiousness. But Charlotte Brontë, with her driving imagination giving free rein to the deep emotions of her ardent nature, then divined the truth about love and restored its nobility and depth, its power and magic, without the least hypocrisy and with a frankness of language which was bound to shock some readers and critics of the Victorian period, and also sometimes with child-like candour which was like a breath of pure fresh air in a sultry atmosphere.

'Experience is not necessary to a writer. Its place is taken by the imagination which creates fictions more alive and more true than life and truth. It sees them naked, whereas truth and life are decked with a mask.'[1]

'A humble life with easy monotonous tasks is a deliberate choice which demands a great deal of love,' said the French poet, Verlaine. And such was the life of the three sisters: busy, wisely disciplined, of necessity undertaking the most menial jobs with a love born of a submission to duty, to maintain harmony at the heart of a home stricken by misfortune.

But since their extraordinary gifts found no employment in day-to-day life, they and their brother lived a double existence: the real life, the life of vicar's children in an isolated parsonage,

1. *La vie des soeurs Brontë*, E. and G. Romieu (Gallimard, Paris, 1929), p. 10.

and then the imaginative life revealed to us by the *Juvenilia* – the 'world below', this dream which dazzled Charlotte, and which Emily was never to be willing nor able to tear herself away from.

What excitement, what passion in these long chronicles with their innumerable episodes in which the fate of cities, states and high-ranking personages is at stake. What richness of invention; what disconcerting and moving psychology.

While these exemplary daughters did the housework and the cooking, sewing and ironing, taught one another, and gave up their time, Charlotte especially, to the Sunday School, they breathed powerful life into the heroes figuring in their stories and poems; a great number of Charlotte's poems celebrated *Angria*, nearly all of Emily's celebrated *Gondal*. Charlotte leads an exciting life in sumptuous marble palaces, near rivers with enchanting banks, Emily and Anne on islands lost far out in the oceans, or on the shore of lakes which in high summer mirror the mesmerising purple of a moor.

Did Charlotte feel no perturbation, no regret in abandoning her imaginative life in which everything obeyed her laws, to face real life where everything is subordinated to strict rules of conduct which protect by domination?

In the imaginary world, Mina Laury, caught in the pleasant trap of love, will love none but Zamorna, and her fidelity will do her credit. In real life, it will be to Charlotte Brontë's credit that she sacrificed everything, including love, to duty. Moving from one world to the other, what a gulf there was to cross, what giddiness to overcome!

Many passages of the letters to Ellen Nussey, as we shall presently see, reveal at some point the scruples and fears of the perceptive Charlotte, whose conscience was as rigorous as her artistic gifts were outstanding. Nothing of her scruples and fears was understood by Ellen, a simple soul with no complexes, as one would say today. Of average intelligence, unoriginal, passive and submissive in her piety as in her affections, gentle and kind, calm and reasonable, loyal and devoted, Ellen was in spite of her limitations the perfect confidante for Charlotte. Their friendship, born of a sympathy which had drawn them to one another in the classroom at Roe Head on the day they arrived, was life-long.

Charlotte could not dream of letting Ellen – no more than her other friend Mary Taylor – glimpse the strange and weird spectacle in which they might have recognised themselves under the features of one or other of the incredible creatures who moved about there. Ellen would have been thunderstruck. So, never having been allowed to share the secret of the young Brontës, how could she have guessed or even suspected that her friends, under the surface appearance of a life of exemplary routine, were feverishly absorbed within themselves and went so far as to lose their identity in a world of incredible fancies which they were for ever creating and keeping alive?

When Charlotte writes to Ellen: 'after tea I either read, write, do a little fancywork, or draw, as I please', it is only one aspect of the truth. Charlotte's secret literary output was never more intense than in the years 1832–4, when the two friends exchanged letters and visits.

Later, Ellen was unaware, like everyone else, of who 'Currer Bell'[2] was until the moment when it was no longer a secret to anyone.

Mary Taylor, a very open, lively personality, and an original one, was no nearer to guessing the riches of her friend's mind. In one of her letters she says ingenuously to Charlotte, who has become the author of *Jane Eyre*, 'It seems incredible to me that you have really written a book'.

The fact is that 'the two eldest Brontë daughters only *seemed* to be nothing more than modest, shy young ladies. In spite of their frail physique, they were capable of violence, which they at once suppressed. Within them, unknown to anyone, seethed an almost savage ardour. These strictly disciplined creatures were to have to confess their real selves in novel writing for their powerful passion to become apparent.'[3]

Through their double celtic inheritance the Brontës belonged to both Irish and Cornish stock. While Anne remained purely celtic, and Branwell had none of the energy and strength of character of the Yorkshire people, Charlotte and Emily shared the violent sentiments and passions of the other natives.

Jane Eyre, arguing against St John Rivers, will say: 'I know no medium. I never in my life have known any medium in my dealings with positive hard characters, antagonistic to my own,

2. Pseudonym of C. Brontë. Cf. p. 163.
3. Robert de Traz, *La Famille Brontë* (Albin Michel, Paris, 1939).

Charlotte Brontë, painting by J. H. Thompson

Emily Brontë, 1833, painting by Branwell Brontë

Branwell Brontë,

Anne Brontë, 1834,

between absolute submission and determined revolt. I have always faithfully observed the one, up to the very moment of bursting, sometimes with volcanic violence, into the other.'[4]

'Thus the combination of celtic blood and Yorkshire upbringing in the Brontës is a most singular and striking mixture of violently contrasting elements.'[5]

In 1834, the year when Charlotte wrote *The Spell*, Mr Brontë, always anxious to see his children's talents being developed, got a drawing master for them from Leeds: a Mr Robinson who had worked in Sir Thomas Lawrence's studio and soon showed himself to be 'a man of considerable talent, but very little principle'. (G)

They all showed great enthusiasm through their continual need to express themselves. In the summer of the same year, 1834, Branwell went to Leeds to see an exhibition of painting and sculpture. There he was able to see some portraits painted by Mr Robinson as well as the huge Satan by the sculptor, Joseph Bentley Leyland, twenty-three years old, who later became his friend, and made a medallion of him which is in the Haworth museum. This Satan, full of hatred and dread, evoked for Branwell the Satan of Milton's *Paradise Lost* addressing the sun; the same passage had, in fact, inspired the artist. This made a sudden and decisive impact on Branwell. In an enthusiastic surge of ambition his vocation seemed to become clear: he wanted to be a painter. He was almost eighteen.

Their father, never weakening in his task, had kept to his decision to teach Branwell himself. But when the day's lessons were over, while the vicar, careful about the claims of his parish, devoted himself to them, Branwell, the only boy in the family, was left to his own whims.

Unfortunately for him, he had not been forced as his sisters had to stick to the fixed timetable drawn up by Miss Branwell. Lacking in energy, disliking the effort imposed by the realities of life, when he didn't go to the village in the hope of relief for his listlessness or boredom in one place or another, he let himself be caught up again by the Angria of his day-dreams in which, now

4. *Jane Eyre* (Collins edition), p. 491.
5. P. Bentley, *The Brontës* (Home and van Thal Ltd, London, 1947), p. 18.

minister, now leader of the army, duke, prince, king, he pursued his dangerously mad adventures. He was seized again by 'a desire to live out victoriously an imaginary series of events, in the face of which one would doubtless prove inadequate if they were true. It is pleasant to feel fear when the reason for it does not really exist.'[6] Then, sooner or later, he found that he was Branwell Brontë once more, with his future to establish in a world that was nothing like the one in which he had been taking refuge for too long. Soon he could no longer distinguish truth from fiction and that led to his ruin.

'Branwell's talents were readily and willingly brought out for the entertainment of others. Popular admiration was sweet to him. And this led to his presence being sought at "arvills"[7] and all the great village gatherings. . . . "Do you want someone to help you with your bottle, sir?" the landlord of the Black Bull would say to any chance traveller. "If you do, I'll send up for Patrick." And while the messenger went, the landlord entertained his guest with accounts of the wonderful talents of the boy, whose precocious cleverness, and great conversational powers, were the pride of the village.' (G) Mr Brontë was to some extent unaware of how his son spent his time outside his lessons. What did he know about Angria? Little, possibly nothing at all. Yet he could not have been ignorant of what was happening around him. But, if he was more observant than Miss Branwell, the microscopic writing kept its secrets successfully. He judged Branwell by himself and could not put him on his guard against a danger he did not foresee.

Charlotte, endowed with great commonsense, and Emily and Anne were saved by their zeal for study and especially by the discipline imposed by their aunt, which was for them a source of equilibrium.

'They were, moreover, grateful to her for many habits she had enforced upon them, and which in time had become a second nature: order, method, neatness in everything; a perfect knowledge of all kinds of household work; an exact punctuality, and obedience to the laws of time and place . . . with their impulsive

6. J.-L. Barrault, *Nouvelles réflexions sur le théâtre* (Flammarion, Paris, 1959), p. 12.
7. Funeral feasts (dialect).

natures, it was positive repose to have learnt implicit obedience to external laws.' (G)

It was probably at this time that Branwell did the portrait of his three sisters which is in the National Portrait Gallery. Everyone hoped to see him become a great painter; so his father thought seriously about sending him as a pupil to the Royal Academy in London.

On 6 July 1835, Charlotte wrote to Ellen: 'I had hoped to have had the extreme pleasure of seeing you at Haworth this summer, but human affairs are mutable, and human resolutions must bend to the course of events. We are all about to divide, break up, separate. Emily is going to school, Branwell going to London, and I am going to be a governess. This last determination I formed myself, knowing that I should have to take the step some time . . . knowing well that Papa would have enough to do with his limited income should Branwell be placed at the Royal Academy and Emily at Roe Head. Where am I going to reside? you will ask. Within four miles of you, at Roe Head. . . . Yes, I am going to teach in the very school where I was myself taught. Miss Wooler made me the offer. . . . I am sad, very sad, at the thought of leaving home; but duty – necessity – these are stern mistresses, who will not be disobeyed. . . . Emily and I leave home on the 29th of this month.'

Mrs Gaskell goes into some detail: 'On the 29th of July, 1895, Charlotte, now little more than nineteen years old, went as teacher to Miss Wooler's. Emily accompanied her as a pupil; but she became literally ill from homesickness, and could not settle to anything, and after passing only three months at Roe Head, returned to the parsonage and the beloved moors.' (G)

Charlotte herself gives the reasons for Emily's return to Haworth: 'My sister Emily loved the moors. Flowers brighter than the rose bloomed in the blackest of the heath for her; – out of a sullen hollow in a livid hillside, her mind could make an Eden. She found in the bleak solitude many and dear delights; and not the least and best-loved was – liberty. Liberty was the breath of Emily's nostrils; without it she perished. . . . Every morning when she woke, the vision of home and the moors rushed on her, and darkened and saddened the day that lay before her. Nobody knew what ailed her but me. . . . In this struggle her health was quickly broken; her white face, attenuated form, and failing strength, threatened rapid decline. I felt in my heart she would die, if she did not go home, and with this conviction obtained her recall.'

With her health sapped by a homesickness that she was powerless to overcome in spite of her strength of will, Emily, that flower of the moors torn from her natural soil, would certainly have withered and died if the perceptive concern of her sister Charlotte had not rescued her in time.

Isolated by her reserved nature, Emily confided only in her poems:

For the moors, for the moors where the short grass
Like velvet beneath us should lie!
For the moors, for the moors where each high pass
Rose sunny against the clear sky!

For the moors where the linnet was trilling
Its song on the old granite stone;
Where the lark, the wild skylark was filling
Every breast with delight like its own.

What language can utter the feeling
That rose when, in exile afar,
On the brow of a lonely hill kneeling
I saw the brown heath growing there.

It was scattered and stunted and told me
That soon even that would be gone;
It whispered, 'The grim walls enfold me,
I have bloomed in my last summer sun.'

It was to be proved later that Emily, brave as she was, could not live far from Haworth, from her moors and her imaginary world.

Charlotte and Anne decided not to let their sister repeat an experiment that might cost her dear. In future, Emily would be the one to stay at home.

Once, later on, Emily, anxious like her sisters to earn her living, left Haworth to go as governess to the boarding-school run by Miss Patchett, near Halifax. She was unable to stay more than six months.

Apart from another passage in Mary Taylor's letter of 18

January 1856 to Mrs Gaskell, already quoted, no detail has reached us of Charlotte's second stay at Roe Head and Dewsbury Moor, except in her letters to Ellen Nussey. Charlotte ends the one dated 10 May 1836 in this way:

'If you knew my thoughts, the dreams that absorb me, and the fiery imagination that at times eats me up, and makes me feel society, as it is, wretchedly insipid, you would pity and I dare say despise me. But I know the treasures of the *Bible*. I love and adore them. I can see the Well of Life in all its clearness and brightness; but when I stoop down to drink of the pure waters they fly from my lips as if I were Tantalus. . . . Goodbye. Charlotte.

'Come and see me soon; don't think me mad, this is a silly letter.'

A series of letters, undated, follow at the end of this year, 1836. Here are a few passages from them:

'Roe Head. . . . I will no longer shrink from answering your questions. I DO wish to be better than I am. I pray fervently sometimes to be made so, I have stings of conscience, visitings of remorse, which formerly I used to be a stranger to. . . . I am in that state of horrid, gloomy uncertainty that, at this moment, I would submit to be old, grey-haired, to have passed all my youthful days of enjoyment, and to be settling on the verge of the grave, if I could only thereby ensure the prospect of reconciliation to God. . . .'

'Roe Head. . . . I am a very coarse, commonplace wretch, Ellen. I have some qualities which make me very miserable, some feelings that you can have no participation in, that few, very few people in the world can understand. I don't pride myself on these peculiarities, I strive to conceal and suppress them as much as I can, but they burst out sometimes, and those who see the explosion despise me and I hate myself for days afterwards.'

'Roe Head 1836. . . . My life since I last saw you has passed on as monotonously and unvaryingly as ever, nothing but teach, teach, teach, from morning till night. The greatest variety I ever have is afforded by a letter from you, or a call from the Taylors, or by meeting with a pleasant new book. . . .

'My own dear Ellen, goodbye; I can write no more, for I am called to a less pleasant avocation.'

9

Christmas 1836 – Branwell's failure at the Royal Academy – His literary ambition revives – Charlotte writes to the poet Southey – Branwell writes to Wordsworth – Dewsbury Moor – Mary Taylor's evidence – Charlotte's sensibility and her scruples – Christmas 1837 – Branwell the portrait painter

At Christmas 1836 all the children were at home again with their father and aunt, happy to be together again and enjoying their freedom. The three sisters anxiously discussed their future. Branwell, who left for London in 1835 to attend classes at the Royal Academy, had come back almost at once. It is not even certain that he went to the Academy. It is only known that he visited the city, saw its buildings, including Westminster Abbey, the Castle Tavern in Holborn; all the rest is a mystery. Would the wretched Branwell ever be able to adapt himself to real life? Mr Robinson, the Leeds teacher, continued his lessons and undertook to initiate him into the art of portrait-painting.

After the failure of his great project of entering the Royal Academy, the artist's career, as it were, eluding him, Branwell returned to his early literary ambitions. Convinced that he really was a writer, a poet, he wanted to convince the world as well, and set about this without hesitation. It was on *Blackwood's Magazine* that he made his first assault: towards the end of 1835 he addressed a long letter to its editor with these words in capital letters on the first page: 'SIR, READ WHAT I WRITE.'

'I have addressed you twice before, and now I do it again.' Branwell then praises the contributors to *Blackwood's Magazine*, James Hogg, who had died recently, and John Wilson, and then goes on, 'My resolution is to devote my ability to you, and for God's sake, till you see whether or not I can serve you, do not coldly refuse my aid. . . . PROVE ME; and if I do not stand the proof, I will not further press myself on you. If I do stand it – why – You have lost an able writer in James Hogg, and God grant you may get one in – Patrick Branwell Brontë.'

This letter was kept but not answered.

Branwell wrote a fourth letter, with which he sent a long poem,

'Misery', and he received no reply to that either. Extremely disappointed, he then asked for an interview, declaring that he would not hesitate before a journey of three hundred miles, but this final letter continued in such a tone that it could bring him nothing but contempt, rebuff and rejection. In this way he closed against himself for ever the doors of *Blackwood's*, which had provided his greatest pleasures when he was a child.

Happiness at being home restored Charlotte's self-confidence. Hope banished fear. Had not she also always eagerly aspired to authorship? But how could she venture on that dangerous path without knowing what her writing was worth, especially her poems? More severe judges than her brother and sisters were absolutely indispensable. She had to put her trust in a poet of repute whose opinion would carry weight. After certainly discussing with Branwell and her sisters, Charlotte decided to submit some of her poems to Southey, the Poet Laureate, to whom she wrote on 29 December. Her letter does not seem to have been preserved.

The holidays ended without bringing a reply and Charlotte had to return to Roe Head still not knowing whether Southey had received her letter and her poems.

As for Branwell, having drawn a blank with *Blackwood's Magazine*, he turned to Wordsworth to whom he wrote on 19 January 1837:

'Sir, I most earnestly entreat you to read and pass your judgement upon what I have sent you. . . .

'Do pardon me, sir, that I have ventured to come before one whose works I have most loved in our literature, and who most has been with me a divinity of the mind, laying before him one of my writings, and asking of him a judgment of its contents. . . .

'My aim, sir, is to push out into the open world . . . surely in this day, when there is not a *writing* poet worth a sixpence, the field must be open, if a better man can step forward.'

But Wordsworth did not reply. The fact that he kept the letter is perhaps due to chance. However, he remembered it when the name of the Brontës became famous, which would lead one to think that Branwell's prose had made an impression on him. The poem he sent was dull and full of affected sentimentality, but what accompanied and introduced it had a curious kind of interest.

January and February passed. Charlotte, still receiving no reply from Southey, was giving up hope when, at the beginning of March, the long-awaited letter reached her. It has been included in the *Life of Southey* by his son, Charles Cuthbert Southey.

Only a long absence had been the cause of his delay, the poet explained at the beginning. Then he went on:

'You evidently possess, and in no inconsiderable degree, what Wordsworth calls "the faculty of verse". I am not depreciating it when I say that in these times it is not rare . . . whoever, therefore, is ambitious of distinction in this way ought to be prepared for disappointment. . . .

'The daydreams which you habitually indulge are likely to induce a distempered state of mind . . . literature cannot be the business of a woman's life, and it ought not to be. The more she is engaged in her proper duties, the less leisure will she have for it, even as an accomplishment and a recreation. . . .

'But do not suppose that I disparage the gift which you possess, nor that I would discourage you from exercising it. I only exhort you so to think of it, and so to use it, as to render it conducive to your own permanent good. Write poetry for its own sake; not in a spirit of emulation, and not with a view to celebrity. . . . So written, it is wholesome both for the heart and soul; it may be made the surest means, next to religion, of soothing the mind, and elevating it. . . .

'Farewell, madam. It is not because I have forgotten that I was once young myself, that I write to you in this strain; but because I remember it. You will neither doubt my sincerity, nor my goodwill. . . . Robert Southey.'

Charlotte was to say to Mrs Gaskell long afterwards:

'Mr Southey's letter was kind and admirable; a little stringent, but it did me good.' At the time, she was so upset by it that on 16 March, without more delay, she replied to the poet with her usual frankness:

'. . . At the first perusal of your letter I felt only shame and regret that I had ever ventured to trouble you with my crude rhapsody; I felt a painful heat rise to my face when I thought of the quires of paper I had covered with what once gave me so much delight, but which now was only a source of confusion; but after I had thought a little, and read it again and again, the prospect seemed to clear. You do not forbid me to write; you do not say that what I write is utterly destitute of merit. You only warn me against the folly of neglecting real duties for the sake of imaginative pleasures; of writing for the love of fame. . . . I know the first letter I wrote to you was all senseless trash from beginning to end; but I am not altogether the idle, dreaming being it would seem to denote. . . .

'. . . Once more allow me to thank you with sincere gratitude. I trust I shall never more feel ambitious to see my name in print; if the wish should rise, I'll look at Southey's letter and suppress it. It is honour enough for me that I have written to him and received an answer. That letter is consecrated; no one shall ever see it but Papa and my brother and sisters. . . .'

And it is thanks to the fame which she then stoically renounced that we have the unusual privilege of reading the letter from Southey.

At this point, Miss Wooler had to leave Roe Head, with its lawns and delightful woods, to transfer her school to Dewsbury Moor, about three miles away, not set so high, damp and unhealthy, in which the air was neither as pure nor as invigorating, according to Mrs Gaskell.

'Dewsbury is a poisonous place for me' was Charlotte's view. She regretted Roe Head, perhaps especially on account of her sister Anne who had come to replace Emily and whose health was very delicate.

It was at the beginning of 1837 also that Ellen Nussey and her family left The Rydings for Brookroyd.

A letter in which Emily described the conditions of her new life as a governess at Law Hill had added to Charlotte's anxiety:

'My sister Emily', she wrote to Ellen on 2 April 1837, 'is gone into a situation as teacher in a large school of near forty pupils near Halifax. I have had one letter from her since her departure; it gives an appalling account of her duties – hard labour from six in the morning until near eleven at night, with only one half-hour of exercise between. This is slavery, I fear she will never stand it. . . .'

While Emily's life was hard, and she thought of Law Hill as a prison, she found freedom from captivity in her poetry. The numerous poems which she wrote shut away in her room show that she was feverishly immersed in her tumultuous world of Gondal.

Charlotte's letters to Ellen reveal qualms of conscience becoming daily more overwhelming:

'. . . I abhor myself – I despise myself; if the doctrine of Calvin be true, I am already an outcast. . . . when I begin to study on the subject, I almost grow blasphemous, atheistical in my sentiments. Don't desert me, don't be horrified at me. You know what I am. I wish I could see you, my darling . . . if you grow cold, it is over.'

And here is the only evidence, Mary Taylor's, taken from her letter of 18 January 1856 to Mrs Gaskell:

'Three years after, I heard that she had gone as teacher to Miss Wooler's. I went to see her and asked how she could give so much for so little money. . . . She seemed to have no interest or pleasure beyond the feeling of duty, and, when she could get the opportunity, used to sit alone, and "make out". She told me afterwards that she had sat in the dressing room until it was quite dark, and then observing it all at once, had taken sudden fright.

'She told me that one night, sitting alone, about this time, she heard a voice repeat these lines:

Come, thou high and holy feeling,
Shine o'er mountain, flit o'er wave,
Gleam like light o'er dome and shieling

There were eight or ten more lines which I forget. She insisted that she had not made them, that she had heard a voice repeat them. It is possible that she had read them, and unconsciously recalled them. They are not in the volume of poems which the sisters published. She repeated a verse of Isaiah, which she said had inspired them, and which I have forgotten. Whether the lines were recollected or invented, the tale proves such habits of sedentary, monotonous solitude of thought as would have shaken a feebler mind.'

One would have expected Charlotte to be able, with Anne's company, to resign herself to her fate, to be satisfied even, if not happy in it, in spite of the long hours of exhausting work for a very low salary. The people she was with once more were not strangers. Among her pupils were the younger sisters of her old school fellows. Her friends Ellen Nussey and Mary Taylor lived only a few miles away. Miss Wooler, pleasant, kind Miss Wooler whom Charlotte respected and loved, had become a friend with whom she could have pleasant conversation every evening and sometimes late into the night.

'It was about this time that an event happened in the neighbourhood of Leeds, which excited a great deal of interest. A young lady, who held the situation of governess in a very respectable family, had been wooed and married by a gentleman, holding some subordinate position in the commercial firm to which the young lady's employer belonged. A year after her marriage, during which she had given birth to a child, it was discovered that he whom she called husband had another wife. Report now says that this first wife was deranged, and that he had made this an excuse to himself for his subsequent marriage. But, at any rate, the condition of the wife who was no wife – of the innocent mother of the illegitimate child – excited the deepest commiseration: and the case was spoken of far and wide, and at Roe Head among other places. . . .

'I believe I have already mentioned that some of her surviving friends consider that [this] incident which she heard, when at school at Miss Wooler's, was the germ of the story of *Jane Eyre*.' (G)

Until then Charlotte's letters to Ellen had been full of commonsense and playful fun. Why do they show at this period such inner turmoil and agitation, with scruples of conscience severe enough to upset and ruin her health? If Charlotte suffered anguish at Roe Head and more especially at Dewsbury Moor, it was certainly not Miss Wooler's fault; she sympathised with her anxious temperament and delicate health and used her ingenuity to divert her. She invited her to go out, to visit Ellen and Mary, but often in vain.

'Charlotte was always fearful of loving too much, of wearying the objects of her affection; and thus she was often trying to restrain her warm feelings, and was ever chary of that presence so invariably welcome to her true friends. According to this mode of acting, when she was invited for a month, she stayed but a fortnight. . . .' (G)

Charlotte's submission to duty gradually became excessive and finally revealed a worrying instability. What was its cause, if not the fact that she was deeply disturbed at being once more torn from her imaginary world?

She could not fail to be aware of her gifts, to be tortured by the irresistible power of the creative genius which possessed her and found no outlet for its expression. All the vital forces of her being were absorbed by a never-ending toil that she was not made for. Her sensibility, cramped and frustrated in this way, became keener, she grew irritable, her nerves over-tense; then she was really depressed and ill.

Nor could she help knowing the nature of her Angrian dream, that world on which the Genii had left an indelible mark. There, no moral law imposed its control; evil escaped the punishment that usually follows it. There, passions were unleashed without regret or remorse. And this was the world she took pleasure in. She was relishing its poison 'as if it were nectar'.[1]

Charlotte's keen clarity of mind did indeed allow her to measure the extent to which she remained spellbound by the memory of Angria, and that against her will.

She sought help in vain in Ellen's friendship, in religion; but the Calvinistic doctrines terrified her, as they had terrified Byron before her. And her mind, so marvellously well balanced, became a prey to devastating nightmares.

In spite of herself, she had to have recourse to her imaginary world; to it alone, as always, but now with bitter self-reproach, she went in search of refuge and consolation.

'How few', she confided to her journal, 'would believe that from sources purely imaginary such happiness could be derived! . . . What a treasure is thought! What a privilege is reverie! I am thankful I have the power of solacing myself with the dream of creations whose reality I shall never behold. May I never lose that power. . . .'

Since she had started teaching at Roe Head and later at Dewsbury Moor, Charlotte had gone on exchanging letter after letter with her brother, who at home was feverishly continuing the Chronicles of Angria in which she collaborated with the mounting enthusiasm of an imagination of disturbing power.

1. *Jane Eyre* (Collins edition), p. 192.

Branwell's letters, relating the exploits of the Duke of Zamorna, the well-beloved, literally entranced her.

'Never shall I, Charlotte Brontë . . . forget how distinctly I, sitting in the schoolroom at Roe Head, saw the Duke of Zamorna leaning against that obelisk. . . . I was quite gone. I had really, utterly forgot where I was and all the gloom and cheerlessness of my situation. I felt myself breathing quick and short as I beheld the Duke lifting up his sable crest, which undulated as the plume of a hearse waves in the wind. . . . "Miss Brontë, what are you thinking about?" said a voice, and Miss Lister thrust her little rough, black head into my face.'[2]

Time passed, leaving behind it weariness, worry, suffering. It was 1837. Christmas was at hand and the holidays brought the three sisters back to the family home where they dared to be themselves.

The moor, at the mercy of the elements, lay still, as if lifeless beneath a thick white mantle.

From their windows they looked admiring at it, were inspired by it. They waited impatiently for Ellen, who, braving the cold, the snow and the wind, was coming to see them. But suddenly Tabby had an accident which threw their little world into confusion. Going down the steep village street to do some shopping the faithful old servant slipped on the frosty surface, fell and broke her leg.

Charlotte wrote to Ellen on 29 December 1837: 'She now lies at our house in a very doubtful and dangerous state. Of course we are all exceedingly distressed at the circumstance, for she was like one of our own family. Since the event we have been almost without assistance . . . and consequently the whole work of the house . . . falls on ourselves. Under these circumstances I dare not press your visit here at least until she is pronounced out of danger . . . should Tabby die while you are in the house, I should never forgive myself.'

When, thanks to the intelligent, tireless care of her nurses, Tabby's life was no longer in danger, wisdom, expressed once more by Miss Branwell, finally persuaded Mr Brontë, by nature disinterested and generous, to make a decision. He agreed that

2. Margaret Lane, *The Brontë Story* (Heinemann, London), pp. 109–11.

Tabby, almost helpless, should go and live with her sister in the village on the small income from her savings. If she came to be in need, Mr Brontë would see to her.

When they heard this verdict, Charlotte, Emily and Anne rebelled for the first time in their life. How could they have the heart to abandon Tabby when she was old and infirm, Tabby who since their childhood had never stopped loving and caring for them? Sad, silent and filled with indignation, they refused to have tea, or breakfast next morning, and consented to end their fast only when their father, astonished but agreeing with them in his heart, decided that Tabby should remain at the parsonage.

During this time Charlotte was tormented by another serious worry. Since before the holidays, Anne had had a cough and a pain in her side and found difficulty in breathing. Miss Wooler had not been at all alarmed by it, considering it to be just a common cold. It was different for Charlotte, haunted by the memory of her elder sisters, Maria and Elizabeth.

'Miss Wooler thought me a fool', she wrote to Ellen on 4 January 1838, 'and by way of proving her opinion treated me with marked coldness. We came to a little *éclaircissement* one evening. I told her one or two rather plain truths, which set her a-crying, and the next day, unknown to me, she wrote to Papa, telling him that I had reproached her bitterly – taken her severely to task etc etc. Papa sent for us the next day after he had received her letter. Meanwhile, I had formed a firm resolution – to quit Miss Wooler and her concerns for ever – but just before I went away she took me into her room, and giving way to her feelings, which in general she restrains far too rigidly, gave me to understand that in spite of her cold repulsive manners she had a considerable regard for me and would be very sorry to part with me. . . . I gave in and said I would come back if she wished me – . . . but I am not satisfied. I should have respected her far more if she had turned me out of doors instead of crying for two days and two nights together. I was in a regular passion; my *warm temper* quite got the better of me – of which I don't boast, for it was a weakness; nor am I ashamed of it, for I had reason to be angry.

'Anne is now much better, though she still requires a great deal of care. . . .'

Emily, who had returned exhausted from Halifax, had taken her place at home again, shouldering the humblest and heaviest tasks as she had done in the past and caring for Tabby as well.

Under her own roof with her family, and near the moors, whether they lay dormant or were awake, she could attempt anything. While she made the bread – always excellent and light – or did any other work, she was Queen Augusta Geraldine Almeda or some other such person of the world of Gondal which she carried within her. In this perfect harmony, hour after hour wonderful poetry sprang from her boundless imagination.

Branwell, in spite of his diverse talents, was leading an idle and dissipated life that was to end in his ruin. It is true that he had an extraordinary facility for writing: his literary output is astonishing. He was gifted in drawing and no less in music. Without having made much effort, he played the piano and the organ and was enraptured by church music. In this year, 1838, at the age of twenty-one, he decided to try to earn his living as a portrait-painter and installed himself in Bradford in Fountain Street, with Mr and Mrs Kirby, from whom he had rented a room serving as both bedroom and studio. From time to time he painted a portrait but spent the best part of his time in the bar of the George Hotel, the meeting place of business men and also of second-rate painters and poets. At weekends he went back to Haworth.

Few of his paintings have come down to us. In his room at the parsonage are to be seen the portrait of his friend the sacristan, the famous John Brown, Worshipful Grand Master of the Lodge of the Three Graces, of which Branwell had become a member in February 1836; that of Brown's brother, William, the grave-digger – both restored, unfortunately – those also of Mr and of Mrs Kirby and of their niece, Miss Margaret Hartley, which are not bad.

His best-known portraits: his three sisters, and Emily in profile are in the National Portrait Gallery.

If Branwell, with the talent that everyone recognised, had been capable of sustained effort, perhaps he could have made a living by this craft, at a time when photography had just begun. But he would begin a portrait and then leave off for one reason or another. This enterprise did not last long. After a few months his father, no doubt unable to bear such a heavy expense any longer, brought him home.

At the end of the holidays, Charlotte had no choice but to resume her hard task at Dewsbury Moor.

Uncomplaining but struggling with all her courage against a depression which was taking hold of her, she set off again, 'ready to die in harness'. (G)

But her nerves were at breaking point. She started at the slightest sound, everything frightened her and left her trembling; her reason and her life were in danger. The expenditure of nervous energy had been too great, for the mind had worn out the body. The doctor said that the only cure was for her to return home.

10

Charlotte returns to Haworth ill – Her first proposal – Henry Nussey – Charlotte becomes governess with the Sidgwicks at Stonegappe

So Charlotte also came home to Haworth and after a period of complete rest, Mr Brontë, anxious to distract his daughter in her convalescence, invited Mary Taylor and her sister Martha to come and spend a few days at the parsonage.

Charlotte wrote to Ellen, who was then away from home:

'. . . They are making such a noise about me I cannot write any more. Mary is playing on the piano; Martha is chattering as fast as her little tongue can run; and Branwell is standing before her, laughing at her vivacity. . . .'

Freed from a burden that had begun to crush her, Charlotte regained her health and happiness and began to write again. The time was passing by so peacefully, so pleasantly that she would not let herself think of the future. But the future broke into her life in an unexpected way: she received a letter from the young clergyman, Henry Nussey, one of Ellen's brothers, in which he proposed to her.

'Matrimony did not enter into the scheme of her life' according to Mrs Gaskell. Yet it would have been the only way of escaping from the harsh, difficult and dreary existence that awaited her.

Charlotte, who had a very high conception of love, wrote this reply to Henry Nussey:

'Haworth, 5th March, 1839.

My dear Sir,

. . . You are aware that I have many reasons to feel grateful to your family, that I have peculiar reasons for affection towards one at least of your sisters, and also that I highly esteem yourself – do not therefore accuse me of wrong motives when I say that my answer to your proposal must be a *decided negative*. In forming this decision, I trust I have listened to the dictates of conscience more than to those of inclination. I have no personal repugnance to the idea of a union with you, but I feel convinced that mine is not the sort of disposition calculated to form the happiness of a man like you. It has always been my habit to study the characters of those amongst whom I chance to be thrown, and I think I know yours and can imagine what description of woman would suit you for a wife. The character should not be too marked, ardent, and original, her temper should be mild, her piety undoubted, her spirits even and cheerful, and her *personal attractions* sufficient to please your eyes and gratify your just pride. As for me, you do not know me; I am not the serious, grave, cool-headed individual that you suppose; you would think me romantic and eccentric; you would say I was satirical and severe. However, I scorn deceit, and I will never, for the sake of attaining the distinction of matrimony and escaping the stigma of an old maid, take a worthy man whom I am conscious I cannot render happy. . . . Let me say also that I admire the good sense and absence of flattery and cant which your letter displayed. Farewell. I shall always be glad to hear from you as a friend.'

On 12 March she wrote to Ellen:

'. . . You ask me, my dear Ellen, whether I have received a letter from Henry. I have, about a week since. The contents, I confess, did a little surprise me, but I kept them to myself and unless you had questioned me on the subject, I would never have adverted to it. Henry says he is comfortably settled at Donnington, that his health is much improved, and that it is his intention to take pupils after Easter. He then intimates that in due time he should want a wife to take care of his pupils, and frankly asks me to be that wife. . . . Now, my dear Ellen, there were in this proposal some things which might have proved a strong temptation. I thought that if I were to marry Henry Nussey, his sister could live with me, and how happy I should be. But again I asked myself two questions: do I love him as much as a woman ought to love the man she marries? am I the person best qualified to make him happy? alas! Ellen, my conscience answered *no* to both these questions. I felt that though I esteemed, though I had a kindly leaning towards him, because he is an amiable and well-disposed man, yet I had not, and could not have, that intense attachment which would make me willing to die for him; and, if I ever marry, it must be in that light of adoration that I will regard my husband. Ten to one I shall never have the chance again; but, *n'importe*.

Moreover I was aware that Henry knew so little of me he could hardly be conscious to whom he was writing. Why, it would startle him to see me in my natural home character; he would think I was a wild romantic enthusiast indeed. I could not sit all day long making a grave face before my husband. I would laugh and satirise and say whatever came into my head first. And if he were a clever man, and loved me, the whole world weighed in the balance against his smallest wish should be light as air . . . write to me soon and say whether you are angry with me or not. Goodbye, my dear Ellen.'

In order to judge the Reverend Henry Nussey by her own standards, Charlotte had not needed to read his private journal, in which his method of looking for a wife proves that he was, to say the least, unimaginative and cold.

'On Tuesday last received a decisive reply from M.A.L.'s papa; [his former vicar]: a loss, but I trust a providential one. Believe not her will but her father's. All right, but God knows best what is good for us, for his Church, and for His Glory. Write to a Yorkshire friend . . . C.B. Received an unfavorable reply from C.B. The will of God be done.'

Henry Nussey finally found a wife but his marriage was not happy.

'In Henry Nussey we have not in the least Charlotte Brontë's creation, St John Rivers[1]. . . on the whole it is the diary of a dull uninspired person with not sufficient brains to be a high-souled fanatic; and it is a high-souled fanatic that Miss Brontë depicts in her book. That is why I am inclined to think that the real prototype of Rivers existed for her not in life but in literature; that she had read from the Keighley Library Sargent's *Memoir of Henry Martyn*, that devoted missionary from Cornwall, of whom her aunt must have constantly spoken to her, and her father also, for he was practically contemporaneous with him at S. John's College, Cambridge. . . . Martyn, it will be remembered, translated the New Testament into Hindustani. There are points also in the relations with Miss Lydia Grenfell, whom he had hoped to take back with him to India when he died of the plague, that unquestionably recall St John Rivers.'[2]

1. See *Jane Eyre*.
2. Clement Shorter, *The Brontës' Life and Letters,* Vol. I, p. 150.

Charlotte had found no happy refuge in marriage. A literary career was forbidden her; had not Southey's advice been decisive?

An artist's career was also closed to her for she had ruined her weak eyes copying engravings in all their minute detail and applying the same technique of drawing to whatever her imagination suggested in its continual search for self-expression.

The only alternative was teaching. Having no choice, Charlotte and Anne set about looking for posts as governesses, but without enthusiasm and even with apprehension.

'Neither [Charlotte] nor her sisters were naturally fond of children. The hieroglyphics of childhood were an unknown language to them, for they had never been much with those younger than themselves. . . . Consequently teaching very young children was anything but a "delightful task" to the three Brontë sisters.' (G)

Like her elder sisters, the gentle Anne, who was not without courage and will-power, was anxious to earn her living. She left home first. Through the intermediary of Miss Wooler she went to the Inghams of Blake Hall, Mirfield.

'For my own part I am as yet "wanting a situation" like a housemaid out of place,' Charlotte wrote to Ellen on 15 April 1839. 'By the way I have lately discovered that I have quite a talent for cleaning, sweeping up hearths, dusting rooms, making beds etc; so, if everything else fails, I can turn my hand to that if anybody will give me good wages for little labour. I won't be a cook; I hate cooking. I won't be a nurserymaid, nor a lady's maid, far less a lady's companion. . . . I won't be anything but a housemaid.'

A few weeks later, Charlotte in her turn left home to go to the Sidgwicks at Stonegappe. Here is what was written by Mr A. C. Benson, the son and biographer of Archbishop Benson, Mr Sidgwick's cousin:

'Charlotte Brontë acted as governess to my cousins at Stonegappe for a few months in 1839. . . . She was, according to her own account, very unkindly treated, but it is clear that she had no gifts for the management of children, and was also in a very morbid condition the whole time. My cousin, Benson Sidgwick, now vicar of Ashby Parva, certainly on one occasion threw a Bible at Miss Brontë! And all that another cousin can recollect of her is that if she was invited to walk to church with them, she thought she was being ordered about like a slave; if she was not invited, she imagined she was excluded from the family circle. Both Mr and Mrs John Sidgwick were extraordinarily benevolent people, much beloved.' Were they motivated by as kindly feelings towards their subordinates? Wasn't their attitude to them completely different from the one they adopted with their equals?

What Charlotte Brontë recounted later to Mrs Gaskell, reported to us, seems to answer these questions: '... She had been entrusted with the care of a little boy, three or four years old, during the absence of his parents on a day's excursion, and particularly enjoined to keep him out of the stableyard. His elder brother, a lad of eight or nine, and not a pupil of Miss Brontë's, tempted the little fellow into the forbidden place. She followed, and tried to induce him to come away; but instigated by his brother, he began throwing stones at her, and one of them hit her so severe a blow on the temple that the lads were alarmed into obedience. The next day, in full family conclave, the mother asked Miss Brontë what occasioned the mark on her forehead. She simply replied: "An accident, ma'am," and no further inquiry was made. . . . But one day, at the children's dinner, the small truant of the stableyard, in a little demonstrative gush, said, putting his hand in hers, "I love 'ou, Miss Brontë". Whereupon the mother exclaimed, before all the children, "Love the *governess*, my dear!" ' (G)

On 8 June 1839, Charlotte wrote to her sister Emily:

'I have striven hard to be pleased with my new situation. The country, the house and the grounds are, as I have said, divine. But, alack-a day! there is such a thing as seeing all beautiful around you – pleasant woods, winding white paths, green lawns, and blue sunshiny sky – and not having a free moment or a free thought left to enjoy them in. The children are constantly with me, and more riotous, perverse, unmanageable cubs never grew. As for correcting them, I quickly found that was entirely out of the question: they are to do as they like. A complaint to Mrs Sidgwick only brings black looks upon oneself, and unjust, partial excuses to screen the children. . . . I said in my last letter that Mrs Sidgwick did not know me. I now begin to find that she doesn't intend to know me, that she cares nothing in the world about me except to contrive how the greatest possible quantity of labour may be squeezed out of me, and to that end overwhelms me with oceans of needlework, yards of cambric to hem, muslin nightcaps to make, and, above all things, dolls to dress. . . . I now see more clearly than I have ever done before that a private governess has no existence, is not considered as a living and rational being except as connected with the wearisome duties she has to fulfil. While she is teaching the children, working for them, amusing them, it is all right. If she steals a moment for herself she is a nuisance. . . . Mr Sidgwick is in my opinion a hundred times better. . . . It is very seldom that he speaks to me, but when he does I always feel happier and more settled some minutes after. . . . One of the pleasantest afternoons I have spent here – indeed the only one at all pleasant – was when Mr Sidgwick walked out with his children, and I had orders to follow a little behind. . . . He spoke freely and unaffectedly to the people he met and though he indulged his children . . . he would not suffer them grossly to insult others. . . .

'. . . Next week we are going to Swarcliffe, Mr Greenwood's place near Harrogate, to stay three weeks or a month. . . .'

On 1 July she wrote to Ellen:

'. . . I only received your letter yesterday, for we are not now residing at Stonegappe, but at Swarcliffe, a summer residence of Mr Greenwood's, Mrs Sidgwick's father. It is near Harrogate and Ripon; a beautiful place in a beautiful country. As it is, I will only ask you to imagine the miseries of a reserved wretch like me, thrown at once into the midst of a large family – proud as peacocks and wealthy as Jews – at a time when they were particularly gay, when the house was full of company . . . having the charge given me of a set of pampered, spoilt, and turbulent children, whom I am expected constantly to amuse as well as instruct. . . . At times I felt and I suppose seemed depressed. To my astonishment I was taken to task on the subject by Mrs Sidgwick with a stress of manner and a harshness of language scarcely credible. Like a fool, I cried most bitterly, I could not help it. . . . At first I was for giving all up and going home but after a little reflection I determined to summon what energy I had and to weather the storm. I said to myself I had never yet quitted a place without gaining a friend. Adversity is a good school; the Poor are born to labour and the Dependent to endure. I resolved to be patient. . . . I recollected the fable of the Willow and the Oak; I bent quietly and I trust now the storm is blowing over me. Mrs Sidgwick is generally considered an agreeable woman; so she is, I dare say, in general society. Her health is sound, her animal spirits are good; consequently she is cheerful in company. But oh! Ellen, does this compensate for the absence of every gentle and delicate sentiment? . . . I have never had five minutes conversation with her since I came – except while she was scolding me. . . . I don't intend to stay long after they leave Swarcliffe, which they expect shortly to do.'

Then she turned to write tenderly to Emily:

'Mine bonnie love . . . it is a real, genuine pleasure to hear news from home; a thing to be saved till bedtime, when one has a moment's quiet and rest. . . . I could like to be at home. I could like to work in a mill. I could feel mental liberty. I could like this weight of restraint to be taken off. But the holidays will come. Coraggio.'

Charlotte Brontë stayed no more than three months with the Sidgwicks. More than half that time was spent at Swarcliffe. It was there that she had the opportunity, when Mrs Sidgwick's hosts went there, to visit the manor of Norton Conyers.

II

Return to Haworth – A second proposal – The holiday with Ellen – The three sisters are together again – Branwell goes as tutor to Broughton-in-Furness – He writes to Hartley Coleridge – Charlotte writes to Wordsworth – Miss Celia Amelia – Branwell leaves for Sowerby Bridge

One day, about a week after her return to Haworth, Ellen asked Charlotte to go and stay with her at the seaside.

'Your proposal has almost driven me "clean daft",' she replied to Ellen on 26 July 1839. '. . . When do you wish to go? Could I meet you in Leeds? To take a gig from Haworth to Birstall would be to me a very serious increase of expense, and I happen to be very low in cash. Oh, Ellen, rich people seem to have many pleasures at their command which we are debarred from! However, no repining. . . . I left Stonegappe a week since. I never was so glad to get out of a house in my life. . . .'

Miss Branwell and Mr Brontë, surprised and uneasy at Ellen's unexpected invitation, were not at all enthusiastic. They saw in it an adventure which, without quite knowing why, they could not help being apprehensive about. Their long seclusion weighed heavily on them, whereas Charlotte, absolutely thrilled at this incredible pleasure, had her mind on nothing but departure and discovery. How could she dispel the uneasy fears that had invaded the minds of her father and aunt, about to destroy her happiness under the pretext of saving her from imaginary risks? As a complete diversion, Miss Branwell and Mr Brontë decided to take the whole family to spend a fortnight in Liverpool. Ellen would of course be welcome if she agreed to join them.

On 4 August, Charlotte wrote to Ellen:

'The Liverpool journey is yet a matter of talk, a sort of castle in the air. . . . Aunt, like many other elderly people, likes to talk of such things, but when it comes to putting them into practice, she rather falls off. Such being the case, I think you and I had better adhere to our first plan of going somewhere together, independently of other people. . . .

'I have an odd circumstance to relate to you – prepare for a hearty laugh! The other day, Mr Hodgson, Papa's former curate, now a vicar, came over to spend the day with us, bringing with him his own curate. The latter gentleman, by name Mr Bryce, is a young Irish clergyman, fresh from Dublin University. It was the first time we had any of us seen him, but however, after the manner of his countrymen, he soon made himself at home. His character quickly appeared in his conversation: witty, lively, ardent, clever too, but deficient in the dignity and discretion of an Englishman. At home, you know, Ellen, I talk with ease, and am never shy, never weighed down and oppressed by that miserable *mauvaise honte* which torments and constrains me elsewhere. So I conversed with this Irishman and laughed at his jests, and though I saw faults in his character, excused them because of the amusement his originality afforded. I cooled a little, indeed and drew in towards the latter part of the evening, because he began to season his conversation with something of Hibernian flattery which I did not quite relish. However, they went away and no more was thought about them.

'A few days after, I received a letter. . . . Having opened and read it, it proved to be a declaration of attachment and proposal of matrimony, expressed in the ardent language of the sapient young Irishman. Well! thought I, I have heard of love at first sight, but this beats all. I leave you to guess what my answer would be, convinced that you will not do me the injustice of guessing wrong. When we meet, I'll show you the letter. . . . I am certainly doomed to be an old maid. Never mind, I made up my mind to that fate ever since I was twelve years old. Write soon.'

Strangely enough, this young man was to die of tuberculosis six months later.

On 9 August, Charlotte in a panic scribbled a reply to Ellen: '. . . I really cannot go tomorrow – I could not get my luggage and myself to Leeds by ten o'clock tomorrow morning if I was to be hanged for it. You must write again and fix a day which will give me a little more time for preparation. Haworth, you know, is such an out-of-the-way place, one should have a month's warning before they stir from it. . . .'

On 14 August: '. . . I have in vain packed my box, and prepared everything for our anticipated journey. It so happens that I can get no conveyance this week or the next. The only gig let out on hire in Haworth is at Harrogate. . . . Aunt exclaims against the weather, and the roads, and the four winds of heaven. Papa does not say so, but I know he would rather I stayed at home, and Aunt meant well too, I dare say but I am provoked that she reserved the expression of her decided disapproval until all was settled between you and myself. . . .'

Every cloud vanished when the ingenious Ellen came to Haworth in a carriage to fetch Charlotte. 'Everyone rose into high good humour. . . . Charlotte's luggage was speedily prepared, and almost before the horse was rested, there was a quiet but triumphant starting; the brother and sisters at home were not less happy than Charlotte.'[1]

The two travellers were going to Easton, a little inland hamlet, three miles from Bridlington on the North Sea coast, to friends of Ellen's, Mr and Mrs Hudson, who worked a small farm there.

From Leeds to Selby, Charlotte was very excited at taking the train for the first time. The rest of the journey was then still done by stage coach. However, there were too many passengers for the stage and so the two friends had to go in a cab as far as Driffield, where they had an arrangement to meet Mr Hudson, whom they missed. He hadn't found them when the coach arrived and had left after arranging for a carriage to take them on from Driffield to Easton. So it was alone, and in a post-chaise, that they covered the last lap of this adventurous journey. From the top of a hill, coming near the coast, the sea was visible. Poor Charlotte, who did not have her glasses available, could not enjoy this marvellous sight. Ellen then began to describe it to her, but Charlotte interrupted her, saying 'Don't tell me any more; let me wait.'[2]

After spending a month in Easton with their kind and generous hosts, and their niece, Fanny Whipp – 'Little Hancheon' then aged eight – who won Charlotte's heart, the two girls, drawn irresistibly by the sea, went and took lodgings in Bridlington itself, where they spent the last week of their holiday.

Mr and Mrs Hudson fortunately kept an eye on them and, with their protective affection, came every day to see the two girls, who were inexperienced and rather short of money, and also brought produce from their farm.

1. Ellen Nussey's account. Clement Shorter, op. cit., vol. I, p. 169.
2. Ibid.

Charlotte never forgot the impression of beauty and power, of variety and boundlessness which the sight of the sea awoke in her.

Anne, more adaptable and more resigned, conformed more easily than Charlotte to the pressures imposed on them by their position. However, she was to be forced to give up, also, unable to continue an unsuccessful struggle with uncontrollable children without ill effects to herself. In the course of the year 1840 the three sisters were to be together again. For the present, Emily and Charlotte shared a task that almost completely monopolised them. Tabby, more and more crippled, had had to leave them and go to live with her sister in the village. They went to see her very often, making sure that their old friend didn't lack anything, and they refused to have her replaced. It was hard for them to give up hope of seeing her return.

Emily made the bread and busied herself in the kitchen. Charlotte was in charge of the housework and ironing. But, alas! that could not go on for ever. Duty was beckoning her more and more urgently.

'I intend to force myself to take another situation when I can get one, though I *hate* and *abhor* the very thoughts of governess-ship. . . .' she writes to Ellen on 21 December 1839. She was still obsessed by the need to leave home again and could not help saying to Henry Nussey in a letter of 26 May 1840: 'I am still at home, in very good health and spirits, and uneasy only because I cannot yet hear of a situation.'

In January 1840, Branwell had accepted a post as tutor in the family of Mr Postlethwaite in Broughton-in-Furness. A few weeks later he wrote to his crony, John Brown:

'Old knave of trumps . . . if you saw me now, you would not know me, and you would laugh to hear the character the people give me. Oh! the falsehoods and hypocrisy of this world! . . . What do they think I am? A most calm, sedate, sober, abstemious, patient, mild-hearted, virtuous, gentlemanly philosopher. . . . I take neither spirits, wine, nor malt liquors. I dress in black, and smile like a saint or martyr. Everybody says: "What a good young man is Mr Postlethwaite's tutor!" This is a fact, as I am a living soul, and right comfortably do I laugh at them. I mean to continue in their good opinion. I took a half-year's farewell of old friend whisky at Kendal on the night after I left.'

After describing his drinking spree at the Royal Hotel in Kendal, he adds: 'I found myself in bed next morning, with a bottle of porter, a glass, and a corkscrew beside me. Since then I have not tasted anything stronger than milk-and-water, nor, I hope, shall, till I return at Midsummer; then we will see about it. . . .'

How can one be surprised, even without any further explanations, to see him return by June, recalled to Haworth by his father, it is said.

Yet Branwell had not renounced his literary ambitions. It was from Broughton-in-Furness that he wrote to Hartley Coleridge, the eldest son of the great poet, Samuel Taylor Coleridge, submitting a poem, 'Harriet', and two odes of Horace which he had translated.

Was it the similarity of their destinies that thus drew Branwell all unaware towards that strange man, then aged forty-three, with snow-white hair, small and frail like himself? The same amazing gifts, the same childhood full of promise, the same weak nervous system, the same morbid sensibility, the same inability to face reality, the same need to take refuge in an imaginary world – that of Hartley Coleridge was Ejuxria – the same powerful, but mysterious force driving them to drink as an escape from life and its struggles. According to Mrs Gaskell, Hartley Coleridge's reply was favourable and Branwell met him in Ambleside, in the Lake District, as a second letter which he sent to the poet shows.

In all her leisure moments Charlotte returned in spite of herself to Angria with the same delight. After *Caroline Vernon* she undertook another tale or novel – only a few fragments of it are extant – and sent the beginning of it to Wordsworth. The letter which the poet sent her about it has not come down to us, but Charlotte's reply proves that she was not spared criticism: 'I am not so much attached to this but that I can give it up without too much distress. No doubt, if I had gone on I should have made quite a Richardsonian concern of it. I had materials in my head for half-a-dozen volumes. . . . I am pleased that you cannot quite decide whether I am an attorney's clerk or a novel-reading dress-maker. I will not help you at all in the discovery. . . . Seriously, Sir, I am very much obliged to you for your kind and candid letter. I almost wonder you took the trouble to read and notice the novelette of an anonymous scribe, who had not even the manners to tell you whether he was a man or a woman, or whether his "C.T." meant Charles Timms or Charlotte Tomkins.'

As is obvious, Charlotte grew bolder under the cover of anonymity. There is a great difference between her letter to Southey and this one.

Mr Brontë, undertaking on his own the diverse duties of a parish which had become too heavy, was tired and depressed, and had had to ask for the help of a curate. The life of the parsonage was transformed as a result. Charlotte, however, could never take these young men seriously: they were mostly artless, self-centred, almost always so narrow-minded as to make her indignant, and she has described them in *Shirley* with the rather unkind irony that she could not help using.

In spite of her pleasure at being at home, where she had plenty of leisure to create beings 'having no other antecedents than her imagination', Charlotte was looking for a post and it was becoming urgent. She had in vain asked the help of Ellen, of Miss Wooler; she had unsuccessfully replied to 'numerous advertisements'.

And yet it was harder than ever for her to leave the parsonage at a time when a new curate in the full glory of youth and good looks, and tender-hearted too, enlivened it with his dazzling presence. This year, 1840, when the three sisters were together again at home, was the liveliest, the gayest of their life. The Reverend William Weightman, with 'sun-coloured' curls, pink cheeks, blue eyes, not very robust, a little effeminate perhaps, just down from the university, too, but from Durham, had become a friend of Branwell's and of the sisters, who couldn't resist the teasing fun of calling him among themselves 'Miss Celia Amelia'.

Charlotte, attracted like her sisters but without any delusions, wrote to Ellen on 14 July 1840: '. . . I am fully convinced, Ellen, that he is a thorough male-flirt; . . . Sarah Sugden is quite smitten, so is Caroline Drury. . . . I find he is perfectly conscious of his irresistibleness, and is as vain as a peacock on the subject. I am not at all surprised at all this; it is perfectly natural; a handsome, clever, prepossessing, good-humoured young man will never want troops of victims amongst young ladies – so long as you are not among the number it is all right. . . .'

And on 20 August of the same year: '. . . Haworth is not the place for him. He requires novelty, a change of faces, difficulties to be overcome. He pleases so easily that he soon gets weary of pleasing at all. He ought not to have been a parson. . . .'

None of the young man's little stratagems were to escape Charlotte. 'He sits opposite Anne at church, sighing softly, and looking out of the corners of his eyes to win her attention, and Anne is so quiet, her look so downcast. . . .'

When the first signs of the consumption that was soon to carry off William Weightman showed themselves, Charlotte was overcome. '. . . . When he is well, and fat and jovial, I never think of him, but when anything ails him I am always sorry. . . .'

He had indeed been a charming companion – discreet, attentive, always anxious to give pleasure to these lonely girls who knew nothing of the joys of life. He had cleverly succeeded in organising a very decorous little jaunt to Keighley, so that they could hear a lecture he was going to give one evening on the classics. On 14 February, St Valentine's Day, he had walked ten miles to send each of them a valentine specially written, thus outwitting the watchfulness of Miss Branwell and Mr Brontë. He knew that it was the first time they had received such a token of friendship.

Charlotte had not been able to deny herself the pleasure of painting the portrait of the flirtatious curate, and it is enjoyable to imagine the exciting series of sittings that such an undertaking required.

Did he love one of the sisters? Was one of them in love with him? *Agnes Grey* seems to reveal that Anne loved him at first sight. But *Agnes Grey* is only fiction. The truth is that Anne, like her sisters, like Ellen Nussey, kept her secret. At this time, Charlotte tries to caution Ellen against a possible marriage that might disappoint her, be it with William Weightman or a certain Mr Vincent, who was timidly hanging round her.

With regard to the attractive curate, Charlotte paraded before Ellen's simple eyes the continual philandering which he practised with an amazing casualness. As for Mr Vincent, 'If Mr Vincent is a good, honourable, and respectable man, take him, even though you should not at present feel any violent affection for him; the folly of what the French call "une grande passion" is not consistent with your tranquil character.' In fact, Ellen Nussey never did marry.

In September 1840, Branwell was the first to leave home again. Charlotte announced this to Ellen in a playful tone that seems to hide her disappointment: 'A distant relative of mine, one Patrick Boanerges, has set off to seek his fortune in the wild, adventurous, Knight-errant-like capacity of clerk on the Leeds to Manchester Railroad.'

No doubt she was bitterly disappointed that Branwell, a brilliant boy and the pride of the family, should thus renounce the idea of making use of his outstanding literary and artistic gifts. And yet, if we think back to the year 1840 when the railway, still in its early days, was transforming the economic and social life of the country, the post of clerk in the booking-office at Sowerby Bridge station near Halifax, which Branwell had accepted when at a loss about what to do, might offer many prospects for the future.

Branwell's inability to submit to the demands of life destroyed any hopes of that. At Sowerby Bridge, as at Luddenden Foot, a smaller station to which he was transferred in 1841 and where he remained for twelve months, he began to drink whisky again to forget his disappointments and to avoid boredom.

Branwell, like his sister Charlotte, had grown no taller since he was fourteen. According to Grundy, a railway engineer who made his acquaintance at this time and who became his friend, 'He was really very small, which was one of his handicaps in life.'

12

Charlotte goes to the Whites at Upperwood, Rawdon – Plan to start a little school – Preparations for the stay in Belgium – Charlotte returns to Haworth

Charlotte was at last engaged by the Whites, who lived at Upperwood House in Rawdon, a village two miles from Bradford, and set out at the beginning of March 1841. She was to stay there ten months. On the day after her arrival, she wrote to Ellen: 'The house is not very large but exceedingly comfortable, and well regulated; the grounds are fine and extensive . . . my pupils are two in number, a girl of eight and a boy of six. . . . All I can say, therefore, is, both Mr and Mrs White seem to me good sort of people . . . my pupils are wild and unbroken, but apparently well-disposed. I wish I may be able to say as much next time I write to you. . . . No one but myself can tell how hard a governess's work is to me – for no one but myself is aware how utterly averse my whole mind and nature are to the employment. Do not think that I fail to blame myself for this. . . .'

At Upperwood House as at Stonegappe Charlotte had not a free moment. When, at the end of the day, she had finished with the children, she had to spend the evenings sewing, sewing, desperately sewing. Why could she not take up the pen instead of the needle and so lighten the chains of her slavery and calm the suffering caused by the separation from her family and her home? Yet she insisted on saying to Ellen that, in spite of all that, she was much better placed than at Stonegappe. 'The children are not such little devils incarnate as the Sidgwicks; but they are over indulged, and at times hard to manage.'

Delighted at having overcome her shyness and at having restored some of her real personality, she wrote to Emily on 2 April: 'I have got up my courage so far as to ask Mrs White to grant me a day's holiday to go to Birstall to see Ellen Nussey, who has offered to send a gig for me. My request was granted, but so coldly and slowly. However, I stuck to my point in a very exemplary and remarkable manner. I hope to go next Saturday. . . .'

Mrs White, whom Charlotte thought 'a good sort of body in spite of all her bouncing and boasting, her bad grammar and worse orthography', in the end revealed her real character: 'If any little thing goes wrong, she does not scruple to give way to anger in a very coarse, unladylike manner.'

Charlotte felt more and more ill at ease in this artificial world, although she did not fail to appreciate the good qualities of Mr White, a sensible, kindly man who went to the length of writing to Mr Brontë to invite him to come and spend a week at Upperwood House. But Charlotte was too proud to want to be indebted to her employers: 'I don't at all wish Papa to come, it would be like incurring an obligation.' Her homesickness for the parsonage made her write on 9 May to Henry Nussey: 'My home is humble and unattractive to strangers, but to me it contains what I shall find nowhere else in the world – the profound, the intense affection which brother and sisters feel for each other when their minds are cast in the same mould, their ideas drawn from the same source – when they have clung to each other from childhood and when disputes have never sprung up to divide them.

'We are all separated now, and winning our bread amongst strangers as we can – my sister Anne is near York, my brother in a situation near Halifax, I am here. Emily is the only one left at home, where her usefulness and her willingness make her indispensable. . . .'

Anne, no less than her sister Charlotte, had anxiously tried to obtain another post. In desperation, however unexpected it may seem, this shy girl who was nevertheless endowed with energy and resolution, had had advertisements inserted in the newspapers. And so, towards the end of March 1841, she had gone to the Robinsons who lived at Thorp Green Hall, two miles from Little Ouseburn, near York.

Charlotte was worried about Anne. She knew her strength of will, her patience, her powers of endurance, but she would have liked to know more about the state of her health and she was very disappointed that their holidays could not coincide.

From time to time their father and their aunt, feeling that they were all so sad at being separated, had suggested their starting a little school. Was it not, indeed, the best if not the only way for them to be together in pursuit of the same aim? This idea, which had long kept Charlotte going, was the grain of hope which she protected from adverse winds, waiting for favourable weather to make it germinate and grow. Was this not the moment? Would the cruel delay not make destiny relent?

But how were they to find the capital for this enterprise, however modest? Only their aunt could help. But Charlotte thought 'that she was the last person' to risk part of her money, the accumulation of her savings, on such a venture. Under the huge lace-trimmed bonnet, the severe yet kind face was softened. Miss Branwell proved her affection for her nieces better than empty protestations would have done: without waiting to be asked, she offered to help them. All they would have to do was find the house and the pupils. Many questions cropped up, many difficulties loomed. How could they solve these worrying problems?

'. . . I do not expect that Aunt will risk more than £150. . . . As to getting into debt, that is a thing we could none of us reconcile our minds to for a moment. We do not care how modest our commencement be, so it be made on sure ground, and have a safe foundation. . . .'

With little capital, no diplomas proving their knowledge of foreign languages, of music, drawing, etc., with no certificates to produce, how could they attract the children of parents all the more vain and demanding when their wealth was very recently acquired?

No doubt Charlotte had read a considerable number of French books. Between her stays at Stonegappe and at Upperwood House she had written to Ellen in August 1840: '. . . I have got another bale of French books from Gomersall, containing upward of forty volumes. I have read about half. They are like the rest, clever, sophistical, and immoral. The best of it is they give one a thorough idea of France and Paris, and are the best substitute for French conversation that I have met with. . . .'

No doubt Emily and Anne played the piano, but the three sisters knew that all that was insufficient.

It was then that Mary Taylor wrote from Brussels where she was staying with her sister at the home of friends. Her letters kindled Charlotte's imagination, revealing the way, the only way, to be followed. She wrote to Ellen on 7 August 1841:

'Mary's letter spoke of many of the pictures and cathedrals she had seen – pictures the most exquisite, cathedrals the most venerable. I hardly know what swelled to my throat as I read her letter: such a vehement impatience of restraint and steady work; such a strong wish for wings – wings such as wealth can furnish; such an earnest thirst to see, to know, to learn; . . . I was tantalised with the consciousness of faculties unexercised; then all collapsed and I despaired. . . . These rebellious and absurd emotions were only momentary; I quelled them in five minutes. . . . No further steps have been taken about the project I mentioned to you. . . . But Emily, and Anne, and I, keep it in view. It is our polar star, and we look to it under all circumstances of despondency.'

At length, Charlotte could wait no longer. She saw clearly that it only remained for her to tell her aunt of the important decision she had just made, on the pressing advice of Mr and Mrs White, and other people qualified to give it. Before opening a school with her sisters she must go and spend six months in Brussels with Emily – Anne would go later – to improve their foreign languages, so as to ensure their long-term success, for schools of this kind were numerous in England and competition formidable. Why Brussels? Because '. . . Martha Taylor is now staying in Brussels at a first-rate establishment there. I should not think of going to the Château de Kockleburg, where she is resident, as the terms are much too high; but if I wrote to her, she, with the assistance of Mrs Jenkins, the wife of the British Consul, would be able to secure me a cheap and decent residence and respectable protection. . . .

'I feel certain, while I am writing, that you will see the propriety of what I say; you always like to use your money to the best advantage . . . when you do confer a favour, it is often done in style; and depend upon it, £50 or £100 thus laid out, would be well employed. . . . Papa will perhaps think it a wild and ambitious scheme; but who ever rose in the world without ambition? When he left Ireland to go to Cambridge University, he was as ambitious as I am now. I know we have talents and I want them to be turned to account. I look to you, aunt, to help us. I think you will not refuse. I know, if you consent, it shall not be my fault if you ever repent your kindness. . . .'

Miss Branwell did not remain unmoved by this eager and eloquent appeal and her nieces Charlotte and Emily were able to make their preparations with hearts full of hope and gratitude.

Charlotte wrote to Ellen on 2 November 1841: 'Miss Wooler did most kindly propose that I should come to Dewsbury Moor and attempt to revive the school. . . . At first I received the proposal cordially . . . but a fire was kindled in my heart, which I could not quench. I so longed to increase my attainments. . . . Mary cast oil upon the flames – encouraged me. . . . I longed to go to Brussels. . . . In extreme excitement I wrote a letter home. I made an appeal to my aunt for assistance, which was answered by consent. . . . Dewsbury Moor is relinquished. Perhaps fortunately so, for it is an obscure, dreary place, not adapted for a school.' On 10 December following: '. . . My plans advance slowly and I am not yet certain where I shall go, or what I shall do when I leave Upperwood House. Brussels is still my promised land, but there is still the wilderness of time and space to cross before I reach it. . . .'

At last Charlotte left Upperwood House and the Whites. She returned to Haworth and let Ellen know on 10 January 1842:

'. . . I got home on Christmas Eve. The parting scene between me and my late employers was such as to efface the memory of much that annoyed me while I was there, but indeed, during the whole of my last six months they only made too much of me. . . .'

On 20 January she is happy to tell her friend: '. . . We expect to leave England in less than three weeks. . . . Our place of destination is changed. Papa received an unfavourable account from Mr, or rather Mrs, Jenkins of the French schools in Brussels, and on further enquiry, an institution in Lille in the north of France, was recommended by Baptist Noel and other clergymen, and to that place it is decided that we are to go. . . .

'. . . I considered it kind in Aunt to consent to an extra sum for a separate room. . . . I regret the change from Brussels to Lille, on many accounts, chiefly that I shall not see Mary Taylor. Mary has been indefatigably kind in providing me with information. She has grudged no labour, and scarcely any expense, to that end. . . . I have, in fact, two friends, you and her – staunch and true, in whose faith and sincerity I have as strong a belief as I have in the Bible. . . . I have had letters to write lately to Brussels, to Lille, and to London. I have lots of chemises, nightgowns, pocket-handkerchiefs, and pockets to make besides clothes to repair. I have been, every week since I came home, expecting to see Branwell. . . .'

13

Brussels – Madame Heger's boarding-school – M. Heger and his new pupils – Charlotte and Emily accept Mme Heger's proposal – Death of Miss Branwell – Departure for Haworth – Miss Branwell's will – M. Heger's letter to Mr Brontë

In spite of all the obstacles, destiny was to lead Charlotte to Brussels, where the great adventure of her life awaited her. Mrs Jenkins, whose husband was not consul, as Charlotte thought, but chaplain to the British Embassy, had, after careful enquiries, set her heart on urging them to come to Madame Heger's school, in the rue d'Isabelle, Brussels, of which she had heard very good reports. So it was there that Mr Brontë took his two elder daughters in February 1842 along with Mary Taylor and her brother.

They stayed for a few days in London, which Charlotte and Emily were seeing for the first time, and put up at the Chapter Coffee House in the shadow of St Paul's Cathedral, in Paternoster Row, a narrow paved lane closed to vehicles by a barrier stone at each end. There it was pleasantly quiet. The Chapter Coffee House was an old inn, formerly frequented by booksellers and publishers, and a meeting-place of intellectuals. Goldsmith and Dr Johnson had left the memory of their wit, their humour and their learning, and it was there that the letters of the ill-starred Chatterton were found.

Later, the inn was frequented by university men and clergymen and Mr Brontë himself had stayed there when, from Cambridge or Wethersfield in Essex, he had made short visits to London.

Since the last war, unfortunately, there is nothing left of these traces of the past and Paternoster Row is part of an area of reconstruction.

Charlotte dreamed of seeing pictures, statues and public buildings. St Paul's Cathedral made a very powerful impression on her.

After a very bad crossing, they reached Brussels. 'Mr Brontë took his daughters to the rue d'Isabelle, Brussels, remained one night at Mr Jenkins'; and straight returned to his wild Yorkshire village.' (G)[1]

The first letter, which Ellen Nussey received in March 1842, was from Mary Taylor, giving her a vivid description of the teachers at Kockleburg.

On 26 March, Charlotte then wrote: 'You will have heard that we have settled at Brussels instead of Lille. I think we have done well – we have got into a very good school. . . . Just now we are at Kockleburg spending the day with Mary and Martha Taylor – to us such a happy day – for one's blood requires a little warming, it gets cold with living amongst strangers.'

Madame Heger's school was very different from those that Charlotte and Emily had known in England. The street and the seventeenth-century house have now gone, but they still existed when Mrs Gaskell, before writing the *Life of Charlotte Brontë*, went to Brussels in 1856 and visited the school, being shown round by M. Heger.

'In the first [class] were from fifteen to twenty pupils; in the second sixty was about the average number – all foreigners, excepting the two Brontës and one other; in the third there were from twenty to thirty pupils. The first and second classes occupied a long room, divided by a wooden partition; in each division were four long ranges of desks; and at the end was the *estrade*, a platform for the presiding instructor. On the last row, in the quietest corner, sat Charlotte and Emily, side by side, so deeply absorbed in their studies as to be insensible to any noise or movement around them. . . .

'The principal bedroom was over the long *classe*, or schoolroom. There were six or eight narrow beds on each side of the apartment, every one enveloped in its white draping curtain; a long drawer, beneath each, served for a wardrobe, and between

1. However, a new fact, recorded by J. Lock and Canon Dixon in their recent book *A Man of Sorrow* (Nelson, London, 1965), shows that this was not so. A little notebook belonging to Mr Brontë has been found in which he wrote on p. 21: 'I went to Brussels, Lille, Dunkerque and Calais in February 1842.' He adds: 'I was away only two or three weeks.' According to the same sources Mr Brontë mentioned in a sermon after his return the pilgrimage he had made to the field of Waterloo.

each was a stand for ewer, basin, and looking-glass. The beds of the two Miss Brontës were at the extreme end of the room, almost as private and retired as if they had been in a separate apartment. . . .' (G)

Monsieur Heger, a master at the Athénée Royal, gave the French and Literature lessons in his wife's establishment. During the first weeks of Charlotte's and Emily's stay he had tried to get to know them. He had quickly realised their unusual personalities and extraordinary gifts. Emily's genius seemed to disconcert him.

He considered that to teach French to pupils so different from the others he must adopt a new method. So he decided to read to them selected texts of the greatest French writers, to analyse their qualities with them, and the faults, if there were any, in the hope that in this way they would be able to express their thoughts without the help of grammar book or dictionary, in a style that would show traces of that of the masters.

'After explaining his plan to them, he awaited their reply. Emily spoke first; and said that she saw no good to be derived from it; and that, by adopting it, they should lose all originality of thought and expression. . . . Charlotte then spoke; she also doubted the success of the plan; but she would follow out M. Heger's advice, because she was bound to obey him while she was his pupil. . . .' (G)

In May 1842, Charlotte wrote to Ellen: 'I was twenty-six years old a week or two since, and at this ripe time of life I am a school girl, a complete schoolgirl, and on the whole, very happy in that capacity. It felt very strange at first to submit to authority instead of exercising it, to obey orders instead of giving them; but I like that state of things. I returned to it with the same avidity that a cow, that has long been kept on dry hay, returns to fresh grass. Don't laugh at my simile. It is natural to me to submit, and very unnatural to command. . . .

'No less than seven masters attend to teach the different branches of education – French, Drawing, Music, Singing, Writing, Arithmetic, and German. All in the house are Catholics except ourselves, one other girl, and the *gouvernante* of Madame's children. . . . The difference in country and religion makes a broad line of demarcation between us and the rest. We are completely isolated in the midst of numbers. Yet I think I am never unhappy; my pleasant life is so delightful, so congenial to my own nature, compared with that of governess. My time, constantly occupied, passes too rapidly. Hitherto both Emily and I have had good health and therefore we have been able to work well. There is one individual of whom I have not yet spoken – M. Heger, the husband of Madame. He is professor of rhetoric, a man of power as to mind, but very choleric and irritable in temperament; a little black being, with a face that varies in expression. Sometimes he borrows the lineaments of an insane tomcat, sometimes those of a delirious hyena; occasionally, but very seldom, he discards these perilous attractions and assumes an air not above a hundred degrees removed from mild and gentleman-like. He is very angry with me just at present, because I have written a translation which he chose to stigmatise as *peu correcte*. . . . He asked in brief, stern phrase, how it happened that my compositions were always better than my translations? adding that the thing seemed to him inexplicable. The fact is, some weeks ago, in a high-flown humour, he forbade me to use either dictionary or grammar in translating the most difficult English compositions into French. . . . Emily and he don't draw well together at all. When he is very ferocious with me I cry, that sets things straight. Emily works like a horse. . . . The few private lessons M. Heger has vouchsafed to give us are, I suppose, to be considered a great favour, and I can perceive they have already excited much spite and jealousy in the school. 'Brussels is a beautiful city. The Belgians hate the English.'

Having come for six months, until the long holidays of September 1842, Charlotte and Emily had set to work furiously so as to get the most out of their instruction. They thought only of progress. And the prospect of realising their plan sustained not only them but also Anne who had bravely gone back to the Robinsons while she waited to be freed.

The results they achieved amazed M. Heger. No doubt no one ever suspected what this exile cost Emily, an exile which she endured in order to persevere in her resolve. The memory of her failure to stay at Roe Head and then at Halifax pursued her like remorse. To weaken now would have compromised not only her own future but that of her sisters.

It was very nearly the end of their stay. So that they need not abandon their very successful French and German studies too soon, Madame Heger offered them another six months' stay on new and special terms: *au pair*. Charlotte would take the place of the English teacher who would be dismissed and Emily would give music lessons at certain times.

'The proposal is kind,' Charlotte writes to Ellen, '. . . I am inclined to accept it. What think you? . . . Emily is making rapid progress in French, German, Music and Drawing. Monsieur and Madame Heger begin to recognise the valuable parts of her character, under her singularities.

'If the natural character of the Belgians is to be measured by the character of most of the girls in this school, it is a character singularly cold, selfish, animal, and inferior. They are very mutinous . . . and their principles are rotten to the core. We avoid them, which is not difficult to do, as we have the brand of Protestantism and Anglicanism upon us. People talk of the danger which Protestants expose themselves to in going to reside in Catholic countries, and thereby running the chance of changing their faith. My advice to all Protestants who are tempted to do anything so besotted as to turn Catholics is to walk over the sea on to the Continent; to attend Mass sedulously for a time; to note well the mummeries thereof; also the idiotic, mercenary aspect of all the priests; and *then* if they are still disposed to consider Papistry in any other light than the most feeble, childish piece of humbug let them turn Papists at once – that's all. I consider Methodism, Quakerism, and the extremes of High and Low Churchism foolish, but Roman Catholicism beats them all. At the same time, allow me to tell you that there are some Catholics who are . . . better than many Protestants. . . .'

Charlotte and Emily, daughters of an Ulster Protestant father, with all the bitterness that that implies towards their inveterate enemies the Catholics, and a strict Methodist mother, were Protestants to the heart's core. The Spirit, the real essence of the Church of Rome, eluded them completely.

Incapable of disguising the aversion and scorn they felt for those around them, they always kept to themselves, close together, silent, withdrawn, shy and frightened. Both oddly dressed – Emily persisted in wearing old-fashioned 'leg-of-mutton' sleeves, straight unbecoming skirts – they must have appeared very strange to this flock of young, blooming, Belgian girls, easy-going, full of laughter and coquetry.

With their heads full of what they were taught by the dynamic and zealous Monsieur Heger, whose pedagogic and intellectual qualities were so brilliant that they bordered on genius, they cared little about being laughed at. . . . To work under the direction of such a master thrilled Charlotte and gave her life a new zest. At this time Mary Taylor wrote to Ellen: 'Charlotte and Emily are well . . . they are content with their present position and even gay. . . .'

They accepted Madame Heger's proposition, and spent the greater part of their time during the long holidays working in the empty classrooms. Emily discovered the German Romantics; their world matched her own in which her interest was suddenly renewed as she avidly read *The Tales of Hoffmann*, who was to be her inspiration.

They did not live completely alone and cut off from company. Since their arrival in Brussels, they had been regularly invited by the Dixons, cousins of Mary and Martha Taylor, and by Mrs Jenkins whose persistent kindness was, however, discouraged by Emily's silent and impenetrable personality and by Charlotte's, more sociable and no doubt more adaptable, but too timid. Mrs Jenkins confided to Mrs Gaskell that these visits seemed to give them more pain than pleasure.

Most of all they saw an English family, the Wheelwrights, whose five daughters came every day during the holidays to have lessons at the school; one of them, Laetitia, who was then fourteen, became Charlotte's friend.

Seven or eight pupils who had not been able to go home also added some life and animation around them. And finally, they would join Mary and Martha Taylor to see Brussels and the surrounding countryside.

Alas, their interesting life of study could not continue to the end. They had received bad news at the beginning of the holidays: the charming curate, William Weightman, whom they secretly called Celia Amelia, had died on 6 September in Branwell's arms. They grieved deeply, and no doubt felt a sense of revolt at the idea that so many gifts, such charm, were lost for ever.

Next month, at the beginning of October, the lively, eager and happy Martha Taylor suddenly fell ill at Kockleburg Castle and died mysteriously a few days later. Charlotte was later to taste the bitter-sweet pleasure of bringing this charming creature to life again in the person of Jessie York in *Shirley*.

They had barely returned with Mary from visiting the girl's grave when more bad news arrived from Haworth: their aunt was very ill and they must return home quickly. The next morning, when they were preparing to leave, another letter announced hre death. They took the boat at Antwerp, travelled all day and all night but did not arrive until after the funeral. They found Anne and Branwell with their father.

Branwell was greatly shaken by these two deaths. We have evidence of his grief in a letter written to his new friend, Grundy, on 25 October 1842, in which he announced the death of William Weightman, 'one of my dearest friends', and he added, 'and now I am attending at the deathbed of my aunt, who has been for twenty years as my mother.'

On the 29th he wrote again: 'I am incoherent, I fear, but I have been waking two nights, witnessing such agonising suffering as I would not wish my worst enemy to endure; and I have now lost the guide and director of all the happy days connected with my childhood. . . .'[2]

Miss Branwell, who died at sixty-eight of an intestinal obstruction, was by her own wish buried beside her sister.

Branwell had had to return to the parsonage soon after Charlotte and Emily left for Brussels because the auditing of the accounts of his management of the Luddenden Foot station had shown that his ledgers, illustrated with charming sketches in the margins, were not accurately kept. He was probably sunk in despair when he once more faced his father and his aunt whose devoted affection he so ill repaid. To the thought of his guilt was added the humiliation, the incurable injury to his pride.

Nine years earlier, in 1833, Miss Elizabeth Branwell had made a will in favour of Charlotte, Emily, Anne and a fourth niece, Elizabeth Jane Kingston, not mentioning Branwell, her favourite. Her faith in him, her certainty of his brilliant future, had no doubt prevented her from leaving him a share in such a small inheritance. She left him only a little lacquer box.

However, small as it was, the legacy was for her nieces manna from heaven. Soon, they thought, they would be able to open a school. When they had recovered sufficiently from their painful

2. Clement Shorter, op. cit.

emotions, the three sisters, happy to be together, discussed the problem of the future calmly and wisely.

Anne, for the time being, would return to the Robinsons, where Branwell would join her in January 1843. She had praised her brother so much that the Reverend Mr Robinson had engaged him as tutor to his only son, Edmund.

The truth was that Anne, fearful for Branwell with his usual associates, hoped in this way to remove him from their evil influence. In spite of his faults, and his deplorable conduct, Branwell was still for his sisters the much loved brother, their pride and hope. Without hesitation, Emily decided to stay at home and resume her usual task by her father's side. What was Charlotte to do, torn suddenly from her studies, her reason for living?

The letter which M. Heger sent to Mr Brontë decided the matter:

'Saturday, 5th October, 1842.

'Sir, It is a very sad event which compels your daughters to return urgently to England. Their departure, while distressing us very much, has my complete approval; it is very natural for them to seek to comfort you in your loss. . . . I have not the honour of knowing you personally and yet I feel sincere admiration for you, for in judging a father by his children one is not likely to be mistaken, and in this regard the breeding and the feelings your daughters have displayed have indeed given us a very high impression of your qualities and character. You will be pleased to learn that your daughters have made remarkable progress in all the branches of our teaching and that this progress is entirely due to their love of work and their perseverance; we have indeed had an easy task with such pupils.

'In losing our two dear pupils, we must admit that we feel both sorrow and anxiety; we are distressed because this sudden separation cuts off the almost fatherly affection we felt for them and our grief is all the greater to see such hard work broken off, so many things well begun and requiring only a little more time to be brought to a successful conclusion. In a year from now both your daughters would have been completely equipped to face the uncertainties of the future; both were acquiring knowledge and also the skills of teaching. . . . Then we would have been able, if that had been agreeable to you, to offer your daughters, or at least one of them, a situation to her taste which could have given her that sweet independence so difficult for a young lady to achieve. It is not, believe me, sir, it is not a question of personal interest on our part, but of affection; you will forgive me if I speak to you of your children, if we concern ourselves about their future, as if they were part of our own family. Their personal qualities, their willing nature, their outstanding zeal are the only reasons which urge us to make so bold. . . .'[3]

3. Ibid., vol. I, pp. 248–50.

14

Charlotte's second stay in Brussels – Mme Heger's attitude towards Charlotte changes – Charlotte's isolation grows – Her confession in Ste Gudule – Her feelings about Mme Heger

The kindness and concern expressed in this letter from Monsieur Heger, the truth of what he said, quickly overcame their last hesitations and at the end of January Charlotte set out again, alone, for Brussels. It was an eventful journey.

Because the trains were late, once she reached London she had to get herself taken to the quay and hire a boatman to take her directly to the ship which was due to leave for Ostend the next morning.

'She described to me', relates Mrs Gaskell, 'pretty much as she has described it in *Villette*, her sense of loneliness, and yet her strange pleasure in the excitement of the situation, as in the dead of that winter's night she went swiftly over the dark river to the black hull's side, and was at first refused leave to ascend to the deck. "No passengers might sleep on board", they said with some appearance of disrespect. She looked back to the lights and subdued noises of London – that "mighty heart" in which she had no place – and, standing up in the rocking boat, she asked to speak to someone in authority on board the packet. He came and her quiet simple statement of her wish, and her reason for it, quelled the feeling of sneering distrust in those who had first heard her request, and impressed the authority so favourably that he allowed her to come on board and take possession of a berth. The next morning she sailed; and at seven on Sunday evening she reached the rue d'Isabelle once more; having only left Haworth on Friday morning at an early hour. . . .' (G)

At the Hegers' her modest salary was sixteen pounds a year, out of which she had to pay for her German lessons. Madame Heger offered to be present at her English lessons to ensure that discipline was maintained. Charlotte refused, feeling perfectly capable of keeping order herself, which she did in a dignified way without ever raising her voice, and with vigour and success: 'Where there is energy to command well enough, obedience never fails,' Jane

Eyre was to say when the time came for her to stand out against St John Rivers.[1]

As English mistress and supervisor of the First Class, she was henceforth, by M. Heger's orders, called Mademoiselle Charlotte. Her original terror when confronted by the 'insane tomcat', the 'delirious hyena' had been replaced by the enthusiastic admiration shared by all M. Heger's pupils, and by the marvellous delight of having discussions with this intelligent man who had taken an interest in herself and her sister to the extent of giving them private lessons. She thought with gratitude that he had opened her mind to unsuspected beauties and that he had revealed to her the art of writing, recommending plainness, simplicity and clarity.

On 6 March 1843, she wrote to Ellen: '. . . I am not too much overloaded with occupation . . . if I could only keep up my spirits, and never feel lonely, or long for companionship . . . I should do very well. As I told you before, Monsieur and Madame Heger are the only two persons in the house for whom I really experience regard and esteem, and, of course, I cannot always be with them, nor even often. They told me, when I first returned, that I was to consider their sitting room my sitting room also, and to go there whenever I was not engaged in the schoolroom. This, however, I cannot do. In the daytime it is a public room, where music masters and mistresses are constantly passing in and out; and in the evening, I will not and ought not to intrude on Monsieur and Madame Heger and their children. Thus I am a good deal by myself, out of school hours; but that does not signify. I now regularly give English lessons to M. Heger and his brother-in-law, M. Chapelle. M. Heger's first wife was sister of M. Chapelle's present wife. They get on with wonderful rapidity, especially the first: He already begins to repeat English very decently. . . .

'The Carnival was nothing but masking and mummery. M. Heger took me and one of the pupils into the town to see the masks. It was animating to see the immense crowds, and the general gaiety, but the masks were nothing. I have been twice to the Dixons. They are very kind to me. . . . When Miss Dixon leaves Bruxelles I shall have nowhere to go. . . . I have had two letters from Mary . . . her letters are not the letters of a person in the enjoyment of great happiness. She has nobody to be as good

1. *Jane Eyre* (Collins edition), p. 238.

to her as M. Heger is to me; to lend her books, to converse with her sometimes.'

By the tone of this letter, it is easy to see that Charlotte's life during this second stay in Brussels was very different. Emily, her constant companion, was in Haworth; Martha Taylor lay in the cemetery just outside the town. Her sister Mary was at present in Germany. Miss Dixon was about to leave Brussels; so were the Wheelwrights. And, finally, Miss Charlotte was no longer a pupil of M. Heger, but a mistress in the school run by his wife. Alas, the magic was broken, replaced inevitably by regret which gradually filled her solitude. The weather itself took a hand, for an arctic cold reigned through the whole of February and a great part of March, very hard on her delicate health. In spite of her stoical endurance, she felt deeply depressed. On 1 April 1843 she asked her friend Ellen if she was thinking of coming to Belgium and added:

'. . . I did not regret that you had not accompanied me. If I had seen you shivering as I shivered myself, if I had seen your hands and feet as red and swelled as mine were, my discomfort would just have been doubled . . . there was an observation in your last letter which excited, for a moment, my wrath . . . "Three or four people", it seems, "have the idea that the future *époux* of Mademoiselle Brontë is on the Continent". . . . They could not believe that I crossed the sea merely to return as teacher to Madame Heger's. I must have some more powerful motive than respect for my master and mistress, gratitude for their kindness to induce me to refuse a salary of 50 L. in England and accept one of 16 L. in Belgium. I must, forsooth, have some remote hope of entrapping a husband somehow, or somewhere. If these charitable people knew the total seclusion of the life I lead – that I never exchange a word with any man other than Monsieur Heger, and seldom indeed with him – they would, perhaps, cease to suppose that any such chimerical and groundless notion had influenced my proceedings. Have I said enough to clear myself of so silly an imputation? Not that it is a crime to marry, or a crime to wish to be married, but it is an imbecility which I reject with contempt for women, who have neither fortune nor beauty, to make marriage the principal object of their wishes and hopes, and the aim of all their actions. . . .'

In a letter to Branwell a month later, on 1 May, she wrote: 'I

Miss Elizabeth Branwell, *c.* 1835, presumed portrait, artist unknown

Ellen Nussey, drawing by Charlotte Brontë

hear you have written a letter to me. This letter, however, as usual, I have never received, which I am exceedingly sorry for, as I have wished very much to hear from you. Are you sure that you put the right address and that you paid the English postage, 1s 6d? . . . I heard from Papa a day or two since. All appears to be going on reasonably well at home. I grieve only that Emily is so solitary. . . . Are you in better health and spirits and does Anne continue to be pretty well? . . .

'As for me, I am very well . . . I perceive, however, that I grow exceedingly misanthropic and sour. You will say that this is no news. . . . Among 120 persons which compose the daily population of this house, I can discern only one or two who deserve anything like regard. . . . They have not intellect or politeness or good-nature or good-feeling. . . . I don't hate them – hatred would be too warm a feeling. . . . But one wearies from day to day of caring nothing, fearing nothing, liking nothing, hating nothing, being nothing, doing nothing. – Yes, I teach and sometimes get red in the face with impatience at their stupidity. But don't think I ever scold or fly into a passion. If I spoke warmly, as warmly as I sometimes used to do at Roe Head, they would think me mad. Nobody ever gets into a passion here. Such a thing is not known. The phlegm that thickens their blood is too gluey to boil. They are very false in their relations with each other, but they rarely quarrel, and friendship is a folly they are unacquainted with. The black swan, M. Heger, is the only sole veritable exception to this rule (for Madame, always cool and always reasoning, is not quite an exception). But I rarely speak to Monsieur now, for not being a pupil I have little or nothing to do with him. From time to time he shows his kind-heartedness by loading me with books so that I am still indebted to him for all the pleasure or amusement I have. . . . It is a strange metaphysical fact that always in the evening when I am in the great dormitory alone, having no other company than a number of beds with white curtains, I always recur as fanatically as ever to the old ideas, the old faces and the old scenes in the world below.'

Charlotte remained in the grip of her secret world in which, under the names of Marian Hume, Mary Percy, Mina Laury, she had lived, in her imagination, entirely for the Duke of Zamorna. Real life was now lying in wait for her, closing in on every side; how was she to exist in it without him! Was not the moment at hand when her unreal hero was inevitably to become identified with a creature of flesh and blood? What suffering that unconscious, that innocent transformation was to cause her.

Charlotte's dislike for certain mistresses, especially Mademoiselle Blanche, continued to mount: '. . . Mademoiselle Sophie', she wrote to Emily on 29 May, 'also dislikes Mademoiselle Blanche extremely. She says she is heartless, insincere, and vindictive. . . . Also I find she is a regular spy of Madame Heger. . . . Of late days, Monsieur and Madame Heger rarely speak to me. . . . I am convinced she does not like me – Why, I cannot tell . . . she cannot comprehend why I do not make intimate friends of Mesdames Blanche, Sophie and Hausse. Monsieur Heger is wondrously influenced by Madame, and I should not wonder if he disapproves very much of my unamiable want of sociability. He has already given me a brief lecture on universal *bienveillance* and perceiving that I don't improve in consequence, I fancy he has taken to considering me as a person to be let alone – left to the error of her ways. . . . and I get on from day to day in a Robinson Crusoe-like condition – very lonely. . . . In other respects I have nothing substantial to complain of . . . except the loss of Monsieur Heger's goodwill (if I have lost it). I care for none of 'em. . . .'

Though Charlotte, in her innocence, did not sense it, Monsieur Heger was beginning to take up a large part of her thoughts. He had been born in 1809, and was therefore only seven years older than she was. Married first at twenty-one, he had in 1836 married Mademoiselle Claire Zoé Parent, five years his senior. Soon after the arrival of Charlotte and Emily in Brussels the second Madame Heger had had a fourth child; the following year a fifth – which did not prevent her from keeping a brisk and very close control of her large school.

Mrs Gaskell says of Madame Heger: '. . . She was *dévote*, not a warm or impulsive temperament; she was naturally governed by her conscience, rather than by her affections; and her conscience was in the hands of her religious guides.' Mr Clement Shorter adds: 'She was an accomplished spy.' There could not have been greater antagonism than there was between her and the English girl who had a horror of the Papacy and whose frankness was obvious.

Being perceptive and very sensitive, Charlotte quickly realised the change of attitude in Madame Heger, who ceased to be agreeable, and became more and more aggressive. At first she was puzzled, then perturbed by this, and in the end very distressed.

On 6 August 1843, Charlotte complained to Ellen of her depressing solitude, which was soon to get worse. There was a sort of terror in her apprehension as she thought of the five-week holiday that was to begin in a few days:

'. . . Have mercy and don't blame me, for, I forewarn you, I am in low spirits, and earth and heaven are dreary and empty to me at this moment. . . . Alas! I can hardly write, I have such a dreary weight at my heart, and I do so wish to go home.' However, having made wonderful progress in French, as her admirable essay on the death of Napoleon shows, she decided not to leave Brussels until she had perfected her German.

'There was a great internal struggle; . . . and when she conquered herself, she remained, not like a victor calm and supreme on the throne but like a panting, torn, and suffering victim. Her nerves and her spirits gave way. Her health became much shaken.' (G)

It was in this dangerous state of mind that Charlotte endured the solitude of the empty school. Oppressed by the silence, she tried to find peace in long, aimless walks through the town, not returning to rue d'Isabelle until the evening, and then so worn out with fatigue and distress that she could not sleep. If sleep did mercifully come and allow her a few hours' respite from her anguish, she became at once the prey of frightful nightmares.

Later, in *Villette*, under the guise of fiction, she was to write unrestrainedly of these endless days and nights of which she dared not reveal the distress to Ellen, nor even to Emily.

In her letter of 2 September 1843, she told Emily how one evening, returning from a pilgrimage to the cemetery and a long walk in the country, she had been unable to bring herself to enter the school. Walking up and down the nearby streets, she had suddenly found herself in front of Ste Gudule, just when the bell was ringing for Benediction. She went in and joined in the service but still had not the courage to leave the church and go home to rue d'Isabelle. '. . . An odd whim came into my head. In a solitary part of the Cathedral six or seven people still remained kneeling by the confessionals. In two confessionals I saw a priest. I felt as if I did not care what I did, provided it was not absolutely wrong, and that it served to vary my life and yield a moment's interest. I took a fancy to change myself into a Catholic and go and make a real confession to see what it was like. Knowing me as you do, you will think this odd, but when people are by themselves they have singular fancies. . . . I approached at last and knelt down in a niche that was just vacated. I had to kneel there ten minutes waiting, for on the other side was another penitent invisible to me. At last that went away and a little wooden door inside the grating opened, and I saw the priest leaning his ear towards me. I was obliged to begin and yet I did not know a word of the formula with which they always commence their confessions. It was a funny position. I felt precisely as I did when alone on the Thames at midnight. I commenced with saying I was a foreigner and had been brought up a Protestant. The priest asked if I was a Protestant then. I somehow could not tell a lie, and said "yes". He replied that in that case I could not "jouir du bonheur de la confesse"[2]. But I was determined to confess, and at last he said he would allow me because it might be the first step towards returning to the true church. I actually did confess – a real confession. When I had done he told me his address, and said that every morning I was to go to the rue du Parc – to his house – and he would reason with me and try to convince me of the error and enormity of being a Protestant!!! I promised faithfully to go. Of course, however, the adventure stops there, and I hope I shall never see the priest again. I think you had better not tell papa of this. . .'

The tone here is very different from the one Lucy Snowe was to use in *Villette* to describe a similar adventure. 'I was perishing for a word of advice or an accent of comfort. . . . I had a pressure of affliction on my mind of which it would hardly any longer endure the weight.'[3]

Why did Charlotte in her distress yield in this way to a whim to confess? Had she begun to see her inner self clearly? Was she appalled at this introspection? In her innocence she was no doubt continually surprised by the secret torment that she felt increasing day by day.

But Madame Heger, instinctively on the defensive, watched

2. 'Have the joy of confession.'
3. *Villette* (Everyman edition), p. 145.

every hour and every moment, seeing Charlotte as a dangerous enemy.

In her letter of 13 October 1843, Charlotte wrote to Ellen: '. . . Madame Heger is a politic, plausible, and interested person. I no longer trust to her . . . one day, lately, I felt as if I could bear it [the solitude] no longer, and I went to Madame Heger and gave her notice. If it had depended on her I should certainly have soon been at liberty; but Monsieur Heger, having heard of what was in agitation, sent for me the day after, and pronounced with vehemence his decision that I should not leave. I could not, at that time, have persevered in my intention without exciting him to passion; so I promised to stay a little while longer. . . . I have much to say – many little odd things, queer and puzzling enough – which I do not like to trust to a letter, but which one day, perhaps, or rather one evening – if ever we should find ourselves by the fireside at Haworth or at Brookroyd, with our feet on the fender, curling our hair – I may communicate to you. . . .'

On 14 October, she wrote inside the cover of one of her textbooks (the *General Atlas of Modern Geography*, by Russell):

'The first lesson. I am very cold – there is no fire – I wish I were at home with Papa, Branwell, Emily, Anne and Tabby – I am tired of being among foreigners – it is a dreary life – especially as there is only one person in this house worthy of being liked – also another, who seems a rosy sugar plum but I know her to be coloured chalk.'

In November, Charlotte returned to the subject that was obviously obsessing her, and made a sort of appeal for help to her friend.

'. . . You remember the letter she [Madame Heger] wrote me, when I was in England? How kind and affectionate that was? Is it not odd? I fancy I begin to perceive the reason of this mighty distance and reserve; it sometimes makes me laugh, and at other times nearly cry. When I am sure of it, I will tell it you. In the meantime, the complaints I make at present are for your ear only – a sort of relief which I permit myself. . . .' Mrs Gaskell, reduced to silence by a discretion that was imperative with regard to Monsieur and Madame Heger and the Reverend Arthur Bell Nicholls who were all alive when she wrote *The Life of Charlotte Brontë*, tried to explain Madame Heger's altered behaviour by Charlotte's sometimes excessive frankness in her comments about the Roman Catholic religion, which could not fail to shock, even hurt, the devout Madame Heger. For the same reason, Mrs Gaskell did not refer either to the disconcerting incident of Charlotte's confession, which was to become a mine of varied interpretations for later biographers, dangerous ground on which one must venture cautiously.

15

Charlotte returns to Haworth – The boarding-school – Four letters from Charlotte to M. Heger – Failure of the boarding-school plan. Mary Taylor leaves for New Zealand

Towards the end of the year Charlotte received disturbing news; her father had become nearly blind, Branwell's conduct threatened the peace of them all. She felt that her duty was to return home and be beside her father and brother and share with Emily a task that was becoming too heavy.

This time Monsieur and Madame Heger yielded to the reasons she gave them. Monsieur presented her with a diploma bearing the seal of the Athénée Royal dated 29 December 1843, certifying that she was competent to teach French.

Charlotte let Emily know that she was returning for good: '19th December. I have taken my determination. I hope to be at home the day after New Year's Day. . . . Low spirits have afflicted me much lately, but I hope all will be well when I get home. . . .' On her arrival in Haworth on 2 January 1844, Charlotte was welcomed by the whole family, for Anne and Branwell were on holiday. On the 23rd, she wrote to Ellen, then in the south of England; '. . . Everyone asks me what I am going to do, now that I am returned home and everyone seems to expect that I should immediately commence a school. In truth it is what I should wish to do. I desire it above all things. I have sufficient money for the undertaking, and I hope now sufficient qualifications to give me a fair chance of success. . . .' But the three sisters, in the course of elaborating their grand plan, had not been able to avoid thinking of setting up in a place more suitable than their little village lost in the moors, with its formidable climate.

Now it was no longer possible to think of going here or there, to Burlington or elsewhere, and leaving their father alone. His stoical endurance in misfortune had inevitably affected his constitution. He was finding solitude hard to bear, and when his four children were away, he had perhaps let himself be led on unawares by self-indulgent curates to drink a little too much whisky. When she returned from Brussels, Charlotte, by lavishing on him her affectionate but firm attention, soon made him revert to his abstemious habits.

Forced to abandon their search, they could only plan to adapt the parsonage to accommodate five or six boarders. So they required time for reflection. At this juncture, in her letter of 23 January to Ellen Nussey, Charlotte returned to the thoughts that would not leave her:

'. . . I suffered much before I left Brussels. I think, however long I live, I shall not forget what the parting with M. Heger cost me; it grieved me so much to grieve him, who has been so true, kind, and disinterested a friend. . . . I was surprised also at the degree of regret expressed by my Belgian pupils when they knew I was going to leave. . . .

'I do not know whether you feel as I do, but there are times now when it appears to me as if all my ideas and feelings, except a few friendships and affections, are changed from what they used to be; something in me, which used to be enthusiasm, is tamed down and broken. I have fewer illusions; what I wish for now is active exertion – a stake in life. Haworth seems such a lonely, quiet spot. . . .

'Ann and Branwell have just left us to return to York. They are both wondrously valued in their situations.'

In April she wrote to her friend: '. . . Emily and I walk out a good deal on the moors, to the great damage of our shoes, but I hope to the benefit of our health. . . .'

In May she thanked Ellen for having asked her to go and join her in Harrogate, and kept her informed of what she was doing. '. . . I have seriously entered into the enterprise of keeping a school – or rather, taking a limited number of pupils at home. That is I have begun to seek in good earnest for pupils. I wrote to Mrs White, not to ask her for her daughter, I cannot do that, but informing her of my intentions. I received an answer from Mr White expressive of, I believe, sincere regret that I had not informed them a month sooner, in which case, he said, they would gladly have sent me their own daughter, and also Colonel Scott's: but now both were promised to Miss Corkhill. . . . I have written also to Mrs Busfeild, of Keighley, and have enclosed the diploma which M. Heger gave me before I left Brussels. I have not yet received her answer, but I wait for it with some anxiety. . . . As soon as I can get an assurance of only *one* pupil, I will have cards of terms printed, and will commence the repairs necessary in the house. I wish all that to be done before winter. I think of fixing the board and English education at £25 per annum. . . .'

While Charlotte was carefully making contact with various people, trying to make herself known, to inspire confidence, the memory of her master never left her. Absence revealed an anguishing void, and defined the nature of the feelings which then obsessed her.

If she no longer had the privilege of living under his radiant influence she might at least write to her master; did her gratitude not permit that?

So she wrote, and at first M. Heger replied, at long intervals, no doubt in order to give her support and comfort. None of M. Heger's letters have been preserved. They must have been destroyed by Charlotte or her husband.

It was thought for a long time that Charlotte's letters had suffered the same fate, until 1913 when in *The Times* of 29 and 30 July, some articles appeared with these arresting titles:

THE LOST LETTERS OF CHARLOTTE BRONTE
CHARLOTTE BRONTE'S 'TRAGEDY'

Four letters of Charlotte Brontë to Constantin Heger, which *The Times* published, had just been given to the British Museum by M. Heger's son, Dr Paul Heger, former President of the Academy of Medicine of Brussels, who hoped by publishing them to put an end to a legend.

'These letters', writes Dr Paul Heger, 'reveal the soul of the gifted author whose genius is the pride of England. . . . There is nothing in them which is not entirely honourable to their author as to him to whom they are addressed. It is better to lay bare the very innocent mystery than to let it be supposed that there is something to hide.'

Mr Angus Mackay[1] was right in the conclusion he drew: 'When this part of Charlotte Brontë's history is disclosed we shall pity her more, but I trust we shall not love or esteem her less.'[2]

It was also a happy occasion for Mr Clement Shorter to say: 'Charlotte Brontë is one of the noblest figures in life as well as in

1. Cf. p. 41.
2. *The Times*, 29 and 30 July 1913.

literature and the publication of these letters places her on a higher pedestal than ever before.'

The remarkable teacher, Constantin Heger, a very unpretentious man, absorbed by his various duties, must have torn up most of Charlotte's letters at once on receiving them. He was perhaps embarrassed at being the object of a cult of which he did not feel worthy. In his infrequent replies, he never failed to reproach Charlotte for her 'exaltation' and her 'black thoughts'. In the margin of the most moving of these four letters, this simple man had jotted down the address of a cobbler.

These letters, carefully repaired, had been kept with care. And so it was that seventeen years after the death of M. Heger, time having stilled the delicate scruples of his son and daughters, those who loved and admired Charlotte Brontë were to feel a profound shock at reaching the heart of her secret, now brought to life.

Here are some sizeable extracts from these four letters, which were written in French.[3] The first is dated 24 July 1844:

'Sir, I realise that it is not my turn to write to you, but since Mrs Wheelwright is going to Brussels and is willing to take a letter – I feel that I must not miss such a favourable opportunity of writing to you.

'I am very glad that the school year is almost over and that the holiday period is approaching – I am glad for you, Sir – for I have been told you are working too hard and that your health is a little affected as a result – that is why I do not allow myself to utter a single complaint about your long silence – I would rather remain six months without hearing from you rather than add an atom to the already too heavy load that overwhelms you. . . . Ah, Sir, I once wrote you a very unreasonable letter, because of the anguish gripping my heart, but I shall not do so again – I shall try never to be selfish again and, while thinking of your letters as one of the greatest joys I know, I shall wait patiently to receive them until it pleases and suits you to send one. At the same time I may surely write a short letter to you from time to time. You did give me permission.

'I am very afraid of forgetting my French, for I am sure I shall see you again one day – I do not know when or where – but it must happen since I desire it so much, and then I should not want

3. The translations of the letters which follow retain Charlotte Brontë's curious punctuation.

to stand silent before you . . . every day I learn half a page of French by heart from a book in colloquial style – and it is a pleasure to me to learn this lesson – sir – when I pronounce the French words I feel I am talking to you.

'I have just been offered a post as first mistress in a big boarding-school in Manchester with a salary of £100 – i.e. 2,500 francs, yet I cannot accept it – for accepting means leaving my father and that is impossible. – However I have my own plan. . . . Our parsonage is a fairly large house – with a few alterations – there will be room for five or six boarders – if I could find that number of children of good family I would devote myself to their education – Emily is not very fond of teaching but she would always see to the housework and, although a little withdrawn, she is too kind not to do all she can for the children's wellbeing – she is also very generous-hearted . . . so I have only to find the pupils – rather a difficult thing – for we live far from towns and people are not very anxious to cross the mountains which shut us off – but a task without difficulty is almost without merit . . . the very effort will do me good – There's nothing I fear like laziness – idleness – listlessness – lethargy of the mental powers – when the body is lazy the mind suffers cruelly.

'I would not experience this lethargy if I could write – formerly I spent days, weeks, whole months, writing . . . but just now my sight is too poor for writing – if I wrote much I should become blind. This weak sight is a terrible hardship to me – but for that do you know what I would do, Sir? I would write a book and dedicate it to my literature master – the only master I ever had . . . to you Sir. I have often told you in French how much I respect you – what a debt I owe to your kindness, your advice, I would like to say it once in English – I cannot – I must not think of it – the literary career is closed to me – only that of teaching is open – it doesn't offer the same attractions – it doesn't matter.

'Please give Madame Heger my kind regards – I am afraid Marie – Louise – Claire have already forgotten me. Prospère and Victorine never really knew me – I remember all five well – especially Louise – she had so much character – so much artlessness – so much truth in her little face.

Good-bye, Sir
Your grateful pupil
C. Brontë'

'July 24th

'I have not asked you to write to me soon, because I am afraid of intruding upon you – but you are too kind to forget that I desire it all the same – yes I desire it greatly – that is enough – after all do as you wish Sir – if I did receive a letter and thought that you had written it out of pity – that would hurt me very much. . . .

'Once again good-bye Sir it hurts me to say good-bye even in a letter – Oh it is certain that I shall see you again one day – I must – since as soon as I have earned enough money to get to Brussels I shall come and see you again if only for a moment.'

On 29 July, that is a few days later, Charlotte wrote to Ellen, letting her guess nothing of the tumult in her heart: '. . . Mrs Busfeild was exceedingly polite; regretted that her children were already at school at Liverpool; thought the undertaking a most praiseworthy one, but feared I should have some difficulty in making it succeed on account of the *situation*. Such is the answer I receive from almost everyone. . . .'

Charlotte did everything she could, but in vain, to try to persuade the parents of prospective pupils that the disadvantages of the isolated position of the parsonage would be an advantage: not only would the boarding fees be much lower than elsewhere, but she and her sisters would be able to devote to each of their few pupils a greater part of their time and attention.

After receiving certain suggestions, Charlotte fixed the cost of boarding at £35 per year, as too low a fee would only remove any chances they had of success. Then she had cards printed, not waiting, as she had first intended to, until she was assured of having at least one pupil.

August and September passed without any reply to her letters nor any request for information being sent to her. Who would have wished to come to this dull village, to live in this parsonage surrounded by gravestones, on the edge of a bare moor where at night the howling wind made you shudder?

On 2 October 1844, Charlotte thanked Ellen for all she had done to help them, adding: 'We have no present intention, however, of breaking our hearts on the subject, still less of feeling mortified at defeat. The effort must be beneficial whatever the result may be, because it teaches us experience and an additional knowledge of the world. . . .'

On 24 October she wrote the second of these letters to Monsieur Heger:

'I am very happy this morning – which has not happened often these last two years – this is because a gentleman I know is passing through Brussels and has offered to take charge of a letter for you which he will hand to you himself, or else his sister will, so that I shall be certain that you have received it.

'It isn't a long letter I am going to write to you – first I do not have time – it must leave at once and then I am afraid of boring you. I should just like to ask you if you got my letters at the beginning of the month of May and then in August? I have been waiting now for six months for a letter from you, Sir – six months is a long time to wait! However, I do not complain and I shall be richly rewarded for a little unhappiness if you will now write me a letter and give it to this gentleman or his sister who would give it to me without fail.

'Goodbye Sir I hope to hear from you soon – this thought delights me for the memory of your kindness will never fade from my memory.

Your very devoted pupil,
C. Brontë.

'I have just had all the books bound which you gave me while I was still in Brussels. I love *looking* at them – they make quite a little library – First there are the complete works of Bernadin de Saint-Pierre – the Pensées of Pascal – a volume of poetry, two German books and (what is worth all the rest) two addresses by Monsieur Heger given at the prize-giving ceremony at the Athénée Royal.

'Oct[br] 24th 1844.'

In November, Charlotte gave Ellen the following details: '. . . We have made no alterations yet in our house. It would be folly to do so while there is so little likelihood of our ever getting pupils. I fear you are giving yourself too much trouble on our account. . . . We are glad that we have made the attempt, and we will not be cast down because it has not succeeded. . . .'

The facts of the situation could not be defied. Gradually Charlotte, Emily and Anne had to give up the plan which had sustained them through so many difficult days. All the efforts and sacrifices they had made with a view to achieving it proved to have been useless. Was it not after all better that this was so? Gradually Branwell was going to turn their home into a hell to which Charlotte would no longer dare to invite even Ellen. What would she have done with her school boarders?

There is no doubt that Anne was cruelly disappointed. Although she had been very much appreciated during her three years at the Robinsons', her heavy task disheartened her and she was eager to come home to Haworth.

What was Emily's reaction to this lack of success? We may venture to guess that she felt a sort of liberation as a result.

For Charlotte, the defeat was hard. It removed the weapons she had been counting on in her struggle against herself, against an emotion whose increasing force was destroying her vital energy and creative powers just when all her circumstances were overwhelming her.

Her father's sight was deteriorating daily, plunging him into sadness, depression and anxieties.

'. . . I feel reluctant to leave papa for a single day,' she wrote to Ellen . . . 'I try to cheer him; sometimes I succeed temporarily, but no consolation can restore his sight, or atone for the want of it. Still he is never peevish, never impatient; only anxious and dejected.'

She herself was afraid of going blind also, as she confided to M. Heger several times.

Branwell's strange behaviour at Thorp Green was torture to Anne. His mysterious conduct when he was on holiday puzzled Charlotte and Emily and filled them with anxiety. They could not understand his eagerness to be away again and his changeable moods. He went from extreme excitement to deep dejection, from disturbing gaiety to dark melancholy and had sudden attacks of bad temper.

On 3 January 1845, in the third letter to M. Heger – Charlotte had been back in Haworth for a year – her bitter disappointment at having received no letter from him is freely expressed:

'Mr Taylor has returned, I asked him if he had not a letter for me – "No, nothing". "Have patience" I say – his sister will soon be back. Miss Taylor did return. "I have nothing for you from Monsieur Heger" she says, "neither a letter nor a message." I struggled hard to keep from crying, from being sorry for myself.

But when one does not complain, and when one wishes to control oneself like a tyrant, one's faculties rebel – and one pays for outer calm with an almost unbearable inner struggle.

'Day and night I find neither rest nor peace – if I sleep I have harrowing dreams in which you are always harsh, gloomy, angry with me. . . . I know that you will lose all patience when you read this letter – you will say again that I am over-emotional, that I have black thoughts etc. Granted Sir – I am not trying to justify myself, I submit to all sorts of reproach – all that I know is that I cannot – I will not resign myself to losing my master's friendship completely – I prefer to endure the most intense physical pain rather than have my heart always torn by bitter regrets. If my master withdraws his friendship completely, I shall be utterly without hope – if he gives me a little – very little – I shall be content, happy, I shall have a motive for living – for working.

'Sir, the poor do not require much to keep them alive – they ask only for the crumbs that fall from the rich man's table – but if they are refused these crumbs – they die of hunger – And I do not require much affection from those I love, I would not know what to do with a complete and perfect friendship – I am not accustomed to it – but formerly you showed *a little* interest in me when I was your pupil in Brussels – and I am anxious to keep *that little* – I value it as I would life.

'I refuse to reread this letter – I am sending it as I have written it – yet I have a feeling that there are cold, sensible people who would say on reading it "She is raving". As my only revenge I wish these people just one day of the torments I have suffered for eight months – then we should see whether they too would not lose their reason.

'One suffers in silence as long as one has the strength and when this strength fails one speaks without weighing one's words carefully.

[Here there are two lines crossed out by Charlotte and illegible.]

'I wish you happiness and prosperity, Sir

C.B.'

The imminent departure of Mary Taylor for New Zealand, where she was going to join her brother after the death of her father and the ruin of the family, added still another to Charlotte's sorrows. How could she but be sad at the departure, perhaps for ever – she had a sort of presentiment of it – of a friend like Mary, who, as Charlotte said, 'was full of feelings noble, warm, generous, devoted and profound. . . . She would *die* willingly for one she loved. Her intellect and attainments are of the highest standard. . . .' (G)

Mary, an understanding and attentive friend, and witness of Charlotte's solitary life during her stay in Brussels in 1843, had continually urged her at that time to return to Haworth. She now had doubts about leaving Charlotte, whose eyesight was very strained, her health more and more delicate: liver upsets, headaches, lassitude, lack of energy and strength. Seeing her, in addition, pining away with grief, disappointment, idleness depression, she made a final effort this time to get her away from Haworth.

'When I last saw Charlotte [January 1845] I told her very warmly . . . that to spend the next five years at home . . . in solitude and weak health, would ruin her. . . . Such a dark shadow came over her face when I said, "Think of what you'll be five years hence", that I stopped, and said, "Don't cry, Charlotte." She did not cry, but went on walking up and down the room, and said in a little while, "But I intend to stay, Polly".' (G) Staying was more difficult than leaving; so she would stay. That was her guiding principle.

On 24 March 1845, a few weeks after Mary's departure, Charlotte wrote sadly to Ellen: '. . . In Haworth one day resembles another. . . . I shall soon be thirty; and I have done nothing yet. . . . There was a time when Haworth was a very pleasant place to me; it is not so now. I feel as if we were all buried here. I long to travel, to work, to live a life of action. . . .'

Then Anne and Branwell were at home again, and Charlotte felt released. At last she was able to accept Ellen's invitation. She wrote to her on 18 June 1845:

'. . . Anne, I am rejoiced to say, has decided not to return to Mr Robinson's; . . . Then, dear Ellen, if all be well, I will come and see you at Hathersage. . . . I have no desire to see your medical-clerical curate. I think he must be like most other curates I have seen; and they *seem to me* a self-seeking, vain, empty race. At this blessed moment we have no less than three of them in Haworth parish, and God knows, there is not one to mend another. The

The moors near Haworth

The Reverend Arthur Bell Nicholls

other day, they all three, accompanied by Mr Smidt dropped, or rather rushed, in unexpectedly to tea. It was Monday (baking day), and I was hot and tired; still, if they had behaved quietly and decently, I would have served them out their tea in peace; but they began glorifying themselves and abusing Dissenters in such a manner, that my temper lost its balance, and I pronounced a few sentences sharply and rapidly, which struck them all dumb. Papa was greatly horrified also. I don't regret it. . . .'

On 23 July 1845, Charlotte, on her return from Hathersage, wrote to her friend:

'. . . It was ten o'clock at night when I got home. I found Branwell ill; he is so very often owing to his own fault. . . . When Anne informed me of the immediate cause of his present illness, I was greatly shocked. He had last Thursday received a note from Mr Robinson sternly dismissing him, intimating that he had discovered his proceedings which he characterised as bad beyond expression, and charging him on pain of exposure to break off instantly and for ever all communication with every member of his family. We have had sad work with Branwell since. He thought of nothing but stunning or drowning his distress of mind. No one in the house could have rest. At last we have been obliged to send him from home for a week with someone to look after him; he has written to me this morning . . . he promises amendment on his return, but so long as he remains at home I scarce dare hope for peace in the house. . . .'

In August, she confirms this: 'His bad habits seem more deeply rooted than I thought.'

In September: 'Branwell makes no effort to seek a situation and while he is at home I will invite no one to come and share our discomfort.'

Charlotte had hoped for a situation for her brother, but it was unfortunately given to someone else. So it is always the same refrain that she is forced to repeat to Ellen:

4 November 1845: '. . . Branwell still remains at home, and while he is here – you shall not come. I am more confirmed in that resolution the more I know of him. I wish I could say one word to you in his favour, but I cannot, therefore I will hold my tongue. . . .'

On 18 November, more and more dejected, in still greater distress, Charlotte wrote the fourth and last letter to M. Heger.

'The six months of silence have passed . . . so I can write to you again without breaking my promise.

'The summer and autumn have seemed very long to me; to tell you the truth I have required painful efforts to endure until now the privation I imposed on myself. . . . I must tell you frankly that, in the meantime, I tried to forget you, for the memory of a person that one thinks one must not see again and whom, however, one has a great admiration for, tortures the mind too much, and when one has endured that kind of unhappiness for one or two years one is ready to do anything, to find peace. I have done everything, I have tried to find things to do, I have absolutely forbidden myself the pleasure of speaking of you, even to Emily; but I have been unable to overcome either my sadness or my impatience – that is humiliating – not to succeed in controlling one's own thoughts, to be a slave to a sorrow, to a memory, a slave to a ruling obsession, which has complete power over one's mind. Why cannot I feel for you just as much friendship as you have for me – neither more nor less? then I would be so calm, so free – I could keep silent for ten years without any effort. My father is well, but his sight has almost gone – he rarely complains. I admire his patience – If Providence has the same calamity in store for me – may it at least grant me as much patience to endure it!

'Sir, I have a favour to ask you: when you answer my letter, say something about yourself – not about me for, I know, that if you speak of me it will be in order to scold me and this time I should like to see your kindly side; so tell me about your children; you never had a severe expression when Louise and Claire and Prosper were beside you . . . to write to a former pupil cannot be a very interesting occupation for you – I know that – but it is life to me. Your last letter was a support to me – nourishment for six months – now I need another and you will give it me – not because you feel friendship towards me – you cannot feel much – but because you have a compassionate soul and would not condemn anyone to long suffering in order to save yourself a few moments' boredom. To forbid me to write to you, to refuse to answer me will be to snatch from me the only joy I have in the world, to deprive me of my last privilege – a privilege which I shall never agree to relinquish willingly. Believe me, master, by writing to me you do a good deed – as long as I feel you are fairly pleased with me, as long as I hope to have a letter from you

I can be calm and not too sad, but when a prolonged and dreary silence seems to warn me that my master is drawing away from me – when day after day I await a letter and day after day disappointment comes to cast me into cruel despondency and when the sweet joy of seeing your handwriting, of reading your advice flies from me like an empty illusion, then I am feverish, I cannot eat or sleep, I begin to pine.

'May I write to you again next May. I would have liked to wait a whole year – but that is impossible – it is too long.

C. Brontë.'

[What follows is in English in her letter.]

'I must say one word to you in English. I wish I could write to you more cheerful letters, for when I read this over, I find it to be somewhat gloomy – but forgive me my dear master – do not be irritated at my sadness – according to the words of the Bible: "Out of the fullness of the heart, the mouth speaketh," and truly I find it difficult to be cheerful so long as I think I shall never see you more. You will perceive by the defects in this letter that I am forgetting the French language – yet I read all the French books I can get, and learn daily a portion by heart – but I have never heard French spoken but once since I left Brussels – and then it sounded like music in my ears – every word was most precious to me because it reminded me of you – I love French for your sake with all my heart and soul.

'Farewell my dear master – may God protect you with special care and crown you with peculiar blessings.

C.B.'

16

Concerning Charlotte's letters and her confession – Branwell and Mrs Robinson – Charlotte discovers Emily's poems

Charlotte's letters to M. Heger, her confession in Ste Gudule, have been interpreted in various ways. For some people, her letters are love letters, like any love letters, and in her confession Charlotte must have tried in a practical way to ease her conscience by confessing the forbidden love she felt for M. Heger.

'It seems far more likely, all things considered,' writes Miss Ratchford in *The Brontës' Web of Childhood*, 'that her confession, if it was anything more than a "whim", a "freak", as she herself declares, was an effort to ease her mind of a conflict far older than her acquaintance with M. Heger, and rid her conscience of the sin confessed in her Roe Head diary – idolatry, the worship of the creatures of her own imagination.'

'And yet', as Mr C. W. Hatfield[1] wrote to Miss Ratchford, 'it is useless to say that the letters are not love letters. They are; but they are just as certainly not the kind of letters that a woman writes to her lover.'

In them Charlotte expresses her emotions with an innate reserve coupled with profoundly moving spontaneity and naïveté. 'To discuss them', says the anonymous writer in one of the articles in *The Times*, 'one needs a purity of thought and language equal to her own; and one can only understand them if one remembers always that it is a particular woman, Charlotte Brontë, writing to a particular man, Constantin Heger. . . .'

Charlotte Brontë, with her ardent and passionate nature, could not live without having an ideal to love. In real life, into which she had now plunged, this ideal, this being of her choice was no longer the magnificent and imposing Zamorna, the born seducer, but a little dark man, short-tempered and fiery, transfigured in her eyes because he was the only man she had ever met capable of thrilling her imagination by the sweep of his intelligence, his brilliant conversational exchange, his power of stimulation, his

1. Cf. p. 156.

complete integrity, his lack of self-interest, his kindness, his naturalness.

What did she expect from M. Heger in return for her ardour? She said in her third letter: 'Sir, the poor do not require much to keep them alive – they ask only for the crumbs that fall from the rich man's table – but if they are refused these crumbs – they die of hunger.'

She said it again in the fourth letter: 'To forbid me to write to you, to refuse to answer me will be to snatch from me the only joy I have in the world, to deprive me of my last privilege.'

Nothing and no one at Haworth could compensate for this marvellous privilege of the unique friendship she had been favoured with. Her sensibility in its awakened state could not do without it.

'There can be no question here of "unrequited love" in the ordinary acceptation of the words,' said Dr Paul Heger in his letter of 1913, 'but, besides a warm display of gratitude and respect, of a rather despairing friendship and devotion, all-absorbing and passionate to an extraordinary degree, in revolt against undeserved unappreciation.'[2] When Monsieur Paul in *Villette* suddenly shows Lucy his undisguised friendship, Charlotte makes her heroine say what she must have felt herself for Monsieur Heger, who is himself Monsieur Paul: 'It seemed to me that life could offer nothing more or better. . . . I was become strong, and rich: in a moment I was made substantially happy. . . . If he would but prove reliable, and he *looked* reliable, what, beyond his friendship, could I ever covet?'[3]

Confronted by this silence of M. Heger, a man of principle – a wise, cautious silence, no doubt, but inhumanly cruel – Charlotte finally lost faith in the reliability of friendship. It was a painful ordeal for her and left her in despair.

> He saw my heart's woe, discovered my soul's anguish,
> How in fever, in thirst, in atrophy it pined,
> Knew he could heal, yet looked and let it languish –
> To its moans spirit-deaf, to its pangs spirit-blind.
>
> And once a year he heard a whisper low and dreary
> Appealing for aid, entreating some reply;

2. *The Times*, 29 and 30 July 1913.
3. *Villette* (Everyman edition), pp. 370–1.

Only when sick, soul worn, and torture-weary,
Breathed I that prayer, heaved I that sigh.

He was mute as is the grave, he stood stirless as a tower;
At last I looked up and saw I prayed to stone:
I asked help of that which to help had no power,
I sought love where love was utterly unknown. . . .

Now, Heaven, heal the wound which I still deeply feel;
The glorious hosts look not in scorn on our poor race;
Thy King eternal doth no iron judgment deal
On suffering worms who seek forgiveness, comfort, grace.

He gave our hearts to love: He will not love despise,
E'en if the gift be lost, as mine was long ago;
He will forgive the fault, will bid the offender rise,
Wash out with dews of bliss the fiery brand of woe.[4]

Whereas Madame Heger refused to see Mrs Gaskell who had come to Brussels to get information for her *Life of Charlotte Brontë*, Monsieur Heger received her graciously.

This 'kindly, wise, good, and religious man . . . has furnished me with some interesting details . . . of the two Miss Brontës during their residence in Brussels.' (G)

With a candour matching that of his illustrious pupil, he even showed her the famous letters which Charlotte had written to him. Had he ever understood their agonisingly intense and sublime passion? What an enriching light these letters would have shed on the book which Mrs Gaskell was about to undertake. But hardly two years had passed since Charlotte's death and Mrs Gaskell, who could not think of exposing her friend's private tragedy, merely quoted a few harmless and quite unrevealing passages of these letters.

Besides, was there not Mr Nicholls, always alert and cautious about everything concerning Charlotte's memory, which was sacred to him?

In Mrs Gaskell's opinion, the case of Branwell, whose dissipation and degradation were notorious, did not demand such reserve. 'The story must be told', she wrote. 'If I could, I would have avoided it . . . [but it is] so well known to many living as to be, in a manner, public property.' (G)

4. *The Professor,* edited by Phyllis Bentley (Collins), p. 410.

'Branwell, I have mentioned, had obtained a situation as a private tutor. Full of available talent, a brilliant talker, a good writer, apt at drawing, ready of appreciation, and with a not unhandsome person, he took the fancy of a married woman nearly twenty years older than himself. It is no excuse for him to say that she began the first advances. . . . He was so beguiled by this mature and wicked woman that he went home for his holidays reluctantly, stayed there as short a time as possible, perplexing and distressing them by all his extraordinary conduct . . . accusing himself of blackest guilt and treachery without specifying what they were; and altogether evincing an irritability of disposition bordering on insanity. . . .'

Eventually, it had all been revealed when, in July 1845, Branwell had received the letter from Mr Robinson, forbidding him in threatening terms ever to return to Thorp Green. His unhappy father and his poor sisters had been utterly shocked by it. 'The blind father sat stunned, sorely tempted to curse the profligate woman, who had tempted his boy, his only son – into the deep disgrace of deadly crime.' (G)

The Reverend Mr Robinson, that pale clerical figure, middle-aged and an invalid, died in 1846, about a year after Branwell was dismissed. His wife, Mrs Robinson, was therefore free and Branwell apparently was at once seized by a mad hope which was not to last for long.

'Mr Robinson had made a will in which what property he left to her was bequeathed solely on the condition that she should never see Branwell Brontë again. . . . She dispatched a servant in hot haste to Haworth. He stopped at the Black Bull, and a messenger was sent up to the parsonage for Branwell. He came down to the little inn, and was shut up with the man for some time. Then the groom came out, paid his bill, mounted his horse, and was off. Branwell remained in the room alone. More than an hour elapsed before sign or sound was heard; then those outside heard a noise like the bleating of a calf, and on opening the door, he was found in a kind of fit, succeeding to the stupor of grief which he had fallen into, on hearing that he was forbidden by his paramour ever to see her again, or, if he did, she would forfeit her fortune. . . .' (G)

During this sad period, Branwell first confided in John Brown, with whom he had gone to Liverpool, as Anne's note of Thursday

31 July 1845 reveals:[5] 'Branwell has left Luddenden Foot, and has been a tutor at Thorp Green, and had much tribulation and ill health. He was very ill on Thursday, but he went to Liverpool where he is now, I suppose; and we hope he will be better and do better in future.'[6] In October 1845, Branwell wrote to his friend Grundy:

'In a letter begun in the spring of 1844 and never finished, owing to incessant attacks of illness, I tried to tell you that I was a tutor to the son of ——, a wealthy gentleman. His wife . . . (though her husband detested me) showed me a degree of kindness which, when I was deeply grieved one day at her husband's conduct, ripened into declarations of more than ordinary feeling . . . although she is seventeen years my senior, all combined to an attachment on my part, and led to reciprocations which I had little looked for. During nearly three years I had daily "troubled pleasure soon chastised by fear". Three months since I received a furious letter from my employer, threatening to shoot me if I returned from my vacation, which I was passing at home. . . . I have lain during nine long weeks utterly shattered in body and broken down in mind . . . eleven continuous nights of sleepless horror reduced me to almost blindness, and being taken into Wales to recover, the sweet scenery, the sea, the sound of music caused me fits of unspeakable distress . . . I have striven to arouse my mind by writing something worthy of being read, but I really cannot do so. . . .'[7]

In another letter to the same friend Grundy, written the following year, in July 1846, he again recalls his wretched love affair: '. . . The gentleman with whom I have been is dead. His property is left in trust for the family, provided I do not see the widow; and if I do, it reverts to the executing trustees with ruin to her. She is now distracted with sorrows and agonies; and the statement of her case, as given by her coachman who has come to see me at Haworth, fills me with inexpressible grief. Her mind is distracted to the verge of insanity, and mine is so wearied that I wish I were in my grave.' To his friend, the sculptor, J. B. Leyland, he gives curious, often astounding details; he tells him

5. Cf. p. 51.
6. Clement Shorter, op. cit., vol. I, p. 306.
7. Ibid., p. 295.

that he had received a letter from Mrs Robinson's doctor: '. . . He knows me *well*,' he told Leyland, 'and he pities my case most sincerely, for he declared that though used to the rough ups and downs of this weary world, he shed tears from his heart when he saw the state of that lady and knew what I should feel. . . . She wandered into talking of entering a nunnery. . . .'

It is likely that all that was told and written by Branwell, a victim of opium hallucinations, was only a tissue of false dreams which he confused with reality. Mrs Robinson in any case found quick solace for a grief which no doubt existed only in the morbid imagination of Branwell. In November 1848, only three months after the death of Lady Scott, she married Sir Edward Scott, who was also provided with a comfortable fortune. Poor Branwell had died two months before.

To sum up, everything in this lamentable story is mere conjecture. What part did Mrs Robinson really play? Was Branwell really in love with her? Will one ever be in a position to answer these questions?

Mr Brontë, Charlotte, Emily and Anne believed at least a great part of what Branwell told them about Mrs Robinson. Accordingly, how could the father and the eldest sister have helped conveying to Mrs Gaskell their sense of outrage against the woman who, in their opinion, had been Branwell's evil genius, the cause of his misfortunes, of his downfall.

'Mrs Gaskell told Miss Ellen Nussey that she intended to revenge the wrongs of the Brontës upon "that woman" – an admirable piece of chivalry if she had been sure of her facts,' says Mr Shorter.[8]

Mrs Gaskell did not look at these events objectively but rashly adopted the Brontës' point of view without getting any more information and, in her *Life of Charlotte Brontë* she made a strong attack on Mrs Robinson. There were violent reactions: the lady, considering herself libelled, got lawyers to intervene with the threat of legal action. Mrs Gaskell had to remove the offending passages in the third edition of her book, and she published a letter of apology in *The Times*.[9]

8. Ibid., p. 14.
9. But not long afterwards, the passages suppressed in the third edition were reintroduced.

In that dreary autumn of 1845 Charlotte was weeping for her vanished hopes. For her, the future seemed a gloomy winter, with nothing alive or flourishing. She was obliged to stay with a father who was always depressed and almost blind, and to witness her brother's decline get worse daily. She could not forget what he had meant to her when as children and then as adolescents they had taken refuge together in the kingdoms of Glasstown and Angria.

Yet within herself she had what was to save her from despair. Her powerful imagination was at last to show what it was capable of, and ironically enough, quite simply because there were not five or six families willing to send their daughters to the Miss Brontës' school.

And so this failure was fortunate, bitter though it seemed to them. It opened up the possibility of a literary career, a possibility they thought they had relinquished.

In spite of her bad eyesight, Charlotte began to write again. And covering clean white sheets with her fine handwriting, she made slow but steady progress towards fame. She evoked the Brussels experiences by transposing them, deliberately imposing a restraint on herself which unfortunately destroyed her power.

Anne meanwhile set about evoking her recollections of life as a governess.

What was remote, reticent Emily doing? If Anne, who collaborated with her in the Gondal chronicles, knew that Emily was writing poetry, she did not know what it was like.

The three sisters, long separated, had not in fact been able to tell each other what they were writing as they had been in the habit of doing in the past.

While Charlotte was in Brussels and Anne and Branwell at Thorp Green, Emily, a gifted and prolific poet, was industriously completing her poetry and also writing a story in prose. Brave as she was, her brother's pitiful love affair overwhelmed her. She lived in her dream islands, calm and free, a wise virgin, uninvolved with love or hope, with her heart full of compassion for the suffering of her family. Neither did she lose patience with Branwell, although she had ceased to hope in him. In a note of July 1845[10] Emily wrote: 'I am quite contented for myself . . . desiring

10. Cf. pp. 50 and 51.

that everybody could be as comfortable as myself and as undesponding; and then we should have a very tolerable world of it. . . . I have plenty of work on hands, and writing, and am altogether full of business.'

What she was writing might have remained for ever her secret, but for a turning point in the literary life of the sisters, described by Charlotte in the biographical note to the second edition of the novels of Emily and Anne, published in 1850. 'One day in the autumn of 1845, I accidentally lighted upon a MS. volume of verse in my sister Emily's handwriting. Of course, I was not surprised, knowing that she could and did write verse; I looked it over, and something more than surprise seized me – a deep conviction that these were not common effusions, not at all like the poetry women generally write. I thought them condensed and terse, vigorous and genuine. To my ear they had also a peculiar music – wild, melancholy and elevating.

'My sister Emily was not a person of demonstrative character, nor one on the recesses of whose mind and feelings, even those nearest and dearest to her could, with impunity, intrude unlicensed; it took hours to reconcile her to the discovery I had made, and days to persuade her that such poems merited publication. . . . Meantime my younger sister quietly produced some of her own compositions . . . I could not but be a partial judge, yet I thought that these verses, too, had a sweet, sincere pathos of their own.

'We had very early cherished the dream of one day becoming authors. This dream, never relinquished even when distance divided and absorbing tasks occupied us, now suddenly acquired strength and consistency: it *took the character of a resolve*.'

17

The kingdom of Gondal – Emily's tragic genius

Thanks to Miss Ratchford and others who brought to light the little manuscripts of the Brontë children, we possess the chronicles of Glasstown and Angria by Charlotte and Branwell. But we know nothing of the prose chronicles of Gondal by Emily and Anne which, it will be remembered, were destroyed. The secret of the Brontës would therefore be only partly revealed had not Miss Ratchford, pursuing an arduous but thrilling task, and using all possible sources, succeeded after a quarter of a century in reconstructing the verse novel *Gondal's Queen*, by Emily Jane Brontë.

Only twenty-one of Emily's poems were published during her lifetime. More than two hundred were found in various manuscripts after her death. A few had been kept by Charlotte, then by her husband, the Reverend Arthur Bell Nicholls; others were discovered years later by scholars.

In 1910 Clement Shorter published the complete works of Emily Brontë in two volumes, of which the first was devoted to her poetry. Emily's poems had never before been published separately. But, because of the difficulty of deciphering the manuscripts – often tiny pieces of paper – and of separating them from Anne's, several poems which were not by Emily were attributed to her. This edition was revised by C. W. Hatfield in 1923; then, after fresh manuscripts were discovered, the same Mr Hatfield published the definitive edition in 1941: *The Complete Poems of Emily Jane Brontë*.

If nothing remains of the tales of the Kingdom of Gondal, the notes exchanged between Emily and Anne[1] prove that they had written an immense prose saga of which some of the titles: *A History of the First Wars, Gondal Chronicles, Augustus Almeda's Life, The Emperor Julius's Life,* were enough to convince Miss Ratchford that Emily's *Poems of Gondal* had their source in this material.

In her note of 30 July 1845, Emily in fact writes: 'My birthday – showery, breezy, cool. I am twenty-seven years old today. This

1. Cf. pp. 50 and 51.

morning Anne and I opened the papers we wrote four years since. . . .

'Anne and I went our first long journey by ourselves together, leaving home on the 30th of June, Monday, sleeping at York, returning to Keighley Tuesday evening, sleeping there and walking home on Wednesday morning. . . . And during our excursion we were Ronald Macaglen, Henry Angora, Juliet Augusteena, Rosabella Esmaldan . . . escaping from the palaces of Instruction to join the Royalists who are hard driven at present by the victorious Republicans. . . . I am at present writing a work on the First War. Anne has been writing some articles on this. . . .'

The next day Anne wrote: 'Yesterday was Emily's birthday. . . . Emily is engaged in writing *The Emperor Julius's Life*. She has read some of it, and I want very much to hear the rest. She is writing some poetry, too. I wonder what it is about? I have begun the third volume of *Passages in the Life of an Individual*.[2] I wish I had finished it. . . . We have not yet finished our *Gondal Chronicles* that we began three years and a half ago. When will they be done? The Gondals are at present in a sad state. The Republicans are uppermost, but the Royalists are not quite overcome. . . .'

A phrase almost unnoticed in the midst of simple details on the daily routine of the parsonage very much puzzled Miss Ratchford. This phrase appears in the journal fragment of Monday 24 November 1834, signed Emily and Anne, from which I have already quoted.[3] 'Tabby said just now Come Anne pilloputate (i.e. pill a potato) . . . papa opened the parlour door and gave Branwell a letter saying here Branwell read this and show it to your Aunt and Charlotte – The Gondals are discovering the interior of Geraldine [*sic*.].[4] Sally Mosley is washing in the back-kitchin [*sic*.].'

What was the meaning of 'The Gondals are discovering the interior of Gaaldine'? It was the first hint of the existence of the 'play' of Gondal.

Miss Ratchford tirelessly searched, collated, fitted parts together and finally grew convinced that Emily's Gondal poems formed a whole. She has tried to reconstitute the history of Gondal

2. This novel was published under the title of *Agnes Grey*.
3. Cf. p. 50.
4. The MS transcript 'Geraldine' was later seen by Miss Ratchford to be a mistaken reading of the handwritten 'Gaaldine'.

in *Gondal's Queen*,[5] making use of eighty-four poems presented for the first time in a logical order. They reveal an island beleaguered by tumultuous waves, a land of 'mists and moorlands drear' with 'twilight noons and evenings dark' while the long heavy winter lasts; an enchanting land in the sunshine of a summer that is all too short.

I've seen this dell in July's shine
As lovely as an angel's dream;

. . . . .

I've seen the purple heather bell
Look out by many a storm-worn stone;

– a mountainous region furrowed by rivers, studded with beautiful romantic lakes. It is on the shores of the lakes Elderno and Elnor or Elmor, framed in the heather and steep rocks of Elnor Moor that the heroes of Gondal, with their powerful, unbridled passions, their unquenchable hates, come to sigh for love, to breathe their lamentations, to commit their darkest crimes.

Emily was a child of the moors, and it was the moors that inspired her poetry.[6] Here and there in her poems, Emily, who was otherwise so inscrutable, reveals aspects of her philosophy and her beliefs with a simple and frank sincerity.

In the kingdom of Gondal, contrary to what happened in Charlotte and Branwell's kingdom of Angria, evil does not escape punishment. Augusta Geraldine Almeda, the guilty queen cries:

Yet thou a future peace shalt win
Because thy soul is clear;
And I who had the heart to sin
Will find a heart to bear. . . .

Yet Emily believed with all her heart and energy in a God of love who pities his creatures. Fernando de Samara of Areon Hall utters this cry of anguish:

5. *Gondal's Queen*, edited by Fannie Ratchford (University of Texas Press/Nelson, 1955).
6. See Appendix III.

Shall those long, agonising years
Be punished by eternal tears?
No; *that* I feel can never be;
A God of *hate* could hardly bear
To watch through all eternity
His own creations dread despair!

Emily could not live without freedom. She discovered, too, in the course of her meditations that to be truly free one must renounce everything.

A messenger of Hope comes every night to me,
And offers, for short life, eternal liberty.

These lines are quoted from *The Prisoner*.

Emily, 'a mystic, not by religious vocation, but by temperament' as May Sinclair describes her, is the 'prisoner' who escapes in dream and vision. She refers to the spirit with which she is in communion in suggestive but vague terms, such as 'the Invisible' and 'the Unknown'. But in the poem, 'O thy bright eyes must answer now', she addresses the 'God of Visions' in her own name, thus projecting a stream of light on her unique personality.

No, radiant angel, speak and say
Why I did cast the world away;

Why I have persevered to shun
The common paths that others run;
And on a strange road journeyed on
Heedless alike of Wealth and Power –
Of Glory's wreath and Pleasure's flower.

. . . . .

And gave my spirit to adore
Thee, ever present, phantom thing –
My slave, my comrade, and my King!

. . . . .

And am I wrong to worship where
Faith cannot doubt nor Hope despair
Since my own soul can grant my prayer?
Speak God of Visions, plead for me
And tell why I have chosen thee!

On 2 January 1846, two years before her death, Emily wrote this splendid poem in which she puts an affirmation of her faith into the mouth of a citizen of Gondal:

> No coward soul is mine
> No trembler in the world's storm-troubled sphere
> I see Heaven's glories shine
> And Faith shines equal arming me from Fear . . .
>
> Vain are the thousand creeds
> That move men's hearts, unutterably vain,
> Worthless as withered weeds
> Or idlest froth amid the boundless main
>
> To waken doubt in one
> Holding so fast by thy infinity
> So surely anchored on
> The steadfast rock of Immortality. . . .

As the Abbé Dimnet says very sensitively in *The Brontë Sisters*, Death had no terrors for her. 'The many passages in which she evokes ideas of the grave are invariably peaceful, and what is horrible becomes charming by the grace of her rhythm – without dread she sees "The time when my sunny hair shall with grass roots entwined be".

'Believer or pantheist, and probably both at the same time, she faces the greatest problems with serenity.'[7]

Gondal's Queen, like *Wuthering Heights*, shows that Emily possessed a wonderful sense of the tragic. What could she do with it in her simple monotonous life? It became quite naturally the leaven of her writing. 'Unequalled in power, in passion, in vehemence', as Matthew Arnold says, she was unequalled in imagination. In the grip of that astounding imagination, Emily wrote the *Gondal Poems* and *Wuthering Heights*, 'in much the same way as she wrote the *Plays* of their childhood, in which fantasy, the sole creator of their world, took no account of the constraints that operate in real life.'[8]

7. Ernest Dimnet, *The Brontë Sisters,* trans. Louise Morgan Gill (Cape, London, 1910), p. 83.
8. C. Maurat, Preface to translation of *Jane Eyre* (Livre de Poche, Paris).

Emily's very unusual nature could not in fact give free rein to her passionate aspirations, except in a dimension of phantasy, completely unrestricted, and completely artless. Emily 'offers the apparent anomaly of extreme detachment and of an unconquerable love of life,' writes Miss May Sinclair.

'It was the highest and the purest passion that you can well conceive, for life gave her nothing in return. . . . She had . . . neither praise nor fame in her lifetime, nor friendship, nor love, nor visions of love. All these things "passed her by with averted head"; and she stood in her inviolable serenity. . . . It is this superb attitude to life, this independence of the material event, this detachment from the stream of circumstance, that marks her from her sister . . . it was through her personal destitution that her genius was so virile and so rich,' and, I might add, so original and so pure. In her terrible, cruel writing there is freshness and innocence and something elemental. 'A wind keen with the tang of virgin snow blows through its pages.'[9]

9. Lord David Cecil, *Early Victorian Novelists* (Penguin), p. 135.

18

A plan to publish the three sisters' poems – Mr Brontë and his new curate – In search of a publisher for The Professor, Wuthering Heights *and* Agnes Grey *– Mr Brontë in Manchester – Charlotte begins to write* Jane Eyre *– The winter of 1846–7*

Charlotte's acute critical sense had immediately recognised the stamp of genius in Emily's wonderful poems. But 'it took days to persuade her that such poems merited publication'.[1]

While Charlotte, Branwell and even Anne had continued to cherish the dream of a writing career, Emily, absorbed by her world of Gondal, which merged for her into her own existence, was self-sufficient, and felt not the slightest desire to make contact with a public. She had never written, as the two older ones had done, to a famous poet to ask for his opinion.

However Charlotte was made more determined by her feeling of despair. Was this not the last card they had to play? She knew she could withstand any attack, overcome any obstacle. Her irresistible strength would prevail over Emily's stubbornness and prove her sister's confidence in her.

'I knew, however, that a mind like hers could not be without some latent spark of honourable ambition, and refused to be discouraged in my attempts to fan that spark to flame. . . .

'We agreed to arrange a small selection of our poems, and, if possible, to get them printed. . . .'[2] They decided that each of them would send twenty-one poems which they duly selected and carefully copied out.

Emily, according to Miss Ratchford, chose fifteen poems which had no indication of their origin from an untitled notebook dated 1844, and six others from the Gondal poems. She replaced the strange names of the Gondal heroes and their kingdoms and towns, which served to identify the poems, by more ordinary, more English names.

1. Charlotte Brontë's biographical notice, reprinted in Everyman edition of *Wuthering Heights*.
2. Ibid.

Perhaps Charlotte and Anne were afraid of the idea of having to make similar modifications; for Charlotte did not choose any Angrian poems, nor Anne any of her Gondal ones, which put them at a disadvantage, for these poems contained the best work of both of them.

'Averse to personal publicity, we veiled our names under those of Currer, Ellis and Acton Bell; the ambiguous choice being dictated by a sort of conscientious scruple at assuming Christian names positively masculine, while we did not like to declare ourselves women because . . . we had a vague impression that authoresses are liable to be looked on with prejudice. . . . The bringing out of our little book was hard work. . . . The great puzzle lay in getting answers of any kind from the publishers to whom we applied.'[3]

Charlotte, who took charge of the whole business, wrote finally to Messrs Chambers, the Edinburgh publishers, for advice and at their suggestion applied to Aylott & Jones, 8 Paternoster Row, London.

On 28 January 1846, she addressed her first letter to them.

'Gentlemen, may I request to be informed whether you would undertake the publication of a collection of short poems in one volume, 8vo.

'If you object to publishing the work at your own risk, would you undertake it on the author's account?'

After receiving their reply, she wrote to them again on 31 January. 'Since you agree to undertake the publication of the work respecting which I applied to you, I should wish now to know, as soon as possible, the cost of paper and printing. I will then send the necessary remittance, together with the manuscript. . . . The poems will occupy, I should think, from 200–250 pages. They are not the production of a clergyman, nor are they exclusively of a religious character. . . .'

So began between Charlotte and Messrs Aylott & Jones a correspondence which revolutionised the calm parsonage, without however alerting the attention of Mr Brontë, who was almost blind, or of Tabby, who was ill.

As Charlotte knew nothing about publishing, she bought a manual on it and studied it, so that she was soon able to give

3. Ibid., p. 209.

Messrs Aylott & Jones instructions about the choice of type, size of page, and so forth. She felt she must carry out the enterprise successfully, since she had assumed the initiative and the responsibility for it. Their aunt's money was precious and must be wisely used. What a sure inspiration Miss Branwell had had in bequeathing the little inheritance only to her nieces, for it allowed them to realise this great dream.

The correspondence continued between Charlotte and the publisher of Currer, Ellis and Acton Bell. '6th February, 1846. . . . You will perceive that the poems are the work of three persons, relatives. . . .'

'16th February, 1846. . . . The MS will certainly form a thinner volume than I had anticipated. . . . I only stipulate for *clear* type, not too small, and good paper.'

'3rd March, 1846. . . . I send you a draft for £31,10sh, being the amount of your estimate. I suppose there is nothing now to prevent your immediately commencing the printing of the work. When you acknowledge the receipt of the draft, will you state how soon it will be completed?'

Soon they had to correct the proofs of their poems. It was something tangible at last, and exciting as well, but they could not speak of it to anyone, not even their father, until they knew whether success would crown their undertaking. When Charlotte went to visit Ellen Nussey, in whom she had complete confidence, she nevertheless breathed not a word to her of all this adventure. On returning to Haworth she wrote to her friend:

'3rd March, 1846. . . . I reached home a little after two o'clock. . . . I found papa very well, his sight much the same. . . . I went into the room where Branwell was, to speak to him, about an hour after I got home. . . . I might have spared myself the trouble, as he took no notice, and made no reply; he was stupified. My fears were not in vain. I hear that he had got a sovereign from papa while I had been away, under pretence of paying a pressing debt; he went immediately and changed it at a public-house, and has employed it as was to be expected. Emily concluded her account by saying he was a hopeless being; it is too true. In his present state, it is scarcely possible to stay in the room where he is. What the future has in store I do not know. . . .'

On 23 March 1846, Charlotte asked her publishers to address both letters and proofs in future to her in her proper name: Miss

Brontë, and no longer to C. Brontë, Esq., 'a little mistake having occurred yesterday'; but she gave them to understand that she was not acting on her own behalf but on that of the authors.

On 6 April she wrote once more to her publishers: 'C., E., and A. Bell are now preparing for the press a work of fiction, consisting of three distinct and unconnected tales. . . .

'It is not their intention to publish these tales on their own account. They direct me to ask you whether you would be disposed to undertake the work after having, of course, by due inspection of the MS, ascertained that its contents are such as to warrant an expectation of success. . . .' The publishers' answer came without delay: it was a refusal, but followed by valuable advice. On 11 April, Charlotte thanked them 'in the name of C. E., and A. Bell for your obliging offer of advice', and asked for particulars of what should be done.

Aylott & Jones were booksellers rather than publishers, and had only published the occasional classical or theological work, never works of fiction. However, theirs is the honour of having published the first book by Charlotte and her sisters; this collection of their poems.

As the publication date drew near, there was another letter: 'Have the goodness to send copies and advertisements, as *early as possible* to each of the under mentioned periodicals:

Colburn's New Monthly Magazine
Bentley's Magazine
Hood's Magazine
Jerrold's Magazine
Blackwood's Magazine
The Edinburgh Review
Tait's Edinburgh Magazine
The Dublin University Magazine

and then also to the newspapers, such as *The Daily News* and the *Britannia*.'

Messrs Aylott & Jones then suggested also sending copies and advertisements to *The Athenaeum*, *The Literary Gazette*, *The Critic* and *The Times*.

Charlotte had complete confidence in her publishers, who deserved it, and she conscientiously fell in with their advice.

However, the printing cost of the poems had been increased by five pounds through a miscalculation and she wrote to them on 11 May: 'I think the periodicals I mentioned in my last will be sufficient for advertising at present. . . .' She did not want to spend more than two pounds on publicity. The little volume was due to appear towards the end of May. And one can only marvel at the speed with which the enterprise was carried out.

'In *The Athenaeum* of July 4th, 1846 . . . came a short review of the poems of C., E., and A. Bell. The reviewer assigns to Ellis (Emily) the highest rank of the three "brothers", as he supposes them to be; he calls Ellis "a fine, quaint spirit"; and speaks of "an evident power of wing that may reach heights not here attempted". . . . Currer Bell (Charlotte) is placed midway between Ellis and Acton.' (G)

The complimentary criticism of the *Dublin University Magazine* and of *The Critic* must also have cheered the three sisters.

But a year later, on 16 June 1847, Currer Bell wrote to Thomas de Quincey: 'In the space of a year our publisher has disposed but of two copies, and by what painful efforts he succeeded in getting rid of these two, himself only knows.'

This new set-back did not shake their resolve. One would rather have said that they overcame their destiny by submitting to it and that their courage was spurred on rather than cowed by their disappointment. With decision, perseverance and an unquenchable hope, they became absorbed in their novels, so quieting their spirits, a prey to many torments. And so it was that *The Professor*, *Wuthering Heights* and *Agnes Grey* progressed towards conclusion.

Their father, although wonderfully patient and resigned, suffered greatly from the limitations forced on him. Although he could no longer read and write, he could still preach, if taken to church and led up into the pulpit. He had such a keen sense of time that, however carried away he might be by the power of his oratory, he never failed to finish at the exact moment when the hand of the clock face on which his faded eyes were fixed marked the end of the thirty minutes allocated to his sermons.

The curate who was then helping him had been appointed to Haworth in 1844, two years earlier. A few days after his arrival, Charlotte had written to Ellen: 'Papa has got a new curate lately, a Mr Nicholls from Ireland. He did duty for the first time on

Sunday – he appears a respectable young man, reads well, and I hope will give satisfaction.'

Mr Arthur Bell Nicholls was 'the very same gentleman to whom, eight years afterwards, she was united; and who probably, even now, although she was unconscious of the fact, had begun his service to her, in the same tender and faithful spirit as that in which Jacob served for Rachel. . . .' (G)

Charlotte, as circumstances arose, was to confide in Ellen what she thought of him. For example, on 22 October 1844: '. . . Mr Nicholls is returned [from Ireland] just the same; I cannot for my life see those interesting germs of goodness in him you discovered; his narrowness of mind always strikes me chiefly. I fear he is indebted to your imagination for his hidden treasure. . . .'

If Charlotte and her sisters suffered to see their father's sore trials, Branwell's behaviour was torture to them. Charlotte admits it to Ellen on 17 June 1846: '. . . The death of Mr Robinson, which took place about three weeks or a month ago, served Branwell for a pretext to throw all about him into hubbub and confusion with his emotions etc, etc. . . . To Papa he allows rest neither day nor night, and he is continually screwing money out of him, sometimes threatening to kill himself if it is withheld from him. He says Mrs Robinson is now insane. . . . I do not know how much to believe of what he says, but I fear she is very ill . . . good situations have been offered him more than once . . . but he will do nothing, except drink and make us all wretched. . . .'

In July 1846, Ellen had grave problems; could she go and be a governess and thus earn her living or was she to stay at Brookroyd and look after her aged mother? Where did her duty lie? '. . . The right path to follow', writes Charlotte, 'is that which necessitates the greatest sacrifice of self-interest – which implies the greatest good of others. . . . I recommend you to do what I am trying to do myself. Who gravely asked you whether Miss Brontë was not going to be married to her Papa's Curate? I scarcely need say that never was rumour more un-founded. A cold far-away sort of civility are the only terms on which I have ever been with Mr Nicholls. I could by no means think of mentioning such a rumour to him even as a joke. It would make me the laughing-stock of himself and his fellow curates for half a year to come. They regard me as an old maid, and I regard them, one and all, as highly uninteresting, narrow and unattractive specimens of the coarser sex. . . .'

Charlotte was prejudiced against curates, two of whom had proposed to her unsuccessfully. She seemed resigned to the lonely future which awaited her, and wisely chose to look on its favourable aspects.

A few months earlier, on 30 January 1846, she had written to Miss Wooler: '. . . I speculate much on the existence of unmarried and never-to-be married women nowadays, and I have already got to the point of considering that there is no more respectable character on this earth than the unmarried woman who makes her own way through life quietly, perseveringly, without support of husband. . . .'

The Professor, *Wuthering Heights* and *Agnes Grey* were finished and began to go the rounds of the publishers together. They took no interest in them and coldly sent them back to the unknown authors without giving any reason. More than a year later, in the middle of the summer of 1847, one of them, Mr Newby, was eventually to agree to publish *Wuthering Heights* and *Agnes Grey* by Ellis and Acton Bell, on deplorable terms, but was to reject *The Professor* by Currer Bell.

In the preface to this novel, Charlotte reveals her new attitude which explains the successive publishers' rejections: '. . . I had got over any such taste as I might once have had for ornamented and redundant composition, and come to prefer what was plain and homely. . . .'

'I said to myself that my hero should work his way through life as I had seen real living men work theirs. . . . As Adam's son he should share Adam's doom. . . .'

Having been influenced by M. Heger, her literature master, she was more and more wary of the exuberance of her imagination, more wary of romanticism and of all that was exaggerated and complicated.

We are far from the fantastic events of Angria to which, very regretfully, she had said goodbye; and this was no doubt harmful for the success of *The Professor*, as the next part of her preface demonstrates:

'. . . In the sequel, however, I find that publishers . . . would have liked something more imaginative and poetical – . . . indeed until an author has tried to dispose of a manuscript of this kind he can never know what stores of romance and sensibility lie hidden in breasts he would not have suspected of casketing such treasures. Men in business are usually thought to prefer the real . . . a passionate preference for the wild, wonderful, and thrilling – the strange, startling and harrowing – agitates divers souls that show a calm and sober surface. . . .'

The merits of *The Professor*, published in 1857, two years after the author's death, have never been fully recognised. In this novel, which was too short and too restrained for the taste of the period, Charlotte was denying her nature, and her narrative lacked vigour and appeared colourless to the readers. Yet it is of the same stock as *Jane Eyre* and *Villette*, and if the plot is not very interesting, its best passages have not been surpassed, nor could be.

Charlotte and Emily were still very concerned about their father's sight and towards the end of July 1846 they set out for Manchester. Mr Wilson, the famous oculist whom they consulted, asked to see the patient. So, in the second half of August, Charlotte by herself took her father to Mr Wilson, who decided to operate for cataract.

On 21 August, Charlotte wrote to Ellen: '. . . We got into our lodging yesterday . . . our rooms are very good, but there is no mistress of the house (she is very ill, and gone out into the country). . . . For ourselves I could contrive, Papa's diet is so very simple; but there will be a nurse coming in a day or two, and I am afraid of not having things good enough for her . . . give me some hints if you can.'

On 26 August, Charlotte informed her friend that the operation was over: '. . . it took place yesterday. Mr Wilson performed it, two other surgeons assisted. Mr Wilson says he considers it quite successful. . . . The affair lasted precisely a quarter of an hour. . . . Papa displayed extraordinary patience and firmness; the surgeons seemed surprised. I was in the room all the time, as it was his wish that I should be there; of course I neither spoke nor moved till the thing was done. . . . Papa is now confined to his bed in a dark room for four days, he is to speak and be spoken to as little as possible. . . .'

On the very morning of the operation, *The Professor* had been returned to Charlotte for the sixth time and, as usual, without an explanation. 'Currer Bell's book found acceptance nowhere, nor any acknowledgement of merit, so that something like the chill of despair began to invade his heart,'[4] she was to say later. But Charlotte was brave. 'She had the heart of Robert Bruce within her. . . . Not only did *The Professor* return again to try his chance among the London publishers, but she began, in this time of care and depressing inquietude—there and then did the brave genius begin *Jane Eyre*.' (G)

The rejection of *The Professor* was a salutary lesson to her in the long run. For she then came to realise that she must return to the sources of her real inspiration, and to the style which was essentially hers. Assuredly the kingdoms of Glasstown and Angria held out to her treasures heaped together in confusion. Among them there were riches in spite of exaggeration and irrational ideas. The control so painfully achieved by study and suffering must be able to guide her in her difficult choice. Then *Mina Laury*, *The Spell*, *Albion and Marina*, *An Adventure in Ireland*, and others among her passionate tales, came back to her mind. The spring welled up. The plot took shape. During the month of enforced seclusion in Manchester, Charlotte wrote without pause, as if under the power of an irresistible stimulus.

She brought Mr Brontë home to Haworth at the end of September, happy to join her sisters and to learn that Branwell, whom they had had the responsibility of looking after, had behaved better than could have been hoped.

Always attentive to her father, whose sight was improving but still required great care, Charlotte had little time to write during the day. But in the evening, when he had gone to bed, along with Branwell, she and her sisters still felt their old pleasure at being together in the quiet dining-room, where they devoted themselves to their novels and poems. Sometimes they walked about in the room as they used to do, Emily and Anne with their arms around each other. They exchanged ideas about their work in progress.

'. . . Once or twice a week, each read to the others what she had written, and heard what they had to say about it. . . . It was on one of these occasions, that Charlotte determined to make her heroine

4. Biographical notice to *Wuthering Heights* (Everyman edition), also quoted by Mrs Gaskell.

plain, small, and unattractive, in defiance of the accepted canon . . . they [her sisters] replied that it was impossible to make a heroine interesting without beauty. Her answer was, "I will prove to you that you are wrong; I will show you a heroine as plain and as small as myself, who shall be as interesting as any of yours. . . ." ' (G)

'. . . She said, that it was not every day that she could write. Sometimes weeks or even months elapsed before she felt that she had anything to add to that portion of her story which was already written. Then, some morning, she would waken up, and the progress of her tale lay clear and bright before her, in distinct vision.' (G)

However, at the height of her inspiration, Charlotte, writing as if to dictation, neglected none of her duties and remained at everyone's disposal.

This little piece of information, related by Mrs Gaskell, proves it: '. . . It had become necessary to give Tabby, now nearly eighty years of age, the assistance of a girl. Tabby relinquished any of her work with jealous reluctance and could not bear to be reminded, though ever so delicately, that the acuteness of her senses was dulled by age. . . . Among other things, she reserved to herself the right of peeling the potatoes for dinner; but as she was growing blind, she often left in those black specks, which we call the "eyes" of the potato.

'Miss Brontë was too dainty a housekeeper to put up with this; yet she could not bear to hurt the faithful old servant, by bidding the younger maiden go over the potatoes again, and so reminding Tabby that her work was less effectual than formerly. Accordingly she would steal into the kitchen, and quickly carry off the bowl of vegetables, without Tabby's being aware, and breaking off in the full flow of interest and inspiration in her writing, carefully cut out the specks in the potatoes, and noiselessly carry them back to their place. . . .' (G)

However, the work was progressing, and as it advanced, Charlotte's interest in the characters and their adventures grew. But she tired herself out; at the end of three weeks of ceaseless work she had a fever and was forced to stop.

Her thirtieth birthday came and went, and, in spite of the excitement of writing, the future remained gloomy and empty. Sometimes she was offered a governess's post and the temptation to accept, followed by her refusal, always left her feeling bitter regret.

To Ellen, who no doubt had suggested such means of escape to her, Charlotte replied on 14 October 1846: '. . . I know life is passing away, and I am doing nothing, earning nothing . . . but whenever I consult my conscience, it affirms that I am doing right in staying at home. . . . I returned to Brussels after Aunt's death against my conscience, prompted by what then seemed an irresistible impulse. I was punished for my selfish folly by a total withdrawal for more than two years of happiness and peace of mind. I could hardly expect success if I were to err again in the same way.'

The winter of 1846–7 was a terrible one. A biting, icy wind howled up on the hills, it was freezing very hard, and the family in the parsonage could not keep out the penetrating cold. No one could take any steps to prevent the dangerous colds, the worrying coughs, the exhausting toothaches. Anne, suffering severe attacks of the asthma which she had long been subject to, won everyone's admiration by her extraordinary – one might say heroic – endurance, by her gentleness, her truly Christian resignation. Their younger sister's delicate health continually worried Charlotte and Emily.

To the suffering caused by bad weather were added distressing incidents due to Branwell's odious conduct; one of these was the visit of a bailiff who demanded the payment of his debts, with a threat of taking him to York. Charlotte felt 'grey',[5] weary, quite overcome but, like her sisters, she refused to give in. The strength of their inner life sustained them; it kept alive a compassion, a generosity of heart which was always ready to bring help in the needs or misfortunes of others. To please their father, they always visited the village schools regularly, and Charlotte often cut short an already brief stay at Brookroyd with Ellen to come back and take her place in the Sunday School.

Wretched Branwell, in spite of his excesses, thought that he was still robust; he would be suddenly elated by fruitless bursts of energy and announce that he wanted to prepare for a new career. What would in fact become of him if his father were to die? he confided in his letters to his friend Leyland.

5. Her own word.

But his ageing father was to survive him. Although no one among the people round him would have foreseen it, Branwell was to die in the following year. In the course of his numerous attacks, he had some very serious falls. In addition, alcoholism and opium were pursuing their ravages unseen, undermining a constitution predisposed to tuberculosis.

19

Jane Eyre – *Charlotte reveals her secret to her father – Her fame – Charlotte seeks comfort* – Jane Eyre *and Thackeray*

Charlotte could not bring herself to give up *The Professor* at its sixth rejection. In July 1847 she decided to send her novel to Messrs Smith & Elder.

With her lack of sophistication, Charlotte always sent her manuscript from one publisher to the next in the same brown paper she had used the first time, simply crossing out the previous address each time. So Messrs Smith & Elder were in this way aware of all the misadventures of the unlucky novel.

Three weeks later, on 2 August 1847, she wrote to them to ask what they thought of the manuscript which they must have received.

The reply came quickly. As usual, Charlotte was expecting a short, blunt refusal and was very surprised to take from the envelope a two-page letter. Later, in the biographical note on her sisters, she was to write: 'He [Currer Bell] read it trembling. It declined, indeed, to publish that tale, for business reasons, but it discussed its merits and demerits, so courteously, so considerately, in a spirit so rational, with a discrimination so enlightened, that this very refusal cheered the author better than a vulgarly-expressed acceptance would have done. It was added, that a work in three volumes would meet with careful attention.'

Was this not just the moment for *Jane Eyre*?

A few days later, Charlotte answered them: '. . . It appears to me that it [*The Professor*] might be published without serious risk, if its appearance were speedily followed up by another work from the same pen, of a more striking and exciting character. The first work might serve as an introduction. . . . I have a second narrative in three volumes, now in progress, and nearly completed, to which I have endeavoured to impart a more vivid interest than belongs to *The Professor*. . . .'

During this time, Ellen Nussey came to spend a few days at the parsonage. Charlotte had warned her that she would find Branwell changed: he no longer had his old sparkling wit, he was as thin as 'a rake'; 'I have no apprehension of his being at all uncivil to you; on the contrary, he will be as smooth as oil.'

In that wonderful summer, Haworth had grown gracious. The purple heather, in full bloom, clothed moor and hill. The four friends were enchanted by such beauty, made glorious by brilliant sunshine, a real gift from the gods to these unfavoured regions.

What confidences did they not exchange in these propitious lonely places? But the three sisters maintained the same silence about what concerned them most: the fate of their novels, then in London. Nor did Charlotte say anything to Ellen about the almost-completed manuscript of *Jane Eyre*. Her faithful friend certainly suspected something, but with typically Victorian discretion, together with a certain established code, she accepted that she was not told everything. She had an ill-defined impression that she was unable to penetrate the many aspects of the astonishing personalities of her friends.

Mr Brontë did not know either. As he always took a keen interest in what was happening to his children, his daughters feared failure even more for his sake than for themselves, and spoke to him neither of their writing nor of the steps they had taken. If he asked them no questions, he also must have guessed that something was going on: such a coming and going of letters and parcels could not pass unnoticed. The postman, too, puzzled at bringing so many letters to Currer Bell, Esq., c/o the vicar's daughter, finally asked Mr Brontë who this unknown man could be. To which Mr Brontë replied that he knew no one of that name in his parish.

Besides, hadn't Mr Brontë, during his spirited youth, written and published poems and novels? This close resemblance of mind and tastes prepared him to some extent, without his realising it, to meet the shock that Charlotte's sudden fame would give him.

On 24 August, Charlotte addressed to Messrs Smith & Elder 'the manuscript entitled *Jane Eyre*, a novel in three volumes, by Currer Bell'. (G)

'When the manuscript of *Jane Eyre* had been received by the future publishers of that remarkable novel, it fell to the share of a gentleman connected with the firm to read it first. He was so powerfully struck by the character of the tale, that he reported his impression in very strong terms to Mr Smith, who appears to have been much amused by the admiration excited. . . . But when a second reader, in the person of a clear-headed Scotsman, not given to enthusiasm, had taken the MS home in the evening, and became so interested in it as to sit up half the night to finish it, Mr Smith's curiosity was sufficiently excited to prompt him to read it for himself. . . .' (G)

He could not escape the spell of the novel. He began to read it one Sunday morning, thinking that he would stop about midday to go riding in the country with a friend.

'Before twelve o'clock', he afterwards recorded, 'my horse came to the door, but I could not put the book down. I scribbled two or three lines to my friend, saying I was very sorry that circumstances had arisen to prevent me meeting him . . . and went on reading the MS. Presently the servant came to tell me that luncheon was ready; I asked him to bring me a sandwich and a glass of wine, and went on with *Jane Eyre*. Dinner came; for me the meal was a very hasty one, and before I went to bed that night I had finished reading the manuscript.'[1]

The book was accepted.

While it was printing, Charlotte went for a short visit to Ellen at Brookroyd. There she received the proofs, and corrected them without a mention, as she sat beside Ellen who was sewing at the same table. In the thrill of pleasure at knowing that *Jane Eyre* was about to appear, Charlotte, in no way intoxicated by success, maintained an accurate estimate of her capabilities. On 4 October, under the pseudonym of Currer Bell, she answered Mr Smith Williams, the reader at Smith & Elder, the publishers, who must have encouraged her warmly to pursue a literary career. '. . . The eminent writers you mention, Mr Thackeray, Mr Dickens . . . etc, doubtless enjoyed facilities for observation such as I have not; certainly they possess a knowledge of the world, whether intuitive or acquired, such as I can lay no claim to, and this gives their writings an importance and a variety greatly beyond what I can offer the public. . . .'

Jane Eyre appeared on 16 October 1847, barely six weeks after it was accepted. *Wuthering Heights* by Emily and *Agnes Grey* by Anne were still waiting with Newby, the publisher, who published them only after the success of *Jane Eyre*.

If the protection of anonymity kept everything about this

1. Margaret Lane, op. cit., p. 187.

important event from being known at the parsonage, *Jane Eyre* was a source of great excitement in London – in the world of letters, among both critics and readers.

'. . . I feel honoured', wrote Currer Bell to Mr Williams on 28 October 1847, 'in being approved by Mr Thackeray. . . . One good word from such a man is worth pages of praise from ordinary judges. . . .'

No one knew who Currer Bell was, neither Thackeray nor anyone else, not even Mr Smith, the publisher, who learned it only at the beginning of the following summer. The curiosity that had been awakened was at its height; everyone was trying to discover who the mysterious, inspired author was. '. . . If a woman,' wrote Thackeray to Mr Smith, 'she knows her language better than most ladies do, or has had a "classical" education . . . it is a woman's writing, but whose? Give my respects and thanks to the author. . . .'[2]

The critics, more cautious and wary, hesitated to praise an unknown novelist. But *Jane Eyre*, Charlotte Brontë's masterpiece, 'which surprised and delighted, perturbed and even shocked the reader',[3] had enough power in itself to stand on its own in the world, and soon the critics had no longer any need to hide their admiration. The success was such that three months later, in January 1848, a reprint was necessary. Suddenly she was famous.

What effect did this resounding success have on Charlotte and her sisters? We do not really know. Later, Mrs Gaskell asked Charlotte if she had not been surprised by the popularity of her book. 'She hesitated a little and then said, "I believed that what had impressed me so forcibly when I wrote it, must make a strong impression on anyone who read it. I was not surprised at those who read *Jane Eyre* being deeply interested in it; but I hardly expected that a book by an unknown author could find readers." ' (G)

Emily and Anne then urged their sister to tell their father of her success. So one evening, before he retired to his room, Charlotte went to him in his study with the three volumes of *Jane Eyre* and a few review articles, carefully adding one which was unfavourable.

2. Quoted by M. Lane, op. cit., p. 188.
3. C. Maurat, Preface to the translation of *Jane Eyre* (Livre de Poche).

Here are the details of their conversation as Charlotte related it to Mrs Gaskell:

'Papa, I've been writing a book.'

'Have you, my dear?'

'Yes, and I want you to read it.'

'I am afraid it will try my eyes too much.'

'But it is not a manuscript: it is printed.'

'My dear! You've never thought of the expense it will be! It will be almost sure to be a loss, for how can you get a book sold? No one knows you or your name.'

'But, Papa, I don't think it will be a loss; no more will you, if you will just let me read you a review or two, and tell you more about it.' (G)

His eldest daughter's fame was the pride and consolation of his old age. When Mrs Gaskell went to visit him at Haworth after Charlotte's death, she was very touched to see with what piety the grief-stricken father had collected and kept all the newspaper and review articles which mentioned the author of *Jane Eyre*, *Shirley* and *Villette*.

From now on it was an absolute necessity for Charlotte to make more room in her life for Currer Bell, the author, without, however, abandoning any of her routine work. However difficult that seemed, she achieved it, thanks to her remarkable ability to organise.

Her astonishing success straight away opened literary circles in London to her and her world was suddenly widened to an extraordinary extent. She was to have the privilege of exchanging ideas on everything that interested her with contemporary authors. What an opportunity to assert the independence and courageous frankness of her mind! She did so naturally and simply, with astonishing perceptiveness and breadth of outlook, and so showed herself to be an outstanding critic. Her voluminous correspondence with Mr William Smith Williams, her letters to George Henry Lewes (the friend of George Eliot), and to Thackeray, are of very great interest, and form an important part of her literary output. It will be remembered that Mr William Smith Williams, to whom she wrote at least a hundred letters, was publishers' reader with Smith & Elder. His intuition, the sureness of his judgement and his enthusiasm when he had *Jane Eyre* in his hands were the principal reasons for the immediate and immense success of the novel. Charlotte was never to forget this. A remarkable man, very cultured, loyal and likeable, he had known all the famous people of the period. Clement Shorter writes: 'When Keats left England, for an early grave in Rome, it was Mr Williams who saw him off. Hazlitt, Leigh Hunt, and many other well-known men of letters were friendly with Mr Williams from his earliest days. In his association with Smith & Elder he secured the friendship of Thackeray, of Mrs Gaskell, and of many other writers. . . . He attracted the notice of Ruskin by a keen enthusiasm for the work of Turner.'[4]

As well as this ideal correspondent, she soon had George Henry Lewes, who was one of the first to write to Currer Bell of his 'enthusiasm' on reading *Jane Eyre*, and one of the first to praise it in an article in *The Westminster Review*, whose literary critic he was. Mr Williams, complying with Charlotte's wish, never failed to send her the numerous articles which appeared in the newspapers and reviews, whether they were favourable or not. The acclaim that greeted *Jane Eyre* 'was up to a certain point a *succès de scandale*', writes Ernest Dimnet.[5] In Victorian society at that time, vice was as a matter of fact carefully concealed beneath a mask of hypocrisy. And so this story, whose passion and realism suddenly broke with the accepted tradition, was considered disconcertingly bold and shockingly crude by a section of the public, who nevertheless went on reading it!

So Charlotte had to endure the sometimes virulent criticism of surly, prudish, unprogressive minds, in particular the *Spectator* criticism, about which she wrote to Mr Williams on 4 January 1848: . . . 'I know, in the first place, that my intentions were correct, that I feel in my heart a deep reverence for religion, that impiety is very abhorrent to me; and in the second, I place firm reliance on the judgement of some who have encouraged me. You and Mr Lewes are quite as good authorities, in my estimation, as Mr Dilke[6] or the editor of *The Spectator* . . . none but a coward would let the detraction of an enemy outweigh the encouragement of a friend. . . .'

As for *The Quarterly Review*, aggressively spiteful and notori-

4. Clement Shorter, op. cit., vol. I, p. 381.
5. E. Dimnet, op. cit.
6. C. W. Dilke was editor of the *Athenaeum* from 1830 to 1846.

ously stupid, it will be seen that Charlotte, then in the depths of grief, did not feel its mean attacks.

In the same letter of 4 January 1848, the novelist also answered those who were shocked by the character of the mad woman of Thornfield, Mr Rochester's wife, which was considered exaggerated and unnatural. '. . . I agree with them that the character is shocking, but I know that it is but too natural. There is a phase of insanity . . . in which all that is good or even human seems to disappear from the mind and a fiend – nature replaces it. The sole aim and desire of the being thus possessed is to exasperate, to molest, to destroy, and preternatural ingenuity and energy are often exercised to that dreadful end. . . . It is true that profound pity ought to be the only sentiment elicited by the view of such degradation, and equally true is it . . . [that] I have erred in making horror too predominant. . . .'

This touching confession certainly does not justify – rather the contrary – those who deemed it right to create and foster a legend making of Charlotte a sister devoid of maternal feeling, without sympathetic understanding for Branwell. It is very difficult, if not impossible, to imagine her sorrow at the sight of this gifted brother, now an utter wreck. How could the publishers, or the critics, of *Jane Eyre*, of *Wuthering Heights*, of *The Tenant of Wildfell Hall* guess that the portraits of Mrs Rochester, Hindley Earnshaw and Arthur Huntingdon had been painted from nature, from the living reality of a grief which ceaselessly obsessed them? The stories of burning curtains, of kitchen knives stolen and suddenly brandished were suggested by Branwell's behaviour when he was in the grip of frightful hallucinations which he was now powerless to control.

From time to time Charlotte enjoyed telling Mr Williams of the great comfort she derived from his letters: '. . . I cannot thank you sufficiently for your letters, and I can give you but a faint idea of the pleasure they afford me; they seem to introduce such light and life to the torpid retirement where we live like dormice.'[7]

In her letters to Mr Lewes, Charlotte, new to the ranks of literature, never forgot that she was writing to a well-known novelist and critic, which did not prevent her expressing her ideas with fluency, wit and even flippancy. The first letter she sent

7. December 1847, quoted by M. Lane.

him is dated 6 November 1847: '. . . I thank you sincerely both for its cheering commendation and valuable advice. You warn me to beware of melodrama, and you exhort me to adhere to the real. . . .' Then she explains to him the causes of the failure of *The Professor*. The publishers wanted 'startling incident', 'thrilling excitement'; 'I mention this to you not with a view of pleading exemption from censure, but in order to direct your attention to the root of certain literary evils. . . .'

In the letter of 12 January 1848, after telling Mr Lewes that her experience, knowledge and possibilities were not very varied and that she could never write much, she tried to puzzle out the enigma of her correspondent's admiration for Jane Austen, the author of *Pride and Prejudice*. 'Why do you like Miss Austen so very much?'

In the letter of 18 January she continued the same topic:

'. . . You say . . . that Miss Austen is not a poetess, has no "sentiment" . . . no eloquence, none of the ravishing enthusiasm of poetry and then you add, I must learn to acknowledge her as *one of the greatest artists, of the greatest painters of human character*.

'Can there be a great artist without poetry?

'What I call . . . a great artist cannot be destitute of the divine gift. . . .

'You must forgive me for not always being able to think as you do. . . .'

If it is impossible for Charlotte to yield on this point even to Mr Lewes, she is nonetheless tormented by the thought that he is judging her too favourably: she had confided in Mr Williams on 11 December 1847:

'I am afraid if he knew how much I write from intuition, how little from actual knowledge, he would think me presumptuous ever to have written at all. . . .' She had added: 'I am glad and proud to get the bank bill for £100 Mr Smith sent me yesterday, but I hardly ever felt delight equal to that which cheered me when I received your letter containing an extract from a note by Mr Thackeray in which he expressed himself gratified with the perusal of *Jane Eyre*. . . .'

Mr Thackeray's note gave Charlotte courage and confidence and in a warm surge of gratitude she dedicated the second edition of *Jane Eyre* to the famous writer for whom she had the greatest admiration: '. . . Thackeray is a Titan', she wrote to Mr Williams on 29 March 1848, 'so strong that he can afford to perform with calm the most herculean feats; there is the charm and majesty of repose in his greatest efforts. . . . Thackeray is never borne away by his own ardour – he has it under control. His genius obeys him, it is his servant. . . . Thackeray is unique. . . .'

How was Thackeray going to accept this dedication? Such was the question which Charlotte asked herself anxiously. So, when she received the reply which she had feverishly awaited, she hesitated for a few moments before reading it. It was only Thackeray the writer who existed for her: she knew nothing about his private life. Now, by a wicked trick of fate, it happened that the great man, whose wife had been shut away for some years, presented a striking parallel to Mr Rochester.

'. . . His letter is most friendly in its noble simplicity,' Charlotte had written to Mr Williams, on 28 January 1848, 'but he apprises me, at the commencement, of a circumstance which both surprised and dismayed me. . . . It appears that his private position is in some points similar to that I have ascribed to Mr Rochester, that hence arose a report that *Jane Eyre* had been written by a governess in his family, and that the dedication coming now has confirmed everybody in the surmise.

'Well may it be said that fact is often stranger than fiction! The coincidence struck me as equally unfortunate and extraordinary. . . . I am *very*, *very* sorry that my inadvertent blunder should have made his name and affairs a subject for common gossip.

'The very fact of his not complaining at all and addressing me with such kindness, notwithstanding the pain and annoyance I must have caused him, increases my chagrin. I could not half express my regret to him in my answer, for I was restrained by the consciousness that that regret was just worth nothing at all – quite valueless for healing the mischief I had done. . . . Can you guess in what degree the unlucky coincidence would affect him? . . .'

20

Wuthering Heights *and* Agnes Grey – *Branwell and* Wuthering Heights – *The identity of Currer, Ellis and Acton Bell is revealed – Charlotte and Anne go to London*

In December 1847 *Wuthering Heights* and *Agnes Grey* finally appeared.

If *Agnes Grey*, 'the mirror of the author', made little stir, the terrible naked thoughts of most of the characters in *Wuthering Heights*, their violent, brutal passions, like the elements unleashed, the demoniac temperament of Heathcliff, whose wild, rough name so well suits the cruel son of the moors, shocked and frightened the readers.

Mrs Gaskell reflects to some extent the attitude of her contemporaries: '*Wuthering Heights* has revolted many readers by the power with which wicked and exceptional characters are depicted.' But she hastens to add: 'Others, again, have felt the attraction of remarkable genius, even when displayed on grim and terrible criminals.'

Emily Brontë worked outside the bounds of her time, seeking inspiration 'from no model but the vision of her meditations'.[1] How can we be surprised by the lack of understanding in her contemporaries when, after more than a century, she remains such a mysterious personality?

Charlotte herself never completely fathomed the virile mind of Emily, with its disconcerting power, its range and direction of thought. And yet no one understood better the nature of her genius. Better than any critic she realised at once the outstanding qualities of the *Poems of Gondal*, and in her preface to the second edition of *Wuthering Heights* she tried to depict Emily in a way that would illuminate her novel. 'My sister's disposition was not naturally gregarious; circumstances favoured and fostered her natural tendency to seclusion; except to go to church or take a walk on the hills, she rarely crossed the threshold of home . . . and yet she knew them [the local people]; knew their ways, their

1. Charlotte Brontë in her Preface to *Wuthering Heights*.

language, their family histories; she could hear of them with interest, and talk of them with detail, minute, graphic, and accurate, but *with* them she rarely exchanged a word.'[2]

Her gloomy imagination remained especially impressed by the 'tragic and terrible traits'[3] in the characters she perceived. Emily, too, had read Byron, and perhaps enough has not been made of the influence exerted on her by 'the excesses of Byronism with its duality of natural and demoniac forces'.[4]

Gradually, from all these strong impressions, to which were added the memories of Tabby's ghost stories, of the horrifying tales in *Blackwood's Magazine*, always greatly enjoyed by Emily, and finally of the *Tales* of Hoffmann, were born Hindley and Catherine Earnshaw, Heathcliff, and certain scenes which, according to Charlotte, 'banished sleep by night, and disturbed mental peace by day'.[5]

'*Wuthering Heights*', writes Charlotte in the same preface, 'was hewn in a wild workshop . . . the statuary found a granite block on a solitary moor; gazing thereon, he saw how from the crag might be elicited a head, savage, swart, sinister: a form moulded with at least one element of grandeur – power. He wrought with a rude chisel, and from no model but the vision of his meditations. With time and labour, the crag took human shape and there it stands, colossal, dark and frowning, half statue, half rock . . .'[6]

Emily died too soon to reach her potential, and her sister adds feelingly: 'Had she but lived, her mind would of itself have grown like a strong tree – loftier, straighter, wider-spreading, and its matured fruits would have attained a mellower ripeness and a sunnier bloom; but on that mind time and experience alone could work; to the influence of other intellects she was not amenable. . . .'[7]

Some people have attributed *Wuthering Heights* to Branwell. Now Branwell was no more capable of writing this masterpiece, as powerful as it is strange, than he was of becoming a great painter. The *Juvenilia* have shown his extraordinary precocity, his

2. Ibid.
3. Ibid.
4. Charles du Bos, *Byron* (1929), p. 334.
5. Charlotte Brontë in her Preface to *Wuthering Heights*.
6. Ibid.
7. Ibid.

startling fertility of mind. But none of his many stories has the spark of genius and the development of his dazzling gifts stopped at adolescence. Perhaps he had expended them too lavishly. After that, every source of inspiration seemed to dry up in him. If Branwell was not, if he couldn't be, the author of *Wuthering Heights*, there is no doubt that he was the inspiration for one of its characters, Hindley Earnshaw, that drunkard, that madman possessed by the devil. That is his pitiful collaboration in his sister's work.

Besides, it is certain that when Charlotte and Anne were away from Haworth, Emily and Branwell were almost always together. Emily continued the Chronicles of Gondal, Branwell those of Angria. They must often have discussed them and made up more frightening tales while they ranged over the moors in all directions, both drawn by the furthest, the most isolated and hidden of the farms, with their stories of the supernatural.

The domain of Darkwall, described by Branwell in a sketch dated December 1837, has a curious resemblance to the Earnshaws' home in *Wuthering Heights*, and may have cast doubts in some minds.

In her letter to Mr Williams, announcing Branwell's death, Charlotte put an end to vain controversies: 'My unhappy brother never knew what his sisters had done in literature; he was not aware that they had ever published a line. We could not tell him of our efforts for fear of causing him too deep a pang of remorse for his own time misspent, and talents misapplied.'

The world of *Wuthering Heights* is essentially the same as that of Gondal. Those who thought that Branwell was its author failed to consider this piece of evidence; that the same genius animates the *Poems of Gondal* and *Wuthering Heights*: 'Whoever wrote the poems wrote *Wuthering Heights*', remarks Charles Morgan in his essay on Emily Brontë;[8] 'the same unreality of this world, the same greater reality of another, being in them both, and in nothing else that the human mind has produced. The poems and the novel are twins of a unique imagination.'

The anonymity of Currer, Ellis and Acton Bell had been well kept. No one had yet been able to discover their identity. Charlotte and Ellen continued to correspond as they used to, but still with-

8. C. Morgan, *The Great Victorians* (Nicholson & Watson), pp. 63–79.

out the slightest allusion by Charlotte to her growing fame. However, as she had written in *The Spell*, 'Time reveals all secrets'; one day Ellen, having heard that Charlotte had written and published a novel, lost no time in telling her. Charlotte replied sharply:

'3rd May, 1848 . . . I have given *no one* a right either to affirm, or hint, in the most distant manner, that I am publishing – (humbug!). . . . Though twenty books were ascribed to me, I should own none. . . . If then any Birstallian or Gomersallian should presume . . . to ask you what "novel" Miss Brontë has been "publishing", you can just say . . . that you are authorised by Miss Brontë to say, that she repels and disowns every accusation of the kind. . . . Should you hear anything more, let me know. . . .'

This one and only lie told by Charlotte, who was honesty itself, is surprising. There is no other explanation, Mrs Gaskell rightly thinks, than her loyalty to her sisters: she had, in fact, given them her word never to betray their anonymity. It is known that Emily, with her shyness, could not bear the idea of such a revelation. And it must be added that Charlotte was as anxious as her sisters to preserve this anonymity. Thanks to it, Branwell remained ignorant of a success that would have made him experience vain regrets and plunge him again into despair. And lastly, the mask of Currer Bell, which protected her from unkind judgements and cruel ridicule, allowed her to express herself with complete freedom: '. . . What author would be without the advantage of being able to walk invisible?' she wrote to Mr Williams on 4 January 1848. 'One is thereby enabled to keep such a quiet mind. I make this small observation in confidence. . . .'

The critics were growing more and more puzzled. They tended to think that Currer Bell was at the same time Currer, Ellis and Acton Bell, whose *Wuthering Heights* and *Agnes Grey* must be youthful works, merely early efforts that preceded the masterpiece, *Jane Eyre*. Newby, the publisher, about whom Emily and Anne had never had much to congratulate themselves, adopted this hypothesis, hoping to turn it to advantage sooner or later. After the publication of *Agnes Grey*, Anne Brontë (Acton Bell) had at once begun another novel, *The Tenant of Wildfell Hall*, which she finished in June of the same year, 1848. She offered it to Mr Newby, who accepted it and published it without any delay this time. He did not even wait for the printing to be finished before he signed a contract with an American firm, saying that this novel was by Currer Bell, the author of *Jane Eyre*.

However Charlotte had given the key of the enigma to her friend Mary Taylor, probably because she was so far away. Was not New Zealand in the Antipodes? On 4 September 1848 she wrote: '. . . About two months since I had a letter from my publishers – Smith and Elder – saying that *Jane Eyre* had a great run in America, and that a publisher there had consequently bid high for the first sheets of a new work by Currer Bell, which they had promised to let him have.

'Presently after came another missive from Smith and Elder; their American correspondent had written to them complaining that the first sheets of a new work by Currer Bell had been already received, and not by their house, but by a rival publisher and asking the meaning of such false play; it enclosed an extract from a letter from Mr Newby [A. and E. Bell's publisher] affirming that to the best of his belief *Jane Eyre*, *Wuthering Heights* and *Agnes Grey* and *The Tenant of Wildfell Hall* (the new work) were all the production of one author. . . .

'The upshot of it was that on the very day I received Smith and Elder's letter, Friday, 7th July, Anne and I packed up a small box, sent it down to Keighley, set out ourselves after tea, walked through a snowstorm to the station, got to Leeds, and whirled up by the night train to London with the view of proving our separate identity to Smith and Elder, and confronting Newby with his *lie*. We arrived at the Chapter Coffee-House . . . about eight o'clock in the morning. We washed ourselves, had some breakfast, sat a few minutes, and then set off in queer inward excitement to 65 Cornhill. Neither Mr Smith nor Mr Williams knew we were coming – they had never seen us – they did not know whether we were men or women, but had always written to us as men.

'We found 65 to be a large bookseller's shop, in a street almost as bustling as the Strand. . . . There were a great many young men and lads here and there; I said to the first I could accost, "May I see Mr Smith?" He hesitated, looked a little surprised. . . . At last we were shown up to Mr Smith. "Is it Mr Smith?" I asked, looking up through my spectacles at a tall young man. "It is." I then put his own letter into his hand directed to Currer Bell. He looked at it and then at me again. "Where did you get this?" he said. I laughed at his perplexity – a recognition took place. I gave my real name: Miss Brontë . . . explanations were rapidly gone into; Mr Newby being anathemised, I fear, with undue vehemence. Mr Smith hurried out and returned quickly with one whom he introduced as Mr Williams, a pale, mild, stooping man of fifty. . . .'

Mr Smith urged the two young ladies to stay at his home, but they refused. '. . . We returned to our inn, and I paid for the excitement of the interview by a thundering headache and harassing sickness. Towards evening, as I got no better and expected the Smiths to call, I took a strong dose of sal volatile. It roused me a little; still I was in grievous bodily case when they were announced. They came in, two elegant young ladies, in full dress, prepared for the Opera – Mr Smith himself in evening costume, white gloves, etc. We had by no means understood that it was settled we were to go to the Opera, and were not ready. Moreover, we had no fine, elegant dresses with us, or in the world. However, on brief rumination, I thought it would be wise to make no objections – I put my headache in my pocket, we attired ourselves in the plain high-made country garments we possessed, and went with them to their carriage, where we found Mr Williams. They must have thought us queer, quizzical-looking beings, especially me with my spectacles. I smiled inwardly at the contrast, which must have been apparent, between me and Mr Smith as I walked with him up the crimson-carpeted staircase of the Opera House and stood amongst a brilliant throng at the box-door which was not yet open. Fine ladies and gentlemen glanced at us with a slight, graceful, superciliousness quite warranted by the circumstances. Still, I felt pleasantly excited in spite of headache and sickness and conscious clownishness, and I saw Anne was calm and gentle, which she always is.

'The performance was Rossini's opera of the *Barber of Seville* . . . very brilliant, though I fancy there are things I should like better. We got home after one o'clock; we had never been in bed the night before . . . you may imagine we were tired. The next day, Sunday, Mr Williams came early and took us to church. . . . In the afternoon Mr Smith came in his carriage with his mother, to take us to his house to dine. Mr Smith's residence is in Bayswater, six miles from Cornhill; the rooms, the dining-room especially, looked splendid to us. There was no company – only his mother, his two grown-up sisters, and his brother, a lad of twelve or thirteen, and a little sister, the youngest of the family, very like himself. We had a fine dinner, which neither Anne nor I had appetite to eat, and were glad when it was over.

'On Monday we went to the Exhibition of the Royal Academy and the National Gallery, dined again at Mr Smith's. . . . On Tuesday morning we left London laden with books which Mr Smith had given us, and got safely home. . . . We saw Mr Newby, but of him more another time, Goodbye. God bless you. Write. C.B.'

Charlotte, still anxious not to reveal that she and her sisters were the authors of the three novels which had created a sensation in London, England and America, had begged Mr Smith and Mr Williams to introduce Anne and herself in the name of Brown. 'All this time those who came in contact with the "Miss Browns" seem only to have regarded them as shy and reserved little country-women, with not much to say.' (G)

21

Return to Haworth – Death of Branwell – Illness and death of Emily

Charlotte came home exhausted from this visit. Unfortunately the house she came back to was not exactly a haven of peace. 'Papa, and sometimes all of us have sad nights with him [Branwell]', she wrote to Ellen on 28 July 1848. 'He sleeps most of the day, and consequently will lie awake at night. But has not every house its trial?'

Now she was back with Emily, Charlotte felt a sort of remorse. On 31 July she wrote to Mr Williams: '. . . I committed a great error in betraying his identity to you and Mr Smith. It was inadvertent – the words "we are three sisters" escaped me before I was aware. I regretted the avowal the moment I had made it; I regret it bitterly now, for I find it is against every feeling and intention of Ellis Bell. . . .' Then, in a different tone, she goes on: '. . . I smile at you again for supposing that I could be annoyed by what you say respecting your religious and philosophical views; that I could blame you for not being abler, when you look amongst sects and creeds, to discover any one which you can exclusively and implicitly adopt as yours. I perceive myself that some light falls on earth from Heaven – that some rays from the shrine of truth pierce the darkness of this life and world; but they are few, faint, and scattered, and who without presumption can assert that he has found the *only* true path upwards?'

During the last three years of his life, Branwell took opium continually and drank as often as he had the opportunity. He had to endure frightful attacks of delirium tremens and, as he slept in his father's room, he sometimes declared that one of them would be dead before morning. 'The poor old man and I have spent a terrible night.'

Yet his death was sudden: '. . . The past three weeks have been a dark interval in our humble home', Charlotte wrote on 9 October to Ellen who was then away from home. 'Branwell's constitution has been failing fast all the summer; but still, neither the doctors nor himself thought him so near his end as he was. He was entirely confined to his bed but one single day, and was in the village two days before his death. He died, after twenty minutes' struggle, on Sunday morning, September 24th. He was perfectly conscious till the last agony came on. His mind had undergone the peculiar change which frequently precedes death, two days previously; the calm of better feelings filled it; a return of natural affection marked his last moments. He is in God's hands now; and the All-powerful is likewise the All-merciful. A deep conviction that he rests well after his brief, erring, suffering, feverish life, fills and quiets my mind now. . . . Till the last hour comes, we never know how much we can forgive, pity, regret a near relation. . . . Papa was acutely distressed at first, but, on the whole, has borne the event well. Emily and Anne are pretty well, though Anne is always delicate, and Emily has a cold and cough at present. . . .'

Charlotte, who would so much have wanted to have enough strength to be the support of her family, fell ill through the emotional strain, the very day of Branwell's death. Her usual headaches, nausea, loss of appetite, and finally a liver infection forced her to stay in bed for a week. 'A dreary week. But, thank God, health seems now returning.'

A few days earlier, on 2 October, she had written to Mr Williams: 'Branwell was his father's and his sisters' pride and hope in boyhood, but since manhood the case has been otherwise. It has been our lot to see him take a wrong bent; to hope, expect, wait his return to the right path: to know the sickness of hope deferred, the dismay of prayer baffled: to experience despair at last – and now to behold the sudden early obscure close of what might have been a noble career . . .' On 6 October, another letter to Mr Williams: '. . . I believe you are too prone to think too highly of your fellow-creatures in general – to see too exclusively the good points of those for whom you have a regard. Disappointment must be the inevitable result of this habit. Believe all men, and women too, to be dust and ashes – a spark of the divinity now and then kindling in the dull heap – that is all. When I looked on the noble face and forehead of my dead brother (nature had favoured him with a fairer outside, as well as a finer constitution, than his sisters) and asked myself what had made him go ever wrong, tend ever downwards, when he had so many gifts to induce to, and aid in, the upward course, I seemed to receive an oppressive revelation of the feebleness of humanity – of the inadequacy of even genius to lead to true greatness if unaided by religion and principles.'

Now the awful alarm bell rang. In her letter of 29 October 1848, Charlotte tells Ellen of her terrible fears: '. . . I feel much more uneasy about my sisters than myself just now. Emily's cold and cough are obstinate. I sometimes catch a shortness in her breathing, when she has moved at all quickly. She looks very, very thin and pale. Her reserved nature occasions me great uneasiness of mind. It is useless to question her; you get no answers. It is still more useless to recommend remedies; they are never adopted. Nor can I shut my eyes to the fact of Anne's great delicacy of constitution. . . . The weather has been most unfavourable for invalids of late; sudden changes of temperature, and cold penetrating winds have been frequent here.'

It was very painful to describe so many anxieties, such great suffering. Charlotte felt that she was being hunted down by a relentless enemy: '. . . I am better,' she wrote to Mr Williams on 2 November 1848, 'but others are ill now. Papa is not well, my sister Emily has something like a slow inflammation of the lungs, and even our old servant, who has lived with us nearly a quarter of a century, is suffering under serious indisposition. . . . Emily is a real stoic in illness: she neither seeks nor will accept sympathy. . . . You must look on and see her do what she is unfit to do, and not dare to say a word – a painful necessity for those to whom her health and existence are as precious as the life in their veins. When she is ill there seems to be no sunshine in the world for me. The tie of sister is near and dear indeed, and I think a certain harshness in her powerful and peculiar character only makes me cling to her more. . . .'

Smith & Elder, in a chivalrous impulse, had bought up the *Poems* of Currer, Ellis and Acton Bell (whose failure will be recalled) from the publisher Aylott & Jones, to make a new edition of them. On 16 November 1848, Charlotte wrote about this to Mr Williams: '. . . Today I have received the *Spectator* and the *Revue des Deux Mondes*. The *Spectator* consistently maintains the tone it first assumed regarding the Bells. . . . Blind he is as any bat, insensate as any stone, to the merits of Ellis. He cannot feel, or will not acknowledge that the very finish and *labor limae* which Currer wants, Ellis has; he is not aware that the "true essence of poetry" pervaded his compositions. – Because Ellis's poems are short and abstract, the critics think them comparatively insignificant and dull. They are mistaken. . . . That will seem to me a happy day when I can announce to you that Emily is better. . . .'

In the *Revue des Deux Mondes*, Eugène Forcade praised *Jane Eyre* highly, but Charlotte was too worried about Emily to get any enjoyment from praise.

She wrote to Mr Williams on 22 November: '. . . I put your most friendly letter into Emily's hands as soon as I had myself perused it, taking care, however, not to say a word in favour of homeopathy – that would not have answered. It is best usually to leave her to form her own judgment, and *especially* not to advocate the side you wish her to favour; if you do she is sure to lean in the opposite direction. . . . Hitherto she has refused medicine, rejected medical advice; no reasoning, no entreaty, has availed to induce her to see a physician. After reading your letter she said, "Mr Williams's intention was kind and good, but he was under a delusion: homeopathy was only another form of quackery."

'*The North American Review* is worth reading: there is no mincing the matter there. What a bad set the Bells must be! what appalling books they write! Today, as Emily appeared a little easier, I thought the *Review* would amuse her, so I read it aloud to her and Anne. As I sat between them at our quiet but now somewhat melancholy fireside, I studied the two ferocious authors. Ellis, the "man of uncommon talents, but dogged, brutal, and morose", sat back in his easy chair drawing his impeded breath as he best could, and looking, alas! piteously pale and wasted; it is not his wont to laugh, but he smiled half-amused and half in scorn as he listened. Acton was sewing, no emotion ever stirs him to loquacity, so he only smiled too, dropping at the same time a single word of calm amazement to hear his character so darkly portrayed. I wonder what the reviewer would have thought of his own sagacity could he have beheld the pair as I did. Vainly, too, might he have looked round for the masculine partner in the firm of "Bell and Co.". How I laugh in my sleeve when I read the solemn assertions that *Jane Eyre* was written in partnership, and that it "bears the marks of more than one mind and one sex".'

The next day, 23 November, Charlotte wrote to Ellen: 'Emily is very ill. I believe, if you were to see her, your impression would be that there is no hope. . . . In this state she resolutely refuses to see a doctor. . . . God knows how all this will terminate. More

N

than once, I have been forced boldly to regard the terrible event of her loss as possible and even probable. But nature shrinks from such thoughts. I think Emily seems the nearest thing to my heart in this world. . . .'

Mr Brontë was very worried. In spite of everything, Charlotte and Anne still retained a vestige of hope which they tried to get him to share. 'My father shakes his head', she wrote to Mr Williams on 7 December, 'and speaks of others of our family once similarly affected, for whom he likewise persisted in hoping against hope, and who are now removed where hope and fear fluctuate no more. . . . Would that my sister added to her many great qualities the humble one of tractability. . . .'

What bitter regret it brought for Charlotte and Anne not only to remain powerless, but to be condemned to do nothing to fight the destructive illness as it steadily progressed. Emily felt nothing but scorn for such efforts to struggle against destiny. As Charlotte foresaw, this great poet, the author of an extraordinary novel, was bound to be hurt by harsh criticism which showed utter lack of understanding of her work and of herself; and the death of her brother had been a severe blow to her.

She became more than ever entrenched in her refusal to accept help, surrendering pitilessly to her fate, so that the tuberculosis, finding no further resistance from her inner vitality, freely continued its ravages. To the end Emily remained silent, resolute, adamant, with no fear of death, which would give her 'for short life, eternal liberty'.[1]

On 10 December 1848, Charlotte wrote to Ellen: '. . . I have written, unknown to her, to an eminent physician in London giving as minute a statement of her case and symptoms as I could, and requesting an opinion. I expect an answer in a day or two. . .'

In the memorable biographical notice on her sisters, from which several passages have already been quoted, Charlotte describes Emily's last days with very moving eloquence: 'But a great change approached. . . . My sister Emily sank rapidly. . . . Day by day, when I saw with what a front she met suffering, I looked on her with an anguish of wonder and love. I have seen nothing like it; but, indeed, I have never seen her parallel in anything. Stronger

1. Emily's poem 'The Prisoner'. See Chapter 17 quoted there; also Appendix III.

than a man, simpler than a child, her nature stood alone. The awful point was that, while full of ruth for others, on herself she had no pity; the spirit was inexorable to the flesh; from the trembling hand, the unnerved limbs, the fading eyes, the same service was exacted as they had rendered in health. To stand by and witness this, and not dare to remonstrate, was a pain no words can render.' In fact, the Sunday following Branwell's death was the last time Emily went out. Mrs Gaskell was to say later: 'I remember Miss Brontë's shiver at recalling the pang she felt when, after having searched in the little hollows and sheltered crevices of the moors for a lingering spray of heather – just one spray, however withered – to take in to Emily, she saw that the flower was not recognised by the dim and indifferent eyes. . . . One Tuesday morning, in December, she arose and dressed herself as usual; making many a pause, but doing everything for herself, and even endeavouring to take up her employment of sewing: the servants looked on, and knew what the catching, rattling breath, and the glazing eyes foretold; but she kept at her work. . .'

That morning (it was 19 December), Charlotte who was no doubt sitting with her dying sister, wrote to Ellen: 'She grows daily weaker. The physician's opinion was expressed too obscurely to be of use. He sent some medicine, which she would not take. Moments so dark as these I have never known." ' (G)

'The morning drew on to noon. Emily was worse. . . . Now, when it was too late, she said to Charlotte: "If you will send for a doctor, I will see him now." About two o'clock she died.' (G)

On 23 December, Charlotte again wrote to Ellen: '. . . Emily will never suffer more in this world. She is gone, after a hard, short conflict. She died on *Tuesday*, the very day I wrote to you. There is no Emily in time or on earth now. . . . We feel she is at peace. . . .

'God has sustained me, in a way that I marvel at . . . I now look to Anne, and wish she were well and strong, but she is neither; nor is Papa. Could you now come to us for a few days? . . . I never so much needed the consolation of a friend's presence. Pleasure, of course, there would be none for you in the visit, except what your kind heart would teach you to find in doing good to others.'

Charlotte tries to draw some courage from Mr Williams too: '25th December, 1848. . . . Emily is nowhere here now. We have laid her cherished head under the church aisle beside my mother's, my two sisters' – dead long ago – and my poor, hapless brother's – . . . Well, the loss is ours, not hers, and some sad comfort I take, as I hear the wind blow and feel the cutting keenness of the frost, in knowing that the elements bring her no more suffering . . . her fever is quieted, her restlessness soothed, her deep, hollow cough is hushed for ever . . . we have not the conflict of the strangely strong spirit and the fragile frame before us – relentless conflict – once seen, never to be forgotten. A dreary calm reigns round us, in the midst of which we seek resignation. My father and my sister Anne are far from well. My father says to me almost hourly: "Charlotte, you must bear up, I shall sink if you fail me." The sight too of my sister Anne's very still but deep sorrow wakens in me such fear for her that I dare not falter. . . .'[2]

'As the old bereaved father and his two surviving children followed the coffin to the grave, they were joined by Keeper, Emily's fierce, faithful bulldog. He walked alongside of the mourners and into the church, and stayed quietly there all the time that the burial service was being read. When he came home, he lay at Emily's chamber door, and howled pitifully for many days.' (G)

Then the father returned to his heightened isolation; Anne to her silent grief from which she could not recover. Charlotte, as always, returned to her duties but sought some comfort from her friends.

2. As was then the custom, Emily was buried the day after she died. As they had done for Branwell three months earlier, they opened the old gate between the little garden and the churchyard.

22

The Quarterly Review – *Illness and death of Anne*

An anonymous article (the author was a certain Miss Rigby) had appeared in *The Quarterly Review* of December 1848. It was a cruel attack on Currer Bell. Fortunately it did not reach Charlotte until after Emily's death, at a time when her grief was so acute that it left her indifferent to injustice and outrage.

'Jane Eyre', writes the author of the article, 'is merely another Pamela'[1] who, by the force of her character and the strength of her principles, is carried victoriously through great trials and temptations from the man she loves . . . it is stamped with a coarseness of language and laxity of tone. . . . It is a very remarkable book; we have no remembrance of another combining such genuine power with such horrid taste. . . . It is true Jane does right and exerts great moral strength, but it is the strength of a mere heathen mind which is a law unto itself still. . . . Altogether the autobiography of Jane Eyre is pre-eminently an anti-Christian composition. There is throughout it a murmuring against the comforts of the rich and against the privations of the poor. . . .

'Whoever it be, it is a person who, with great mental powers, combines a total ignorance of the habits of society, a great coarseness of taste, and a heathenish doctrine of religion, and as these characteristics appear more or less in the writings of all three, Currer, Acton, and Ellis alike, we are ready to accept the fact of their identity or of their relationship with equal satisfaction. . . .

'. . . If we ascribe the book to a woman at all, we have no alternative but to ascribe it to one who has, for some sufficient reason, long forfeited the society of her own sex. . . .'[2]

On 2 January 1849, Charlotte wrote to Mr Williams: '. . . The lash of *The Quarterly*, however severely applied, cannot sting me. . . . Their censure has no bitterness for him [Currer Bell].' On 4 February: '. . . I read *The Quarterly* without a pang, except that I thought there were some sentences disgraceful to the critic.' On

1. See p. 37.
2. *The Quarterly Review*, December 1848 (John Murray, London).

2 March: 'Your generous indignation against *The Quarterly* touched me. . . . However, slander without a germ of truth is seldom injurious: it resembles a rootless plant and must soon wither away.'

In her distress, Charlotte had not appealed in vain to Ellen, for Ellen was a true friend, unselfish, eager to help, and steadfast. She arrived at Haworth without delay.

Mr Brontë, extremely concerned about Anne, had asked Dr Teale of Leeds, a lung specialist, to come to see her. His visit took place at the beginning of January – on the 5th, it is believed. After carefully examining the patient, he followed Mr Brontë into his study to inform him of the result of his examination.

'Mr Brontë joined us after Dr Teale's departure and, seating himself on the couch, he drew Anne towards him and said, "My *dear* little Anne". That was all – but it was understood.'[3] Both lungs were too seriously affected to allow any hope of a cure and the treatment aimed only at lessening the suffering and slowing down the progress of the disease. Faced with such evidence Dr Teale insisted that Ellen should return to Brookroyd and imposed certain precautions which had not been taken during Emily's illness.

Anne, this frail creature of twenty-nine, was however a Brontë, a steadfast spirit. Aware of the fate which awaited her, she was seized not by fear of death, but by overwhelming regret at a task which remained unfinished. Realising that the earthly ties were breaking, unsure as she confronted the Unknown, she had to endure the inevitable struggle; then followed renunciation and peace; she now thought of nothing but proving worthy of her fate, of earning the right to be counted among 'the brave and strong'[4] like her sister Emily, whose death had snapped the spring of life in her.

During Ellen's visit, Charlotte had given her a copy of *Wuthering Heights* in memory of her sister – with Emily dead, Charlotte had now no secret to keep. Her lie was completely forgiven and forgotten: rather it impressed Ellen, who saw in it the token of the tender and steadfast loyalty towards her sister. Pitiless death had lifted the veil of anonymity.

3. W. Gérin, *Anne Brontë*, p. 298 (Nelson, London, 1959).
4. Ibid., quoting from a poem by Anne Brontë.

Throughout Anne's illness, Charlotte had the comfort of being able to speak quite openly to her. Unusually sweet and pliable, Anne punctually took her medicines, however unpleasant they were, especially cod liver oil. She patiently endured blistering, and everything else that was prescribed for her.

In her letter of 10 January 1849, after giving Ellen news of Anne, Charlotte expressed the great comfort she derived from her friendship: 'I see few lights through the darkness of the present time; but amongst them the constancy of a kind heart attached to me is one of the most charming and serene. . . .' On 18 January, she wrote to Mr Williams: 'Anne is very patient in her illness, as patient as Emily was unflinching. I recall one sister and look at the other with a sort of reverence as well as affection – under the test of suffering neither has faltered. . . . Since September sickness has not quitted the house. . . . I suspect now all this has been coming on for years. Unused, any of us, to the possession of robust health, we had not noticed the gradual approaches of decay: we did not know its symptoms: the little cough, the small appetite, the tendency to take cold at every variation of atmosphere have been regarded as things of course. I see them in another light now. . . .'

Anne was now the great concern of Charlotte and her father. The depressing and dangerous winter was slow in passing, and made it impossible for them to think of taking the invalid to a better climate to get a little sun. The doctors had absolutely forbidden it; they had to wait for good weather. Charlotte nursed her with a mother's care, anxiously watching for the coming of spring, then of summer so that Anne's only desire could be realised: to breathe the sea air at Scarborough where she had stayed several times with the Robinson family.

Ellen and her family had invited Anne to Brookroyd, but wisely and with very great tact she refused their generous offer. She dreamed only of going to the seaside, in the belief that that alone could save her; and, putting off her extreme reserve, she wrote to Ellen to ask her to go to Scarborough with her, Charlotte being unable to leave their father.

Charlotte, in spite of her growing anxiety and her tireless energy, could not succeed in mastering the grief she felt for the death of Emily. Yet she struggled against it all the time, sustaining her strength to help those who could not do without her. On 12

April 1849 she wrote to Ellen: 'I read Anne's letter to you; it was touching enough, as you say. . . . I am glad your friends object to your going with Anne, it would never do. To speak the truth, even if your mother and sisters had consented, I never could. . . . If, a month or six weeks hence, she continues to wish for a change as much as she does now, I shall go with her myself. . . . I have consulted Mr Teale, he does not object, and recommends Scarborough, which was Anne's own choice. . . .'

Mr Brontë, whose health was better, rid Charlotte of her scruples and decided that she was to accompany Anne, while he would remain with his two faithful and devoted servants.

On 1 May 1849, Charlotte wrote to Ellen: 'I am glad to hear that when we go to Scarboro', you will be at liberty to go with us; but the journey and its consequences still continue a source of great anxiety to me; I must try to put it off two or three weeks if I can; perhaps by that time the milder season may have given Anne more strength. . . . She wonders, I believe, why I don't talk more about the journey. . . . She is very much emaciated . . . her arms are no thicker than a little child's. The least exertion brings a shortness of breath. . . .'

'20th May: . . . We have engaged lodgings in Scarboro'. We stipulated for a good-sized sitting room and an airy double-bedded lodging-room, with a sea-view. . . . Anne says it is one of the best situations in the place. . . . Miss Outhwaite (her god-mother) left her in her will a legacy of £200, and she cannot employ her money better than in obtaining what may prolong existence, if it does not restore health. We hope to leave home on the 23rd, and I think it will be advisable to rest at York and stay all night there. . . .'

The two sisters left Haworth on Thursday, 24 May. They had arranged to meet Ellen at Leeds station the previous day but Anne was so ill on the Wednesday morning that they were unable to set off, and unable to inform Ellen, who had waited anxiously for them for hours at the station in Leeds where she had arrived at the agreed time. The next day, too anxious to wait any longer, Ellen set out for Haworth. She arrived just in time to help to carry the invalid into the post chaise which had pulled up at the gate.

Ellen Nussey wrote an account of these events for Mrs Gaskell: '. . . The first stage of our journey was to York: and here the dear invalid was so revived, so cheerful, and so happy, we drew consolation. . . .

'By her request we went to the minster. . . . On the 25th we arrived at Scarborough; on the 26th she drove on the sands for an hour . . . and drove the donkey-cart herself.

'On Sunday, the 27th, she wished to go to church . . . we thought it prudent to dissuade her from the attempt. . . .

'She walked a little in the afternoon . . . the evening closed in with the most glorious sunset ever witnessed. . . .

'The night was passed without any apparent accession of illness. She rose at seven o'clock and performed most of her toilet herself. . . .

'Nothing occurred to excite alarm till about 11 a.m. She then spoke of feeling a change. "She believed she had not long to live. Could she reach home alive, if we prepared immediately for departure?"

'A physician was sent for. . . . She begged him to say "how long he thought she might live; – not to fear speaking the truth, for she was not afraid to die". The doctor reluctantly admitted that the angel of death was already arrived, and that life was ebbing fast. She thanked him for his truthfulness, and he departed to come again very soon. She still occupied her easy chair. . . . She clasped her hands, and reverently invoked a blessing from on high; first upon her sister, then upon her friend, to whom she said, "Be a sister in my stead. Give Charlotte as much of your company as you can." She then thanked each of us for her kindness and attention.

'Ere long the restlessness of approaching death appeared, and she was borne to the sofa. . . . "Take courage, Charlotte; take courage." Her faith never failed, and her eye never dimmed till about two o'clock, when she calmly and without a sigh passed from the temporal to the eternal. . . .'

All through these months, Charlotte had been preparing herself for the final separation. Anne's gentle, peaceful death did not break her heart as Emily's pitiless end had done.

So she was left alone, desolate but brave, the sole support of her aged father. On the Tuesday she wrote to him, telling him all that had been done and begging him not to undertake the long journey to Scarborough to be at the funeral, for he would arrive too late.

Grief-stricken, thinking now only of Charlotte, his one reason for living, Mr Brontë begged her to prolong her stay at the seaside for a few weeks with Ellen, so as to try to regain her strength through rest.

Charlotte and Ellen therefore went to Filey, then to Easton, near Bridlington, to Ellen's friends. At the end of June, Charlotte came home to Haworth, while Ellen returned to Brookroyd. On 25 June 1849, Charlotte wrote to Mr Williams: 'I am now again at home, where I returned last Thursday. I call it home still – much as London would be called London if an earthquake should shake its streets to ruins. . . . In the daytime effort and occupation aid me, but when evening darkens, something in my heart revolts against the burden of solitude. – The sense of loss and want grows almost too much for me. I am not good or amiable in such moments. I am rebellious, and it is only the thought of my dear father in the next room, or of the two kind servants in the kitchen, or some caress from the poor dogs which restores me to softer sentiments and more rational views. As to the night – . . . waking, I think, sleeping, I dream of them; and I cannot recall them as they were in health, still they appear to me in sickness and suffering. . . .'

'Labour is the only radical cure for rooted sorrow. . . . Total change might do much; where that cannot be obtained, work is the best substitute. . . .'

On 1 July, she wrote to Ellen: 'I got home a little before eight o'clock. All was clean and bright, waiting for me. Papa and the servants are well; and all received me with an affection which should have consoled. The dogs seemed in strange ecstasy. I am certain they regarded me as the harbinger of others. The dumb creatures thought that as I was returned, those who had been so long absent were not far behind.

'I left papa soon and went into the dining-room . . . I felt that the house was all silent, the rooms were all empty. I remembered where the three were laid – in what narrow dark dwellings – never more to reappear on earth. So the sense of desolation and bitterness took possession of me. The agony that *was to be undergone* and *was not* to be avoided, came on. . . . Today, I am better. I do not know how life will pass, but I certainly feel confidence in Him who has upheld me hitherto. . . . Let me thank you once more, dear Ellen, for your kindness to me, which I do not mean to forget.'

On 14 July: 'My cold, wherever I got it, whether at Easton or elsewhere, is not vanished yet. . . . The pains between my shoulders likewise annoyed me much. Say nothing about it, for I confess I am too much disposed to be nervous. This nervousness is a horrid phantom. I dare communicate no ailment to papa, his anxiety harasses me inexpressibly. . . . Sometimes, Ellen, I have a heavy heart of it. But crushed I am not yet. . . . Still I have some strength to fight the battle of life. . . . [Do] not take alarm or think me in any way worse off than I am. . . .'

23

Shirley – *Charlotte plans to go to London*

After the brilliant success of *Jane Eyre*, publishers and readers had continued to praise the famous Currer Bell, urging her to write a second novel.

Charlotte wanted nothing better than to continue a career so brilliantly begun; but, if she enjoyed the pleasures of fame, she nevertheless felt its demands. As Mrs Gaskell has said: 'Whatever be the value of fame, he [the author] has it in his possession and is not willing to have it dimmed or lost.' *Noblesse oblige.*

As soon as *Jane Eyre* was published, Charlotte had begun to search for a new subject. She began three novels and dropped them at once. Then she had the idea of starting again with the elements of *The Professor*, her first book, paying attention to the wise remarks of Smith & Elder when they refused to publish it; she planned to make it a three-volume novel. She submitted this plan to Mr Williams, knowing very well that she could rely on getting a candid, straight answer.

Charlotte knew her limitations, and in her letters she very naturally emphasised them, not only as a matter of honesty but also for fear of raising too great hopes. We remember her first letter to Mr Williams, who had just congratulated Currer Bell and encouraged him on his way, when *Jane Eyre* was still on the press. Now she told him and, through him, Mr Smith of the deficiencies due to her solitary, secluded life, in which subjects for observation were limited. '. . . I must guess and calculate and grope my way in the dark, and come to uncertain conclusions unaided and alone where such writers as Dickens and Thackeray, having access to the shrine and image of Truth, have only to go into the temple, lift the veil a moment, and come out and say what they have seen. . . .'

In the end she found a promising subject in the Luddite riots, which had taken place in the district round Roe Head, where she had been at boarding-school as a pupil, and later as a teacher. She had been told many stories about them by Miss Wooler and by her father.

So as to enter into the spirit of these troubled times, she sent to Leeds for the *Mercury*[1] of the years 1812–13–14 and set to work with her usual enthusiasm and thoroughness.

'. . . As to my next book, I suppose it will grow to maturity in time, as grass grows or corn ripens; but I cannot force it. It makes slow progress thus far', she wrote to Mr Williams on 15 February 1848.

It was then that Branwell died. 'My book, alas! is laid aside for the present; imagination is pale, stagnant, mute. This incapacity chagrines me', she admits on 18 October 1848. Then followed Emily's illness and death; and finally Anne's illness. However, during the quieter days, when her young sister was resting, Charlotte took up her work again and in February 1849 she sent the first volume of the manuscript of *Shirley* to Cornhill.

'Oh! if Anne were well,' she wrote on 2 April 1849, 'if the dreary word *nevermore* would cease sounding in my ears, I think I could yet do something.'

On her return from Bridlington, after Anne's death, she again began to work steadily. Mr Williams and Mr Smith, sympathetic and affectionate, kept urging her to do so. 'But it was dreary to write without anyone to listen to the progress of her tale, – to find fault or to sympathise – while pacing the length of the parlour in the evenings, as in the days that were no more. Three sisters had done this – then two . . . and now one was left desolate, to listen for echoing footsteps that never came, – and to hear the wind sobbing at the windows, with an almost articulate sound. . . .' (G)

On 23 August 1849, she wrote to Ellen: 'Papa . . . has had another attack of bronchitis. I felt very uneasy about him for some days. . . . After what has happened, one trembles at any appearance of sickness; and when anything ails papa I feel too keenly that he is the *last*, the *only* near and dear relation I have in the world. . . .

'For myself I should be pretty well, but for a continually recurring feeling of slight cold, slight hoarseness in the throat and chest, of which – do what I will – I cannot quite get rid. . . . I wish the atmosphere would return to a salubrious condition. . . . English cholera has been very prevalent here. . . .'

1. *The Leeds Mercury* was the most important weekly in the North (1800–1850); it became a daily when the tax on paper was abolished.

On 29 August 1849, she announced to Mr Williams that she had finished *Shirley*: 'The book is now finished, thank God, and ready for Mr Taylor, but I have not yet heard from him. I thought I should be able to tell whether it was equal to *Jane Eyre* or not, but I find I cannot – it may be better, it may be worse. I shall be curious to hear your opinion, my own is of no value. . . .

'Whatever now becomes of the work, the occupation of writing it has been a boon to me. It took me out of dark and desolate reality into an unreal but happier region. The worst of it is, my eyes are grown somewhat weak and my head somewhat weary. . . . You can write nothing of value unless you give yourself wholly to the theme, and when you do so give yourself you lose appetite and sleep. . . .'

Mr Taylor, to whom Charlotte was to submit the manuscript of *Shirley*, had an important position with Smith & Elder, the publishers. He was the man Mrs Gaskell had referred to when she spoke of the second person to read *Jane Eyre*, 'a clear-headed Scotchman, not given to enthusiasm', who had spent half the night finishing the reading of this sensational novel. On his return from Scotland, Mr Taylor called at Haworth to get the precious manuscript of *Shirley* which he took to Cornhill. Mr Taylor was to be Charlotte's third suitor.

The author of *Jane Eyre* had tried to get out of herself, basing the action of her new novel on real events. *Shirley* does not spring from Charlotte's own emotions and reactions, as *Jane Eyre* does. So it does not have the same interest or charm. The events which Charlotte brought to life again had occurred in her native West Riding of Yorkshire about twenty miles from Haworth, in a region very different in appearance. We recall the old Roe Head house at Birstall, surrounded with verdure: 'Here, the park of Kirkleas, full of sunny glades.' A region of meadows, with mills strung along the banks of rivers which kept them turning profitably; thick woods sheltering beautiful homes; old manor houses like Fieldhead where Shirley Keeldar, the proud, well-born heiress had come to live. Charlotte enjoyed describing these familiar landscapes which she loved. She also enjoyed describing from real life the characters who were going to people her landscape: the three curates to begin with, so alive beneath the biting humour of the caricature that the young clergymen of Haworth recognised themselves immediately. Furious at first, then amused, and bearing her no resentment, they went the length of calling each other by the names Charlotte had given them, names which inmortalised them.

'The whole family of the Yorkes were, I have been assured, almost daguerreotypes. . . . From those many-sided sons, I suspect, she drew all that there was of truth in the characters of the heroes of her first two works. They, indeed, were almost the only young men she knew intimately, besides her brother.' (G) The Yorke family was, in fact, the Taylor family, whose two daughters Mary and Martha, as we have seen, had been the friends of Charlotte and her sisters. 'Shirley is none other than Emily, but an Emily living in wealth and prosperity: *Shirley* is a memorial to Emily. Shirley is less a portrait than a romantic figure in which Emily's outline has played a determining role.'[2]

Though it may please people to find the models for many of the characters in *Shirley*, Charlotte strongly denied having given exact descriptions of persons she had met, as she explained to Ellen: '. . . You are not to suppose any of the characters in *Shirley* intended as literal portraits. It would not suit the rules of art, nor my own feelings, to write in that style. We only suffer reality to *suggest*, never to *dictate*. The heroines are abstractions, and the heroes also. . . .'

Charlotte had invited Ellen to come to Haworth, but she was unable to do so. Charlotte was not sorry for at that time both servants, Tabby and young Martha, fell ill. One day when Martha's condition was very bad, Charlotte, on hearing a cry, went to the kitchen and found Tabby lying near the fireplace. She had fallen when trying to get up from her chair. Charlotte, depressed by headaches and poor health, overburdened by the variety of duties that weighed on her, experienced a moment of complete dejection. '. . . I sat and cried like a fool,' she confided to Ellen. 'That day I hardly knew what to do, or where to turn. Thank God! Martha is now convalescent; Tabby, I trust, will be better soon. Papa is pretty well. . . .'

Charlotte received five hundred pounds for the copyright of *Shirley*. The three novels, *Jane Eyre*, *Shirley*, and *Villette*, for each of which she received the same sum, earned her only fifteen hundred pounds. It is little, and surprises us today, especially as

2. M. Lane, op. cit., p. 231.

her publishers thought highly of her. And yet Charlotte was very glad of the five hundred pounds she got for *Shirley*, for the railway shares which she had bought with her aunt's legacy had fallen so far that she had hardly anything of her little income left. She accepted this stroke of fate with resignation, thinking of those who were completely ruined by this disastrous affair. 'When I look at my own case,' she wrote to Mr Smith on 4 October 1849, 'and compare it with that of thousands besides, I scarcely see room for a murmur. . . . The thought that *Shirley* has given pleasure at Cornhill yields me much quiet comfort. No doubt, however, you are, as I am, prepared for critical severity; but I have good hopes that the vessel is sufficiently sound of construction to weather a gale or two, and to make a prosperous voyage for you in the end.'

Already in 1846 Charlotte had foreseen the catastrophe in which almost all her assets were lost. She had wanted to sell her shares when the market was favourable but had relinquished the idea when she realised her sisters were opposed to it. She preferred to risk losing everything rather than act against the wishes of Emily.

Although the publishers had assured Charlotte of the pleasure they had had in reading *Shirley*, this second novel was not what they had expected after *Jane Eyre*. At the very beginning of the book the author derided curates and they did not like it. They thought they must discuss this and certain other points with her, to obtain some modifications. But Currer Bell, having finished her book, refused:

'I can work indefatigably at the correction of a work before it leaves my hand, but when once I have looked on it as completed and submitted it to the inspection of others, it becomes next to impossible to alter or amend.'[3]

Shirley appeared on 26 October 1849. Charlotte was worried and more anxious than ever to preserve her incognito, and when the critics in the first reviews affirmed that the mysterious Currer Bell, author of *Jane Eyre* and *Shirley*, was a woman, she was very upset.

In her reply to Mr Lewes on 1 November 1849, she emphasised her continuing concern not to be taken for a woman: '. . . I wish

3. Quoted by M. Lane, ibid., p. 232.

all reviewers believed "Currer Bell" to be a man, they would be more just to him. . . . All mouths will be open against that first chapter, and that first chapter is as true as the Bible . . . still, I earnestly conjure you to say honestly what you think [of *Shirley*].'

Towards the end of October, Charlotte felt free to spend a week at Ellen's. As she was not well, she was not able to enjoy this long-anticipated visit to the full. In addition she was very anxious to know how her second novel would be received by the public.

Seeing that her listlessness continued, along with headaches, nausea, hoarseness, and pains in her chest, Charlotte decided to catch the illness in time by going to London to consult a doctor. Her first intention had been to pay no visits, but the anxious care of her publishers prevailed and it was decided that she would be Mrs Smith's guest.

On 15 November 1849, she wrote to Mr Williams: 'As far as I can judge from the tone of the newspapers, it seems that those who were most charmed with *Jane Eyre* are the least pleased with *Shirley*; they are disappointed at not finding the same excitement, interest, stimulus. . . . Mere novel readers, it is evident, think *Shirley* something of a failure. Still the majority of the notices have on the whole been favourable. . . .'

On 22 November 1849, she wrote to Ellen: '. . . *Shirley* works her way. The reviews shower in fast. . . . The best critique which has yet appeared is in the *Revue des Deux Mondes*, Eugène Forcade, the reviewer in question, follows Currer Bell through every winding, discerns every point, discriminates every shade, proves himself master of the subject. . . . With that man I would shake hands if I saw him. I would say: "You know me, monsieur, I shall deem it an honour to know you." I could not say so much to five hundred men and women in all the millions of Great Britain. That matters little. My conscience I satisfy first; and having done that, if I further content and delight a Forcade, a Fontblanque, and a Thackeray, my ambition has had its ration. . . .'

Four days later Charlotte announced her departure to Ellen: '. . . If all be well, I go to London this week probably on Wednesday. The dressmaker has done my small matters pretty well, but I wish you could have looked over them, and given a dictum. I insisted on the dresses being made quite plainly. . . .'

Charlotte had had a copy of *Shirley* sent to Mrs Gaskell, then another to Miss Harriet Martineau[4] for whom she felt 'lively admiration, a deep esteem'[5] adding a few lines: 'Currer Bell offers a copy of *Shirley* to Miss Martineau's acceptance in acknowledgement of the pleasure and profit she [crossed out] he has derived from her works. . . . In his mind *Deerbrook* ranks with the writings that have really done him good.'

On 29 November, just before leaving, Charlotte wrote to Mr Williams: '. . . The note you sent yesterday was from Harriet Martineau; its contents were most gratifying. I ought to be thankful, and I trust I am for such testimonies of sympathy from the first order of minds. . . .'

Through a sort of intuition, Miss Martineau, while she addressed her letter to Currer Bell, Esq., began it: 'Dear Madam'.

4. Social and historical writer (1802–1876). She did much to popularise economics, was a propagandist for religious liberalism and for the abolition of slavery. She became an adherent of the positivist philosophy of Comte.

5. A phrase from a letter of Charlotte Brontë to Mr Williams, 20 November 1849.

24

Charlotte's first visit alone to London (1849) – Charlotte calls on Harriet Martineau – Back in Haworth – Ellen Nussey – Winter again – Charlotte's fame in her own village – Charlotte and Mr Lewes – Sir James Kay-Shuttleworth

Charlotte set out alone for London with a heavy heart. The dream she had always cherished was coming true, but she was emotionally unresponsive to it. Without those who were now dead, Emily especially, the beams of fame had lost their life-giving warmth.

However, during the five years that were to follow, she was to accept admiration and homage from her equals, from Thackeray in particular, and from the public with unaffected gratitude. She was to draw from fame the strength necessary to continue her solitary way, to struggle against her ill-health, against loneliness and despair.

It was in the most brilliant literary circles of London that the powerful, the amazing Currer Bell was to undergo her transformation, appearing suddenly in the shape of a tiny creature, self-effacing and almost trembling: Charlotte Brontë. She was entertained first at Westbourne Place by Mr George Smith, her kind publisher, and his mother, and then at Phillimore Gardens, Kensington, by Dr Wheelwright, whose daughter Laetitia had been her friend since they met in Brussels.

After the first few days, Charlotte wrote to Ellen: '. . . I came to this great Babylon last Thursday and have been in what seems to me a sort of whirl ever since . . . I like [Mr Smith] even better as a son and brother than as a man of business. Mr Williams, too, is really most gentlemanly and well informed. His weak points he certainly has, but these are not seen in society. Mr Taylor – the little man – . . . is rigid, despotic and self-willed. He tries to be very kind and even to express sympathy sometimes, but he does not manage it. . . . I have seen Thackeray. . . .'

It had been understood that she would meet few people. After being used to living very quietly, she always found it a great effort to meet new people, to strive to keep a conversation going. But she was extremely anxious to meet the authors whose books she had admired. Mr Smith, always very attentive, knowing Charlotte's worship of Thackeray, the Titan, the Lion of Juda, as she called him, invited him to dinner at Westbourne Place. Ill-luck would have it that that morning Charlotte had gone sightseeing in London and did not get back to her friend's house until after the midday meal.

'... At the moment Mr Thackeray presented himself,' she wrote to Ellen on 10 December 1849, 'I was thoroughly faint from inanition, having eaten nothing since a very slight breakfast, and it was then *seven* o'clock in the evening. Excitement and exhaustion together made savage work of me that evening. What he thought of me I cannot tell. . . .

'. . . If Mrs Smith were not kind, I should sometimes be miserable. . . . I have seen many things. I hope some day to tell you what. . . .'

Once home again, her first letter to Ellen from the parsonage was a tribute to Thackeray: '. . . Thackeray is a Titan of mind. His presence and powers impress me deeply in an intellectual sense; I do not see him or know him as a man. All the others are subordinate. I have esteem for some, and, I trust, courtesy for all. . . . I believe most of them expected me to come out in a more marked, eccentric, striking light . . . I felt sufficiently at my ease with all except Thackeray; and with him I was painfully stupid. . .'

Charlotte Brontë told Mrs Gaskell how difficult it had been, in the course of this first interview, to know whether Thackeray was joking or speaking seriously. The great man's irony disconcerted her. What Thackeray thought of her he was to say later in his preface to the fragment *Emma* which Charlotte Brontë wrote after her marriage, and which was broken off by her death.

'I remember the trembling little frame, the little hand, the great honest eyes. An impetuous honesty seemed to me to characterise the woman. . . . New to the London world, she entered it with an independent, indomitable spirit of her own; and judged of contemporaries, and especially spied out arrogance or affectation, with extraordinary keenness of vision. . . . I fancied an austere little Joan of Arc marching in upon us, and rebuking our easy lives, our easy morals.' As for the others, on the whole, Charlotte made a strong impression on them. In spite of her shyness, her reserve, when the conversation took a turn which aroused her enthusiasm or her scorn, the real Charlotte Brontë was suddenly revealed. Quivering with emotion she would become eloquent, her eyes would shine with unusual intelligence and power. Then, as if exhausted by too great an effort, she would assume once more the still, timid look that was habitual to her, shutting within herself the treasures of a nature that one had to learn how to discover but which was revealed by her novels. '[She had] peculiar eyes, of which I find it difficult to give a description, as they appeared to me in her later life. They were large, and well shaped; their colour a reddish brown; but if the iris was closely examined, it appeared to be composed of a great variety of tints. The usual expression was of quiet, listening intelligence; but now and then, on some just occasion for vivid interest or wholesome indignation, a light would shine out, as if some spiritual lamp had been kindled, which glowed behind those impressive orbs. I never saw the like in any other human creature. . . .' (G)

It was during her stay with Mrs and Mr Smith that *The Times* published a harsh, savage criticism of *Shirley*. Charlotte was very hurt by it, especially for the sake of her publishers, although the exaggeration and unfair bitterness of the article greatly reduced its importance. She was very sensitive to the kindness and tact of her hosts on this occasion.

Charlotte, having learned that Miss Martineau was staying in London, with friends who lived near Westbourne Place, had written telling her that Currer Bell would like to meet her.

On 10 December, Charlotte accordingly went alone in a carriage to the house of Miss Martineau's friends, where she was expected about six o'clock for tea. Everyone present was very excited. When Currer Bell was announced who would appear? A man or a woman? In the bloom of youth or in declining years?

Every time the bell rang, all the guests looked towards the door. Soon a gentleman, six feet tall, came in. Was he the famous Currer Bell, the author of *Jane Eyre*? No, he was not. Soon after, at the appointed time, 'Miss Brogden' was announced. Then appeared in the doorway 'the smallest creature I had ever seen, except at a fair', relates Miss Martineau. It was Charlotte Brontë, still anxious to remain incognito, 'in a deep mourning dress, neat as a Quaker's, with her beautiful hair smooth and brown, her fine eyes blazing with meaning and her sensible face indicating a habit of self control'. Mrs Gaskell in her turn writes: 'She came – hesitated one moment . . . then went straight to Miss Martineau with intuitive recognition . . . she soon became as one of the family seated round the tea-table; and before she left, she told them, in a simple, touching manner, of her sorrow and isolation.' (G)

The day before she was to leave London, Mr Smith gave a dinner party in her honour. On her return to Haworth, she sent Laetitia Wheelwright an account of this evening: '. . . The evening after I left you passed better than I expected. Thanks to my substantial lunch and cheering cup of coffee, I was able to wait the eight o'clock dinner with complete resignation, and to endure its length quite courageously, nor was I too exhausted to converse, and of this I was glad, for otherwise I know my kind host and hostess would have been much disappointed. There were only seven gentlemen at dinner besides Mr Smith, but of these, five were critics – a formidable band, including the literary Rhadamanthi of *The Times*, *The Athenaeum*, *The Examiner*, *The Spectator*, and *The Atlas*: men more dreaded in the world of letters than you can conceive. I did not know how much their presence and conversation had excited me till they were gone, and then reaction commenced. When I had retired for the night I wished to sleep, the effort to do so was vain – I could not close my eyes. . . .'

When Charlotte was back in Haworth, Mr Brontë had the pleasure, impatiently awaited, of hearing her relate in great detail what she had seen of the wonders of the astonishing capital. She told him of the exhibition of Turner's water colours, which she had greatly admired; of the production of *Macbeth*, and of *Othello*, with the actor Macready, whom she did not like; of the National Gallery; of her visit to the Zoo, willingly describing for him in picturesque detail the most unusual of the animals. Then he sadly recalled Emily's answer when someone urged her to go somewhere: 'What is the use? Charlotte will bring it all home to me.'[1]

Overcome again by the unbearable misery of loneliness, Charlotte invited Ellen to come to Haworth.

On 3 January 1850, she wrote to Mr Williams of her friendship for Ellen and of friendship in general: 'Friendship, however, is a plant which cannot be forced. . . . Affection was first a germ, then

1. M. Lane, op. cit., p. 233.

a sapling, then a strong tree – now no new friend, however lofty or profound in intellect – not even Miss Martineau herself – could be to me what Ellen is; yet she is no more than a conscientious, observant, calm, well-bred Yorkshire girl. She is without romance. If she attempts to read poetry, or poetic prose aloud, I am irritated and deprive her of the book – if she talks of it, I stop my ears. But she is good; she is true, she is faithful, and I love her.

'Since I came home, Miss Martineau has written me a long and truly kind letter. She invited me to visit her at Ambleside. . . .'

The winter was hard, as always. However, Charlotte's health resisted it better than usual, no doubt because of the change and of the advice of the doctor consulted in London. Perhaps also because Ellen, during her stay with her, had forced her to look after herself.

The anniversary of Emily's death reawakened her grief. After Ellen had left, she was alone again with her father. Mr Brontë, whose habits nothing had been able to change, had his midday meal alone in his study, served by his daughter. After his meal she read to him for an hour; then, always alone, for he refused to have anyone to accompany him, he went wherever his duty called him. He often came back exhausted by his long journeys over the moors, too long for a man of his age, but astonished and dejected at feeling so tired. '. . . His strength of will was the same as ever. That which he resolved to do he did, at whatever cost of weariness, but his daughter was all the more anxious from seeing him so regardless of himself and his health. The hours of retiring for the night had always been early in the parsonage; now family prayers were at eight o'clock; directly after which Mr Brontë and old Tabby went to bed and Martha was not long in following. But Charlotte could not have rested. . . . She stopped up . . . striving to beguile the lonely night with some employment, till her weak eyes failed to read or to sew, and could only weep in solitude over the dead that were not. No one on earth can even imagine what these hours were to her. All the grim superstitions of the North had been implanted in her during her childhood by the servants who believed in them. They recurred to her now, – with no shrinking from the spirits of the dead, but with such an intense longing once more to stand face to face with the souls of her sisters, as no one but she could have felt. It seemed as if the very strength of her yearning should have compelled them to appear. On windy nights, cries, and sobs, and wailings seemed to go round the house, as of the dearly-beloved striving to force their way to her.' (G) How could her nervous system, her delicate health withstand such attacks?

Now that *Shirley* was finished, and since her tasks as mistress of the house in no way absorbed a mind like hers, she lived only for the arrival of the post, the day's only distraction. She soon blamed herself for this. Forcing herself to write less often, she also asked her Cornhill friends to send fewer letters. On 16 February 1850 she confided to Ellen: 'I cannot help feeling something of the excitement of expectation till the post hour comes, and when, day after day, it brings nothing, I get low. This is a stupid, disgraceful, unmeaning state of things ... but it is so bad for the mind to be quite alone, and to have none with whom to talk over little crosses and disappointments, and laugh them away. If I could write, I dare say I should be better, but I cannot write a line....' Then she tells Ellen of the emotion she felt when her father gave her her mother's letters and papers.[2]

The books which she had been receiving regularly from Cornhill since her visit to London with Anne in July 1848 were her one comfort. She often wondered what would become of her all through the silent hours but for the cheer they always provided. She opened every new parcel with the same joyous haste – soon mixed with the bitter regret that she was now left alone to savour this pleasure. However, her father, who had remained a great reader, took a lively interest in what was sent.

The publication of *Shirley* had convinced the majority of its readers that its author must live in the area where the action took place. A certain native of Haworth, who had settled in Liverpool, decided that, judging by the names of the places and the dialect used, the author belonged to his village. But who, apart from the vicar's daughter, could write this book? Proud of his discovery – which to him was the truth – he published it in a Liverpool newspaper. 'Far and wide in the West Riding had spread the intelligence that Currer Bell was no other than a daughter of the venerable clergyman of Haworth ... the village itself caught up the excitement.' (G)

2. See p. 24.

On 19 January 1850, Charlotte wrote to Ellen: '. . . Mr Nicholls having finished *Jane Eyre* is now crying out for the "other book"; he is to have it next week.'

On 28 January of the same year, in a post-script, 'Mr Nicholls has finished reading *Shirley*, he is delighted with it. John Brown's wife seriously thought he had gone wrong in the head as she heard him giving vent to roars of laughter as he sat alone, clapping his hands and stamping on the floor. He would read all the scenes about the curates aloud to papa, he triumphed in his own character. . . .' Charlotte had represented him in the person of Mr Macarthy. 'He proved himself as decent, decorous, and conscientious, as Peter [Malone] was rampant, boisterous. . . . He laboured faithfully in the parish. . . . Being human, of course he had his faults; these, however, were proper, steady-going, clerical faults; the circumstance of finding himself invited to tea with a Dissenter would unhinge him for a week; . . . otherwise he was sane and rational, diligent and charitable.'[3]

On 2 February 1850 to Mr Williams: 'I believe both *Shirley* and *Jane Eyre* are being a good deal read in the north just now; . . . one or two curiosity-hunters have made their way to Haworth parsonage, but our rude hills and rugged neighbourhood will, I doubt not, form a sufficient barrier to the frequent repetition of such visits. . . .'

On 5 February, to Ellen: '. . . Martha came in yesterday, puffing and blowing, and much excited. "I've heard such news," she began. "Please, madam, you've been and written two books, the grandest books that ever was seen. My father has heard it at Halifax. . . ." "Hold your tongue, Martha, and be off." I fell into a cold sweat. . . .'

On 16 February, also to Ellen: 'The Haworth people have been making great fools of themselves about *Shirley*. . . . When they got the volumes at the Mechanics' Institute,[4] all the members wanted them. They cast lots for the whole three, and whoever got a volume was only allowed to keep it two days, and was to be fined a shilling per diem for longer detention. . . .'

Yet Charlotte 'was extremely touched in the secret places of her heart to see how proud those who had known her from her

3. Charlotte Brontë, *Shirley* (World Classics, O.U.P.), p. 632.
4. A 'club' for craftsmen.

childhood were of her success. . . . Strangers came "from beyond Bromley" to see her, as she went quietly and unconsciously into church; and the sexton "gained many a half-crown" for pointing her out.' (G)

If this wonderful tribute made Charlotte forget the stinging, immoderate *Times* articles, the one by Mr G. H. Lewes in *The Edinburgh Review* of January 1850 hurt her deeply. At that time, books written by women were not taken seriously by the critics, and so Charlotte had an urgent desire to be judged as a writer, without her sex having to be taken into consideration. Now, in Mr Lewes's article on *Shirley*, the first two pages were headed 'Mental Equality of the Sexes?' and 'Female Literature'.

A few days after the appearance of this article, Charlotte wrote to Mr Lewes: 'I can be on my guard against my enemies, but God deliver me from my friends!'

Mr Lewes protested against such susceptibility, and Charlotte this time replied with complete sincerity, but in a calm and friendly tone: '19th January, 1850, My dear Sir, I will tell you why I was so hurt by that review in *The Edinburgh* – not because its criticism was keen or its blame sometimes severe; not because its praise was stinted (for, indeed, I think you gave me quite as much praise as I deserve) but because after I had said earnestly that I wished critics would judge me as an author, not as a woman, you so roughly – I even thought cruelly – handled the question of sex. . . .

'However, I shake hands with you; you have excellent points; you can be generous; I still feel angry . . . but it is the anger one experiences for rough play rather than for foul play.'

In March 1850 to Ellen: 'Various folks are beginning to come boring to Haworth, on the wise errand of seeing the scenery described in *Jane Eyre* and *Shirley*; amongst others, Sir J. K. Shuttleworth and Lady Shuttleworth have persisted in coming; they were here on Friday. The baronet looks in vigorous health, he scarcely appears more than thirty-five, but he says he is forty-four; Lady Shuttleworth is rather handsome and still young. They were both quite unpretending. . . .'

They lived in Lancashire on the crest of the moors, about twelve miles from Haworth as the crow flies. They gave Charlotte a pressing invitation to come to their home, Gawthorpe Hall; for Sir James Shuttleworth, proud of knowing Mrs Gaskell, was equally anxious to count the author of *Jane Eyre* and *Shirley* among his friends. After some indecision, urged by her father, who was always anxious to find distractions for her, Charlotte finally agreed to go there for a few days.

Back from this short stay in Lancashire, she wrote to Mr Williams on 16 March 1850: 'The quiet drives to old ruins and old halls situate amongst older hills and woods, the dialogues (perhaps I should rather say monologues, for I listened far more than I talked) by the fireside in his antique oak-panelled drawing-room, while they suited him, did not too much oppress and exhaust me. The house, too, is very much to my taste, near three centuries old, grey, stately, and picturesque. On the whole, now that the visit is over, I do not regret having paid it. The worst of it is that there is now some menace hanging over my head of an invitation to go to them in London during the season. . . .'

In March and April, the very damp weather made Haworth more unhealthy than ever. There was a sort of epidemic there again, in the form of a low fever. The inhabitants of the parsonage did not escape, the contagion being made worse by the unhealthy proximity of the churchyard, in which the graves went on accumulating. Mr Brontë had appealed in vain to the Ministry of Health for a new cemetery on the hillside, to replace the old one. Charlotte, depressed by this feverish infection, worried about how her father would react, was more and more apprehensive about travelling to London with Sir James and Lady Shuttleworth.

On 12 April 1850, she wrote to Ellen: '. . . I then gave notice that I would not be lionised; that is why he talks of "small parties". . . . Sir James has been a physician, and looks at me with a physician's eye: he saw at once that I could not stand much fatigue, nor bear the presence of many strangers. . . . But none, – not the most skilful physician – can get at more than the outside of these things, the heart knows its own bitterness, and the frame its own poverty, and the mind its own struggles. Papa is eager and restless for me to go. . . .'

But Mr Brontë was far from better; Charlotte herself had a bad cold and persistent sore throats, Martha had the fever, Tabby alone kept well. How could she think of leaving for London? On 11 May she told Ellen: '. . . I did not think papa well enough to be left, and accordingly begged Sir James and Lady Shuttleworth to return to London without me. . . .'

The days passed; thanks to careful attention, Mr Brontë regained health and strength. Charlotte thought that she could then, without the least fear, leave her father in the care of the servants.

A new obstacle suddenly appeared. On 22 May, she wrote to Mr James Taylor at Cornhill: 'My journey to London is again postponed and this time indefinitely. Sir James Kay Shuttleworth's state of health is the cause. . . . The longings for liberty and leisure which May sunshine wakens in you, stir my sympathy. . . . For my part, I am free to walk on the moors, but when I go out there alone, everything reminds me of the times when others were with me, and then the moors seem a wilderness featureless, solitary, saddening. . . .'

Charlotte was conducting a voluminous correspondence at this time. As well as having to reply to numerous admirers there were the authors who sent her their books. She had to take care – and it was sometimes difficult – to avoid hurting their touchy susceptibility.

25

Charlotte's second stay in London (1850) – Dinner with Thackeray – Charlotte's journey to Scotland – Visit to the Lakes – Her meeting with Mrs Gaskell – The article by Sydney Dobell – Visit to Miss Martineau

At last, on 3 June, Charlotte wrote to Ellen: 'Gloucester Terrace, Hyde Park Gardens. I came to London last Thursday. I am staying at Mrs Smith's, who has changed her residence as the address will show. . . . I at last explained to Sir James that I had some little matters of business to transact and that I should reside quietly at my publishers. . . . I have seen very few persons, and am not likely to see many. . . . We have been to the Exhibition of the Royal Academy, to the Opera, and the Zoological Gardens. The weather is splendid. I shall not stay longer than a fortnight in London. . . .'

On 12 June, she resumed her story: '. . . Of course I cannot in a letter give you a regular chronicle of how my time has been spent. I can only just notify what I deem three of the chief incidents. A sight of the Duke of Wellington at the Chapel Royal (he is a real grand old man), a visit to the House of Commons . . . and last, and not least, an interview with Mr Thackeray. He made a morning call, and sat about two hours. Mr Smith only was in the room the whole time. . . . The giant[1] sat before me; I was moved to speak to him of some of his shortcomings (literary, of course); one by one the faults came into my mind, and one by one I brought them out, and sought some explanation or defence. He did defend himself, like a great Turk and heathen; that is to say, the excuses were often worse than the crime itself. The matter ended in decent amity; if all be well I am to dine at his house this evening. . . . I have seen Lewes, too. . . .' Thackeray and Charlotte had a profound admiration for one another. But how could the mocking humour of the one come to terms with the gravity of the other?

1. Thackeray was over 6 ft tall.

As for Mr Lewes, Charlotte found that he resembled Emily, which moved her to tears. He remained sitting beside her during a whole evening, very interested by her conversation. 'On parting we shook hands, and she said, "We are friends now, are we not?" "Were we not always, then?" I asked. "No, not always," she said, significantly; and that was the only allusion she made to the offending article.' (G)

He had given her some novels of Balzac and George Sand to take away. When she returned them to him after reading them, she told him shortly that she preferred George Sand to Balzac. She admired Balzac but did not like him.

Here is the portrait which, later on, Mr Lewes was to give George Eliot of Charlotte: 'A little, plain, provincial, sickly-looking old maid, yet what passion, what fire in her!'[2]

Lady Ritchie, one of Thackeray's daughters, gives a humorous description of Charlotte's arrival, accompanied by Mr Smith, at the time fixed for the dinner: '. . . I can still see the scene quite plainly – the hot summer evening, the open windows, the carriage driving to the door. . . . We saw the carriage stop. . . . My father, who had been walking up and down the room, goes out into the hall to meet his guests, and then, after a moment's delay, the door opens wide, and the two gentlemen come in, leading a tiny, delicate, serious little lady, pale . . . our hearts are beating with wild excitement. This then is the authoress, the unknown power whose books have set all London talking . . . some people even say our father wrote the books – the wonderful books . . . the moment is so breathless that dinner comes as a relief to the solemnity of the occasion, and we all smile as my father stoops to offer his arm; for, though genius she may be, Miss Brontë can barely reach his elbow. . . .'[3]

After dinner, during which Thackeray did most of the talking, they all moved into the drawing-room where a select company was gathered in honour of Charlotte Brontë, who was the embodiment of Jane Eyre; the famous Carlyle and Mrs Carlyle were there. They all waited in vain for the brilliant conversation they had hoped to hear. Charlotte withdrew to a sofa and from time to time she exchanged a few kind words with the governess. When

2. J. Clarke, *Haworth Parsonage*, p. 188.
3. Clement Shorter, op. cit., vol. II, p. 93.

Mrs Brookfield asked her if she liked London, 'the little lady' replied with lowered eyes 'yes . . . and no'.

Mrs Procter, one of the guests, said afterwards that it was 'one of the dullest evenings she had ever spent in her life'. After Charlotte Brontë had left, Thackeray, worn out, abandoned his guests to their fate, took French leave and finished the night at the Garrick Club.

On 21 June, Charlotte wrote to Ellen: 'I am leaving London, if all be well, on Tuesday, and shall be very glad to come to you for a few days. . . . My London visit has much surpassed my expectations. . . . Mrs Smith's youngest son is at school in Scotland, and George, her eldest, is going to fetch him home for the vacation; the other evening he announced his intention of taking one of his sisters with him, and proposed that Miss Brontë should go to Edinburgh, and join them there, and see the city and its suburbs. I concluded he was joking, laughed and declined; however, it seems he was in earnest . . . I still refused. Mrs Smith did not favour it; you may easily fancy how she helped me to sustain my opposition, but her worthy son only waxed more determined. His mother is master of the house, but he is master of his mother. This morning she came and entreated me to go. (George wishes it so much); now I believe that George and I understand each other very well, and respect each other sincerely. We do not embarrass each other or very rarely, my six or eight years of seniority, to say nothing of lack of all pretension to beauty etc., are a perfect safeguard. I should not in the least fear to go with him to China. I like to see him pleased, I greatly *dis*like to ruffle and disappoint him, so he shall have his mind, and, if all be well, I mean to join him in Edinburgh. . . .'

When she returned from Edinburgh, Charlotte went straight to Ellen's at Brookroyd to rest a little before going on to Haworth.

She wrote to Mr Williams: '. . . Those were two very pleasant days. I always liked Scotland as an idea, but now, as a reality, I like it far better; it furnished me with some hours as happy almost as any I ever spent. . . . My dear Sir, do not think I blaspheme when I tell you that your great London, as compared to Dun-Edin . . . is as prose compared to poetry. . . . You have nothing like Arthur's Seat, and above all you have not the Scotch national character; and it is that grand character after all which gives the land its true charm, its true greatness.'

On 30 July, it was to her friend Laetitia Wheelwright that she delighted in describing once again this fairytale journey: '... My stay in Scotland was short, and what I saw was chiefly comprised in Edinburgh and the neighbourhood, in Abbotsford and Melrose.... Edinburgh compared to London is like a vivid page of history compared to a huge dull treatise on political economy; and as to Melrose and Abbotsford, the very names possess music and magic....'

While Charlotte was staying in London, Richmond had drawn her portrait which Mr Smith wished to give to Mr Brontë. Mr Nicholls, Charlotte's husband, was to bequeath it later to the National Portrait Gallery.

On the same day, two portraits arrived in Haworth, that of Charlotte by Richmond, for Mr Brontë, and also a reproduction of the Wellington portrait, also by Richmond, for Charlotte. On 1 August 1850, Charlotte wrote to Mr Smith to thank him for these gifts, saying that the portrait of the Duke of Wellington was a treasure to her. Then she added: 'Papa seems much pleased with the portrait, as do the few other persons who have seen it, with one notable exception, viz. our old servant who tenaciously maintains that it is not like – that it is old-looking – but, as she, with equal tenacity, asserts that the Duke of Wellington's portrait is a portrait of "The Master" (meaning papa) I am afraid not much weight is to be ascribed to her opinion....'

Mrs Gaskell considered this pastel drawing 'an admirable likeness'.

Sir James Kay-Shuttleworth and Lady Shuttleworth, who had taken a house in the Lake District, at Windermere, invited Charlotte to stay with them. She accepted unwillingly, and only to please her father. Misfortune had made her fearful and she always felt apprehensive about leaving her 'dear papa'. It was during this visit that Charlotte Brontë and Mrs Gaskell met. Mrs Gaskell at once felt drawn to the little person in a black silk dress who was introduced to her: sad, reserved, with a very soft voice. Charlotte let herself be won over by the charm, the gay, friendly manner and the kind heart of Mrs Gaskell, a happily fulfilled wife and mother. Her shyness was broken down by the warm sympathy shown her by this new friend. During the three days which they spent together, they confided their impressions, their ideas and their feelings to each other, as they sewed in the drawing-room with Lady Shuttleworth and during their drives with Sir James in this magnificent region which Charlotte had formerly only imagined in dreams.

Without suspecting that five years later hers would be the sad honour of writing *The Life of Charlotte Brontë*, Mrs Gaskell was passionately interested by everything concerning the famous author of *Jane Eyre* and *Shirley*.

The contrast between this frail, solitary creature, broken by suffering, a prey to perpetual anxieties, and the vigour, power and daring of her imagination impressed her so much that the echo of her astonishment is heard in the biography of Charlotte.

Immediately she returned home, Mrs Gaskell, as if urged on by some premonition, wrote to her friend, Catherine Winkworth, who was a great admirer of Currer Bell, a letter which was fortunately preserved. Writing while the memory was very fresh, she presented Charlotte Brontë as she had appeared to her. She also gave some moving details supplied by Lady Shuttleworth. When Mrs Gaskell gave an account of this memorable meeting in *The Life of Charlotte Brontë* she quoted a part of her letter to Catherine Winkworth, and so was able to give us her first impressions in all their spontaneity.

After this meeting, the two new friends maintained a regular correspondence and Charlotte sent Mrs Gaskell a copy of the *Poems* by Currer, Ellis and Acton Bell: 'The little book of rhymes was sent by way of fulfilling a rashly made promise; and the promise was made to prevent you from throwing away four shillings in an injudicious purchase. I do not like my own share of the work, nor care that it should be read: Ellis Bell's I think good and vigorous and Acton's have the merit of truth and simplicity. Mine are chiefly juvenile productions, the restless effervescence of a mind that would not be still. . . .' Charlotte had not included in the collection any of the Angrian poems, which are her best – they are full of interest, fire and brilliance. She told tales marvellously in verse as well as prose. Yet a reading of all that she wrote shows that she expressed the poetry of her nature only in the passionate lyricism of her prose.

It was in September 1850 that Sydney Dobell wrote in *The*

Palladium his famous article on the novels of the Brontës. He had been the first to reveal the power, the strange beauty and the high literary merit of *Wuthering Heights*. At last, although too late, justice was done to Emily, and Charlotte's heart was overflowing with gratitude. But Sydney Dobell remained convinced like so many others that *Wuthering Heights* was only a first attempt by the author of *Jane Eyre*. To dispel all misapprehensions and re-establish the truth of the matter, Mr Smith decided to publish a new edition of *Wuthering Heights* and *Agnes Grey* with a preface by Charlotte, accompanied by a biographical notice on her sisters. Since their death, she had not dared to open their books again. She shuddered with terror at the thought of what she was about to undertake, afraid of the depression that was bound to follow: '. . . I found the task at first exquisitely painful and depressing, but regarding it in the light of a *sacred duty*, I went on, and now can bear it better. It is work, however, that I cannot do in the evening, for if I did I should have no sleep at night . . .' she wrote to Ellen on 3 October.

Since her stay in London, followed by the unforgettable visit to Scotland, Charlotte felt her isolation and loneliness more and more. The tribute to the memory of her sisters plunged her into a grief which was made worse by the long nights of a hard, dreary winter. In an effort to rid herself of a persistent nightmare and also to placate her father who was then very well, she accepted the warm and pressing invitation of Miss Harriet Martineau who had returned to Ambleside in the Lake District. Before going, Charlotte sent a copy of the second edition of *Wuthering Heights* to Mr Dobell and wrote to him: '. . . I offer this little book to my critic in *The Palladium* and he must believe it accompanied by a tribute of the sincerest gratitude; not so much for anything he has said of myself as for the noble justice he has rendered to one dear to me as myself – perhaps dearer. . . .'

From Ambleside, Charlotte wrote to Ellen on 18 December: '. . . I shall never forget last autumn! Some days and nights have been cruel; my recollection of my sisters intolerably poignant. I am better now. I am at Miss Martineau's for a week. Her house is very pleasant, both within and without; . . . her visitors enjoy the most perfect liberty; what she claims for herself she allows them. I rise at my own hour, breakfast alone (she is up at five and takes a cold bath, and a walk by starlight, and has finished breakfast and got to her work by seven o'clock). I pass the morning in the drawing-room, she in her study. At two o'clock we meet; work, talk, and walk together till five, her dinner hour; spend the evening together, when she converses fluently and abundantly, and with the most complete frankness. I go to my own room soon after ten; she sits up writing letters till twelve.... She is a great and good woman; of course not without peculiarities ... she is both hard and warm-hearted, abrupt and affectionate, liberal and despotic. I believe she is not at all conscious of her own absolutism....'

In a letter of 15 January 1851 to Mr James Taylor, Charlotte returned to a discussion of Miss Martineau whose personality surprised and impressed her, and also attracted her, illustrating the saying that unlikes attract each other. 'You asked me whether Miss Martineau made me a convert to mesmerism? Scarcely; yet I heard miracles of its efficacy and could hardly discredit the whole of what was told me. I even underwent a personal experiment; and though the result was not absolutely clear, it was inferred that in time I should prove an excellent subject....'

In spite of her admiration for Miss Martineau, Charlotte could not share her philosophical, political or religious opinions. When her friend's new book appeared, written in collaboration with Mr Atkinson, *Letters on the Nature and Development of Man*, the explicit atheism of the authors was to prove unbearable to her. And yet she was to be angry about the scornful criticism it received.

Before returning to Haworth, Charlotte spent a few days with Ellen.

26

Villette – *Charlotte and Mr James Taylor – Charlotte and Mr George Smith – Charlotte's third visit to London (1851) – Return to Haworth via Manchester – Charlotte falls ill – Visit to Scarborough – Charlotte returns to her writing*

During the four or five months which preceded her third stay in London in May 1851, Charlotte, urged by her publishers, started to work again on the theme of *The Professor*, but dealing with it in quite a different way. This became *Villette*. But terrible depressions, violent headaches, frequently recurring attacks of faintness often forced her to break off. She was very annoyed about this. In March she called on Ellen for help. And Ellen hurried to her aid.

Charlotte used all her resources to be a pleasant hostess to Ellen during her several weeks' stay. She grew calmer and more cheerful.

In the meantime Messrs Smith & Elder had decided that, if their publishing business was to prosper, they must start a branch in India and declared that only Mr James Taylor was capable of carrying out such a difficult enterprise successfully. Mr Taylor was obliged to accept this onerous tribute and his departure was fixed for 20 May 1851. That same winter he unsuccessfully courted Charlotte in a manner as persistent as it was timid and deferential. He let her understand that, having to remain in exile for five years, he would be satisfied with the promise that she would marry him when he returned. He was then in Scotland and it had been agreed that he would call at Haworth before returning to London.

'Mr Taylor has been and gone', Charlotte wrote to Ellen on 5 April 1851. 'He looked much thinner and older. . . . He is not ugly, but very peculiar; the lines in his face show an inflexibility, and, I must add, a hardness of character which do not attract. . . . He gave me a book at parting, requesting in his brief way, that I would keep it for his sake. . . .

'And so he is gone, and stern and abrupt little man as he is – his absence . . . leaves me certainly with less support and in deeper solitude than before. . . .' On 9 April she expressed clearly to Ellen what she felt for Mr Taylor: '. . . Would Mr Taylor and I ever suit? . . . Friendship, – gratitude – esteem I have, but each moment he came nearer me, and that I could see his eyes fastened on me, my veins ran ice. Now that he is away, I feel far more gently towards him.'

On the 23rd, she concluded: 'My dear Ellen . . . if Mr Taylor be the only husband fate offers to me, single I must always remain. But yet, at times I grieve for him, and perhaps it is superfluous, for I cannot think he will suffer much. . . .' In any case Charlotte could not envisage marriage without a painful mental reservation: 'The least allusion to such a thing is most offensive to papa.' What is surprising is that Mr Brontë liked Mr Taylor and did not reject him as a suitor for his daughter's hand. No doubt the fact that five years were to pass before his return from Bombay greatly diminished his apprehensions.

How in fact could Charlotte have avoided comparing Mr Taylor with Mr Smith? At the beginning of the new year, on 20 January 1851, she had written to Ellen about Mr Smith: '. . . Meantime, I am content to have him as a friend, and pray God to continue to me the common sense to look on one so young, so rising, so hopeful, in no other light.

'That hint about the Rhine disturbs me; I am not made of stone, and what is mere excitement to him is fever to me. . . . As I see it now, the journey is out of the question, for many reasons. I cannot conceive either his mother or his sisters relishing it, and all London would gabble like a countless host of geese. . . . Dear Nell, Heaven grant us both some quiet wisdom, and strength not merely to bear the pain, but to resist the lure of pleasure when it comes in such a shape as our better judgment disapproves.'

Happiness continued to elude Charlotte. Had happiness been offered to her, she would have turned away and let it go to someone more worthy. This is reflected in a letter she wrote to Mr Smith, on 3 November 1852, when she had almost finished *Villette* and was discussing the characters of Lucy Snowe and Doctor John with him: '. . . Lucy must not marry Doctor John; he is far too youthful, handsome, bright-spirited, and sweet-tempered. . . . His wife must be young, rich, pretty.' Lucy was Charlotte herself, no other, and Doctor John Mr Smith.

At the end of May 1851, in spite of her ill-health and in the hope of improving it by the change, Charlotte accepted the invitation of Mrs Smith and her son, on the occasion of the famous London Exhibition held that year.

She arrived just in time to attend Thackeray's second lecture on 'The English Humourists of the 18th Century'. On 30 May she wrote to her father: '... On Thursday afternoon I went to hear the lecture. It was delivered in a large and splendid kind of saloon.... The walls were all painted and gilded.... The audience was composed of the élite of London society. Duchesses were there by the score, and amongst them the great and beautiful Duchess of Sutherland, the Queen's Mistress of the Robes. Amidst all this Thackeray just got up and spoke with as much simplicity and ease as if he had been speaking to a few friends by his own fireside. The lecture was truly good.... He saw me as I entered the room and came straight up and spoke very kindly. He then took me to his mother, a fine, handsome old lady, and introduced me to her....' Charlotte had hoped to pass unobserved among so many grand people, but Thackeray pointed her out to several friends and many heads were turned towards her. At the exit, all this high society stood forming a passage for her in acknowledgment of their admiration. 'Miss Brontë's hand trembled to such a degree that her companion feared lest she should turn faint.' (G)

Charlotte had come to London for a week but stayed for a month. She went five times to the Crystal Palace erected in Hyde Park, less for her own pleasure than to comply with her hosts' eagerness, for these visits exhausted her. She was nevertheless amazed by all that she saw there, comparing it to 'a mixture of genii palace and a mighty bazaar'. How many things she had to relate, to describe to her father! She was already giving him a foretaste of it in her letters. On 2 June she wrote to Ellen: 'Sunday, yesterday, was a day to be marked with a white stone: through most of the day I was very happy, without being tired or over-excited. In the afternoon I went to hear D'Aubigné, the great Protestant French preacher; it was pleasant – half sweet, half sad – and strangely suggestive to hear the French language once more.' She went to see Rachel acting: she made her 'shudder to the marrow of my bones; ... she is a snake, she is a devil. The great gift of genius she undoubtedly has; but, I fear, she rather abuses it....'

She was also present at a Confirmation in the Spanish Embassy chapel. There she saw Cardinal Wiseman. This appeared to her 'impiously theatrical'. Charlotte and the person who accompanied her were the only two Protestants present at this ceremony.

She was invited to a grand reception by the Marquis of Westminster but refused to go. Thackeray offered several times to introduce her into high society where the great ladies would have welcomed her with open arms. 'But seriously,' she wrote to her father on 14 June, 'I cannot see that this sort of society produces so good an effect on him as to tempt me in the least to try the same experiment, so I remain obscure. . . .' While she was coming and going in the midst of this bustling sociability, which in other circumstances she would no doubt have found enchanting – for Mr Smith had the art of varying the distractions – Charlotte could not let herself be happy without painful reservations; she kept remembering with terror the solitude that was awaiting her. On 11 June she wrote to Ellen: '. . . You seem to think me in such a happy, enviable position; pleasant moments I have, but it is usually a pleasure I am obliged to repel and check, which cannot benefit the future, but only add to its solitude. . . . I pass portions of many a night in extreme sadness. . . .'

On the 19th she adds: '. . . I cannot boast that London has agreed with me well this time; an oppression of frequent headache, sickness, and a low tone of spirits, has poisoned many moments which might otherwise have been pleasant. Sometimes I have felt this hard, and been tempted to murmur at Fate, which compels me to comparative silence and solitude for eleven months in the year, and in the twelfth, while offering social enjoyment, takes away the vigour and cheerfulness which should turn it to account. But circumstances are ordered for us, and we must submit. . . .'

Charlotte travelled back to Haworth by Manchester. She spent two days with Mr and Mrs Gaskell, whose four charming and intelligent daughters filled the house with gaiety. She kept marvelling to see such well behaved children. Julia, the youngest, became her friend and Charlotte spoke of her with a tender, rather timid emotion. This visit comforted her. But when she reached home, the silence of Haworth seemed even heavier. 'It is useless to tell you how I live', she wrote to Ellen on 1 September 1851. 'I endure life . . . the old headaches, and starting wakeful nights are coming upon me again.'

A visit from Miss Wooler did her much good. But after she had gone, she became once more a prey to the frightening monotony, having as her sole distraction only a few letters, always impatiently awaited, and the books sent regularly from Cornhill.

In December the death of old Keeper, the faithful dog which had waited in vain for the return of its mistress, brought back painful memories.

Her health remained very delicate. If the weather was not fine, she could not go out without running the risk of catching colds or bronchitis, from which her recovery was slow. And in spite of her precautions, Charlotte caught cold and fell ill. Always patient, resigned and self-effacing, she could not, however, help calling Ellen to her aid. Her friend's presence was a support to her as always and brought her comfort. But the trouble was too deeply rooted; after Ellen's departure she had a relapse and Mr Brontë had to send for a doctor. He diagnosed only a liver complaint and the strong remedies which he prescribed had a deplorable effect on a hyper-sensitive organism. The patient was unable to take any nourishment for more than a week. Her father lived in mortal anxiety. Finally, although Charlotte felt her chest racked by pain, the doctor declared that there was nothing the matter with her lungs. This assertion was the best of remedies; she regained confidence and hope; there was a slight improvement and gradually, very slowly, her strength returned. Seeing her father unusually well and vigorous, she was happy to go and spend a week with Ellen, and this short visit did her a great deal of good.

For four months now, Charlotte had not been able to get on with *Villette*. All her friends advised her to get away, to try for a time to forget Haworth whose climate and isolation were bad for her. But she would not desert her father or go away anywhere else until she had finished her novel.

However, during the harsh winter of 1851–2, she had not stopped thinking of her sister Anne, an exile in her grave. She felt an irresistible desire to go and find out for herself if everything had been done fittingly, according to her wishes. At the end of spring, she resolved to set out for Scarborough and stay in Filey, where she had gone three years earlier with Ellen. On 2 June 1852 she wrote to her father: '. . . On the whole, I get on very well here, but I have not bathed yet, as I am told it is much too cold. . . . The sea is very grand. . . . There are so very few visitors at Filey yet that I and a few sea-birds and fishing-boats have often the whole expanse of sea, shore, and cliff to ourselves.' Then she explains to Ellen why she had set out alone: 'Do not be angry, the step is right. . . . On Friday I went to Scarborough, visited the churchyard and stone. It must be refaced and re-lettered; there are five errors. I gave the necessary directions. *That* duty, then, is done; long has it lain heavy on my mind; and that was a pilgrimage I felt I could only make alone. . . .' Her three weeks' stay by the sea gave her back her strength and she returned 'sunburnt and weather-beaten as a fisherman'. Towards the end of July her father had a slight stroke, which had a disastrous effect on his sight. Charlotte, completely occupied by the nursing which his condition required, had to lay *Villette* aside once more. Everything was conspiring against her. She grew anxious, and wrote to Mr Smith, begging him not to announce her new novel until he had it in his hands.

However, her devoted care was rewarded: soon Mr Brontë was out of danger, then convalescent, and finally, having recovered his sight, was able to carry out his duties again.

But after these several weeks of fatigue and exhaustion, Charlotte suffered repeated attacks of faintness, followed by the inevitable depressions which paralysed her mind and her inspiration; so Mr Brontë himself asked Ellen to come and distract his daughter a little.

Once again her devoted friend answered the call and did so much good that, after she left, Charlotte no longer felt obsessed by solitude. The weather changed, the wind – to which she was so sensitive – began to blow from the west and the writer of the *Tales of Angria*, once more inspired, shut herself up in the dining-room and gave rein to her lyricism as in the past; her own life became interwoven with that of her characters. Nearly eight years had passed since Charlotte stayed in Brussels, which she called Villette. Time had eventually calmed her suffering and she could now recall it with a detachment which had been dearly bought. *Villette*, like *Jane Eyre*, is the drama of Charlotte Brontë herself, disappointed by the realities of life. Under the guise of Jane or Lucy, she appears before us with her enthusiasms, her aspirations, her noble need for love and adoration, but also with her common-sense, her clear-sightedness, her pride, her self-denial rigorously imposed and accepted.

After she had sent the first part of the novel to Mr Smith, she wrote to him on 30 October 1852: 'You must notify honestly what you think of *Villette*. . . . I can hardly tell you how I hunger to hear some opinion beside my own and how I have sometimes desponded, and almost despaired, because there was no one to whom to read a line, or of whom to ask a counsel. . . . You will see that *Villette* touches on no matter of public interest. I cannot write books handling the topics of the day. . . .'

On 3 November, when Mr Smith had received the first two volumes of *Villette*, Charlotte wrote to him again: 'I feel very grateful to you for your letter; it relieved me much. . . . I feel in some degree authorised to rely on your favourable impressions, because you are quite right where you hint disapprobation. . . . Most of the third volume is given to the development of the "crabbed professor's" character.' This third volume was quickly finished, but Mr Smith did not easily accept the author's point of view and made many comments about the interest of the book being spoiled by the lack of unity in it. Mr Williams, while aware of the great beauties of *Villette*, also had many objections to make. Both of them had been dazzled by *Jane Eyre* to the detriment of the works that followed it.

As for Charlotte, sending off the last part of *Villette* was a relief to her: 'I said my prayers when I had done it', she wrote to Ellen on 29 November. 'Whether it is well or ill done, I do not know. . . . I will now try to wait the issue quietly.'

The conclusion of *Villette* had greatly preoccupied Mr Brontë, who wanted it to be a happy one, as in a fairy tale. All that Charlotte could concede to her father was to leave the reader to wonder if Monsieur Paul Emmanuel, the school master, had or had not perished at sea on his way back from the Antilles, and to come to his own conclusions.

Had not Charlotte been forced to hide in her inmost heart her feelings for Monsieur Heger and, with no help, to bear the emptiness of absence, and resign herself to forgetting? Like her, Lucy Snowe would have to give up Monsieur Paul, after already giving up the charming Doctor John. Monsieur Heger, as we have seen, was the incarnation of a character that took its inspiration from Byron in Charlotte's earliest adolescence. In *Villette*, he is the starting point for a work of art; he is the immortal Monsieur Paul. As for Madame Heger, his wife, she did not forgive the novelist for creating an unforgettable portrait of her as Madame Beck.

Many critics have thought that, without Monsieur Heger, *Villette* would never have been written. There is no doubt that it would not have been written without the *Juvenilia* either. Miss Ratchford who, in the course of her remarkable work on the Brontës, has been able to compare certain sentences of the little manuscripts with sentences of *Villette*, writes that 'from beginning to end, *Villette* is the most Angrian of Charlotte's novels'.

27

The Reverend Arthur Bell Nicholls – His proposal to Charlotte – Mr Brontë and Mr Nicholls – Charlotte's last visit to London (1853) – The huge success of Villette *– Miss Martineau's opposition – The Bishop of Ripon's visit – Charlotte returns to Mrs Gaskell in Manchester – Mr Nicholls leaves – Charlotte decides to marry Mr Nicholls – The marriage – Mrs Nicholls –* Emma *– Charlotte's illness and death*

Charlotte was now thirty-six, and with *Villette* finished she had time to spare to think about the future. In spite of the attraction she felt towards George Smith – there was no doubt she loved him – marriage between the author of *Jane Eyre* and her publisher still appeared impossible to her. She had nothing to offer him but her genius and her fame – no youth, no beauty nor fortune. Mr Smith, man of the world that he was, had enough insight and subtlety to say that he believed that 'Charlotte would have given all her genius and all her fame to be beautiful'.

Mr James Taylor, whom she missed a little since he had gone so far away, had finally stopped writing. She resigned herself to this, of course. But solitude seemed to her like a spectre whose approach she could not bear. And yet for eight years, lodging in the sexton's cottage quite close to Haworth parsonage, there had lived a man who silently watched and loved her. He was the Reverend Arthur Bell Nicholls, Mr Brontë's curate, whose presence Charlotte did not seem even to notice, although he came to talk to her father every day.

Mr Nicholls was two years younger than she was. He had been born in County Antrim in Ireland, of Scottish parents. An orphan since childhood, he was brought up by an uncle and aunt at Banagher where this uncle, Dr Alan Bell, was headmaster of the Royal High School. When he had finished his studies at Trinity College, Dublin, Mr Nicholls left Ireland for Haworth, his first curacy. 'Of middle height, with a pale serious face framed in a long oval by thick dark hair and whiskers, he made an impression of rather dull sobriety. He was unprepossessingly reserved in manner, but anyone who took his calm demeanour for passivity would have been mistaken; his level gaze could have a startling intensity. . . .'[1]

It was not the famous author who had attracted him in Charlotte – quite the reverse – it was the daughter, the sister, the friend whom he so admired. The love of this high-principled, deeply religious man, devoted to his duties, was an enduring tribute to Charlotte's virtues. He had stood aside – knowing how much it cost him – to make way for those who could aspire to seek the hand of the woman all London was talking about: Mr George Smith, Mr James Taylor, perhaps others too. But the years slipped by and in spite of her successes and her fame, everything remained unchanged in Charlotte's lonely life; Mr Nicholls began to hope again. Eight years of waiting had strengthened his love, a deep, unselfish love which had complete possession of him. He had been a distressed witness of all the sorrows that had overwhelmed Charlotte. He could not bear to see her suffer alone. He wished to be the one to sustain, protect and comfort this frail, courageous creature who until now had been concerned only for others.

When *Villette* was finished, his proposal fell like a thunderbolt on Mr Brontë and his daughter, although for some time his unusual behaviour had aroused Charlotte's attention.

On 15 December 1852, she wrote to Ellen: 'I know not whether you have ever observed him specially when staying here. . . . What papa has seen or guessed I will not inquire, though I may conjecture. He has minutely noticed all Mr Nicholls' low spirits, all his threats of expatriation, all his symptoms of impaired health, noticed them with little sympathy and much indirect sarcasm. On Monday evening Mr Nicholls was here to tea. I vaguely felt without clearly seeing, as without seeing I have felt for some time, the meaning of his constant looks, and strange feverish restraint. After tea, I withdrew to the dining-room as usual. As usual, Mr Nicholls sat with papa till between eight and nine o'clock, I then heard him open the parlour door as if going. I expected the clash of the front-door. He stopped in the passage: he rapped: like lightning it flashed on me what was coming. He entered, he stood before me. What his words were you can guess;

1. M. Lane, op. cit., p. 178.

his manner you can hardly realise, nor can I forget it. Shaking from head to foot, looking deadly pale, speaking low, vehemently yet with difficulty, he made me for the first time feel what it costs a man to declare affection where he doubts response.

'The spectacle of one ordinarily so statue-like, thus trembling, stirred, and overcome, gave me a kind of strange shock. . . . I could only entreat him to leave me then and promise a reply on the morrow. I asked him if he had spoken to papa. He said, he dared not. I think I half led, half put him out of the room. When he had gone I immediately went to papa, and told him what had taken place. . . . If I had *loved* Mr Nicholls and had heard such epithets applied to him as were used, it would have transported me beyond my patience; as it was, my blood boiled with a sense of injustice, but papa worked himself into a state not to be trifled with, the veins on his temples started up like whipcord, and his eyes became suddenly bloodshot. I made haste to promise that Mr Nicholls should on the morrow have a distinct refusal. . . . Papa's vehement antipathy to the bare thought of anyone thinking of me as a wife, and Mr Nicholls's distress, both give me pain.'

The result of Mr Nicholls's declaration was that he immediately sent in his resignation as curate of the parish of Haworth: '. . . You ask how papa demeans himself to Mr Nicholls,' Charlotte writes to Ellen on 18 December. 'I only wish you were here to see papa in his present mood; you would know something of him. He just treats him with a hardness not to be bent, and a contempt not to be propitiated. The two have had no interview as yet: all has been done by letter. Papa wrote, I must say, a most cruel note to Mr Nicholls on Wednesday. In his state of mind and health I felt that the blow must be parried, and I thought it right to accompany the pitiless dispatch by a line to the effect that, while Mr Nicholls must never expect me to reciprocate the feeling he had expressed, yet at the same time I wished to disclaim participation in sentiments calculated to give him pain; . . . I am afraid also that papa thinks a little too much about his want of money; he says that the match could be a degradation. . . . In short, his manner of viewing the subject is, on the whole, far from being one [with] which I can sympathise. My own objections arise from a sense of incongruity and uncongeniality in feelings, tastes, principles. . . .'

Mr Brontë, in his paternal pride, could not allow an obscure curate, to whom he gave no more than a hundred pounds a year, to dare cast his eyes on the famous 'Currer Bell'.

Charlotte's indignation in face of her father's violent reaction to Mr Nicholls, soon stirred her interest and her sympathy for this man capable, as she herself was, of loving and suffering. Charlotte's pity could not but be tender-hearted and passionate, forming invisible ties between her and the man whom her refusal had filled with despair.

In these painful circumstances she was glad to accept Mrs and Mr Smith's invitation. As the proofs of *Villette* were ready, she could correct them on the spot and await the publication of her new book. So she made her preparations for this visit to London, which was to last about a month.

'... Papa wants me to go too,' she writes to Ellen on 2 January 1853, 'but I am sorry for one other person whom nobody pities but me. ... Martha and John Brown don't understand the nature of his feelings but I see now what they are. ... He continues restless and ill. ... A few days since, he wrote to papa requesting permission to withdraw his resignation. Papa answered that he should only do so on condition of giving him his written promise never again to broach the obnoxious subject either to him or to me. This he has evaded doing, so the matter remains unsettled. I feel persuaded the termination will be his departure for Australia. ...'

Quite distracted, Mr Nicholls had in fact taken strong measures: he had volunteered to go as a missionary to the Antipodes.

So Charlotte went to London, sorry as always to be leaving her father alone, a father who with old age and sorrow had grown selfish and hard but who nevertheless occupied such a large place in his daughter's heart.

From London she wrote to Ellen: '... 11th January 1853. ... Mrs Smith and her daughters are looking well, but on Mr Smith hard work is telling early. ... One feels pained to see a physical alteration of this kind, yet I feel glad and thankful that it is merely physical; as far as I can judge, mind and manners have undergone no deterioration, rather I think the contrary. ... No news from home, and I feel uneasy to hear how papa is. ...'

All Mr Smith's time was taken up by his publishing business, with its increasing responsibilities. So Charlotte was completely free to go out alone and anxious to get to know certain places which seemed rather astonishing to the Smith family: two prisons – Newgate and Pentonville, the Bank, the Exchange, the Foundling Hospital, the Bethlehem Hospital: a choice which surely revealed the nature of Charlotte's thoughts at a time when she made no mention of the subject in her letters.

Mr George Smith, while remaining a charming friend, possibly no longer showed her the enthusiasm of the publisher for the newly discovered sensational author. Besides, his life was about to take a new direction: he was soon to marry. How could Charlotte with her sensitiveness have been unaware of this change, however subtle it was?

This stay in London, her last, seems to have been the signal to make a break, to submit to what awaited her: a happiness scarcely enjoyed, before it was to be destroyed by the finality of death.

However, an intense joy was still in store for her. *Villette*, published at the end of January 1853, a little more than three years after *Shirley*, was immensely successful. Back in Haworth, she wrote to Ellen on 15 February: '. . . I got a budget of no less than seven papers yesterday and today. The import of all the notices is such as to make my heart swell with thankfulness to Him who takes note both of suffering and work, and motives. Papa is pleased too. . . .'

The only conflicting opinion was that of Miss Martineau, a friend to whom she had remained faithful in spite of radical disagreement on essential matters and whom she had defended against everyone, especially against Miss Wooler. Admittedly, Charlotte had begged Miss Martineau to tell her with complete frankness what she thought of her book. Miss Martineau's article on *Villette* in *The Daily News* and the letter which she sent to Charlotte wounded her deeply and very intimately, for this criticism seemed to her unjust and unfounded: 'I do not like the love, either the kind or the degree of it,' Miss Martineau wrote to her, developing her theme in her review in *The Daily News*. There she condemned the passion which animates all the women in the novel, their need to be loved. Life was not like that, she declared.

In accordance with Miss Martineau's wishes, Charlotte returned her letter, writing to her: 'I enclose it, and have marked with red ink the passage which struck me dumb. All the rest is fair, right, worthy of you, but I protest against this passage;

and were I brought up before the bar of all the critics in England, to such a charge I should respond "not guilty".

'I know what *love* is as I understand it; and if man or woman should be ashamed of feeling such love, then is there nothing right, noble, faithful, truthful, unselfish in this earth. . . . To differ from you gives me keen pain.'

Nothing could hurt her more than the criticism of those who judged her novels to be coarse or vulgar. She herself seemed to suffer a direct attack, and moreover appeared to be as astonished as she was hurt by it.

Miss Martineau went further. On 13 April, Charlotte wrote to Miss Wooler: '. . . "Extremes meet!" . . . Miss Martineau . . . accuses me with attacking popery "with virulence".'

With great reluctance, Charlotte had then to decide to take her friendship with Miss Martineau no further. An abyss separated them in their beliefs, their ways of seeing and feeling. She had the courage to tell her so and refused an invitation to Ambleside. But Charlotte could not withdraw her friendship in this way without suffering; her solitude grew all the greater, yet her health resisted the rigours of the next winter, 1852–53, much better. She went for 'long walks on the crackling snow', in the cold air which she found so bracing.[2]

In March there was a great stir in the parsonage because of the pastoral visit of the Bishop of Ripon, Dr Longley, who later became Archbishop of Canterbury. He spent the night with his hosts, all the clergy of the neighbourhood having been invited to come to tea and supper with him.

'. . . The Bishop has been and is gone,' Charlotte wrote to Ellen on 4 March 1853. 'He is certainly a most charming little Bishop. . . . His visit passed capitally well; and at its close, as he was going away, he expressed himself thoroughly gratified with all he had seen. . . . If you could have been at Haworth to share the pleasures of the company, without having been inconvenienced by the little bustle of the preparation, I should have been *very* glad. . . . All passed, however, orderly, quietly, and well. Martha waited very nicely; and I had a person to help her in the kitchen. . . . My penalty came on in a strong headache and bilious attack as soon as the Bishop was fairly gone. . . . I thought [Mr

2. From a letter of February 1853 to Mrs Gaskell.

Nicholls] made no effort to struggle with his dejection. He dogged me up the lane after the evening service in no pleasant manner, he stopped also in the passage after the Bishop and the other clergy were gone into the room, and it was because I drew away and went upstairs that he gave me that look which filled Martha's soul with horror. She, it seems, meantime, was making it her business to watch him from the kitchen door. . . .' Mr Nicholls shut himself off in his despair which he neither could nor would confide in anyone. '. . . Silent pity is just all I can give him, and as he knows nothing about that, it does not comfort. He is now grown so gloomy and reserved that nobody seems to like him,' she writes on 6 April. John Brown could not accept such an attitude. He was annoyed to see Mr Nicholls refuse all the dishes which his wife prepared for him and sometimes became threatening. He, Martha and many others took sides with their old vicar, without any sense of proportion.

Once again Charlotte tried to escape from this painful atmosphere: she accepted Mrs Gaskell's invitation and went to Manchester.

During these visits the two friends got to know and like one another better. Charlotte's frail health, her very emotional nature, her neurotic temperament, her terror of meeting strangers endeared her to Mrs Gaskell who felt a need to protect her and give her self-confidence.

Since Mary Taylor, the 'Polly' of Roe Head, had told her that she was very ugly, Charlotte had remained convinced of it, imagining that people avoided her because of her plainness. This was not so, except in her imagination, and nearly always the opposite happened. Mrs Gaskell tells us that 'as for the rest of her features, they were plain, large, and ill set' but she hastens to add 'unless you began to catalogue them, you were hardly aware of the fact, for the eyes and power of the countenance overbalanced every physical defect; the crooked mouth and the large nose were forgotten, and the whole face arrested the attention, and presently attracted all those whom she herself would have cared to attract. Her hands and feet were the smallest I ever saw; when one of the former was placed in mine, it was like the soft touch of a bird in the middle of my palm. The delicate long fingers had a peculiar fineness of sensation, which was one reason why all her work – writing, sewing, knitting – was so clear in its minuteness. She was remarkably neat in her whole personal attire; but she was dainty as to the fit of her shoes and gloves.' Never did the slightest breath of jealousy touch these two women who both enjoyed great fame. Mrs Gaskell admired Charlotte Brontë's novels and Charlotte appreciated *Mary Barton*, *Cranford* and *Ruth* of Mrs Gaskell. If their friendship was short – it lasted only five years – it left Mrs Gaskell such a precious memory that it inspired what is perhaps her finest book, *The Life of Charlotte Brontë*.

Charlotte returned from Manchester in a calmer mood. The unpretentious family which she had just left was the image of happiness to her. Even if Mrs Gaskell had a name in literature, her husband was only a clergyman, like Mr Nicholls. The sacred nature of this profession, the renunciation of an easy life that it imposed could not but enhance it in Charlotte's eyes as in those of Mrs. Gaskell. But there was her father, her dear but formidable father.

Mr Nicholls's departure was drawing near. He took the service on Whit Sunday. When Charlotte approached to receive communion, 'He struggled, faltered then lost command over himself,' she wrote to Ellen on 16 May, 'stood before my eyes and in the sight of all the communicants, white, shaking, voiceless. Papa was not there, thank God! . . . He goes either this week or the next. I heard the women sobbing round, and I could not quite check my own tears. . . .'

As a token of their respect and gratitude for eight years of devoted service, the parishioners made him a presentation, 'a gold watch, which Mr Nicholls showed me with natural pride, forty years later . . . at Banagher. . . ' Mr Clement Shorter relates. Charlotte had felt very pleased about it. Mr Nicholls left Haworth on 27 May. Before leaving, he very properly went for a last time to the parsonage to say goodbye to Mr Brontë. He did not find Charlotte in the dining-room, where a thorough cleaning was going on.

That day she told Ellen: '. . . He went out thinking he was not to see me, and indeed, until the very last moment I thought it best not. But perceiving that he stayed long before going out at the gate, and remembering his long grief, I took courage and went out trembling and miserable. I found him leaning against the garden door in a paroxysm of anguish, sobbing as women never sob. Of course I went straight to him. Very few words were interchanged, those few barely articulate. . . . For a few weeks he goes to the South of England, afterwards he takes a curacy somewhere in Yorkshire, but I don't know where. . . . I see no chance of hearing a word about him in future unless some stray shred of intelligence comes through Mr Sowden or some other second-hand source. . . .'

Mr Nicholls finally settled at Kirk Smeaton. After waiting a fairly long time for a reply from the Director of Missions he in his turn had asked for postponements before making a definite decision. He was, in fact, subject to severe attacks of rheumatism but his main reason was that he could not help hoping that the depth and constancy of his love would perhaps in the end overcome the resistance of Charlotte who was in everything else so sensitive and tender-hearted. No doubt he was relying only on Providence to overcome the inflexible father.

It was his successor, Mr de Renzi, a curate so like all those whom Charlotte had satirised in *Shirley*, who was the instrument of this miracle. He unconsciously served Mr Nicholls's cause with Mr Brontë, bringing him by comparison to regret his former curate, whose qualities he finally recognised. No doubt he asked himself if he had been right to reject so pitilessly a man whom it was so difficult to replace.

In the course of the summer Charlotte had a cold, and then influenza; her father's health was also poor and Mr Brontë himself wrote to Mrs Gaskell asking her to postpone until September the visit she was to make to them.

In September Charlotte wrote to her: '. . . Come to Haworth as soon as you can; the heath is in bloom. . . .'

Mrs Gaskell came to Haworth on a dull, dark, rainy day. Two days earlier a storm had ravaged the moor, destroying its splendour. She did not find the parsonage as austere as she had expected. Success had given Charlotte a little affluence, and she had refurnished the dining room, had the walls papered, and hung red curtains. This colour, the dominant note in the room, made a happy warm contrast with the hard grey landscape; in the other rooms, which were unchanged, everything was in keeping.

The meticulous cleanliness of the whole house astonished Mrs Gaskell, who had never seen anything like it. Its silence made an impression on her. 'You catch the ticking of the clock in the kitchen, or the buzzing of a fly in the parlour, all over the house.

. . . Miss Brontë helps in the housework; for one of the servants (Tabby) is nearly ninety, and the other only a girl. . . .'

Mrs Gaskell went for walks with Charlotte over the moors. '. . . Oh! those high wild desolate moors,' she wrote, 'up above the whole world, and the very realms of silence!' She noted how much the visits of her companion were appreciated in all the cottages nestling in the hollows of the moors. Three miles from Haworth, when they saw her arrive, 'the chair was dusted for her, with a kindly "sit ye down, Miss Brontë".'

Back at the parsonage, they relaxed by a bright fire and the two friends exchanged confidences. It was thus that Charlotte spoke to Mrs Gaskell of Mr Nicholls, no longer hiding from her her pain, her distress and her doubts. Later when she wrote *The Life of Charlotte Brontë* it must have been difficult for the novelist in Mrs Gaskell to be compelled to keep silent on such a moving subject. But it concerned Mr Nicholls as well as Charlotte. She ventured to insert just one short sentence: 'I was aware that she had a great anxiety on her mind at this time; and being acquainted with its nature, I could not but deeply admire the patient docility which she displayed in her conduct towards her father.' (G)

However Charlotte, almost in spite of herself, had been led to correspond secretly with Mr Nicholls. The despairing letters which he sent her touched her deeply and, giving way to her pity, she finally replied, thinking in this way to help him to become resigned to his fate. These proofs of friendly feeling did not fail to comfort him; he begged her to write to him again, which she did not have the courage to refuse. Mr Nicholls then became bold enough to accept the invitation of his friend Mr Grant, the curate of Oxenhope, near Haworth. And in secret they met.

Charlotte knew very well that this state of affairs could not last and that she must confront the future. If the correspondence with Mr Nicholls and their secret meetings weighed heavily on her over-scrupulous conscience, they had given her an opportunity to know this faithful suitor really well and to realise that a love like his was too precious a treasure to be rejected. She decided to accept this tribute and to marry the curate whom her father scorned; from esteem and friendship love would be born, she refused to have doubts about it. Charlotte was right and it was love and not fame that was to bring her happiness.

And, did she not belong to Haworth, to the moors that had

inspired her, to the parsonage which she never left without regret, to her father by whose side she would remain, to all her dead whose invisible presence sustained her in the difficulties of her life? There were two quite distinct persons in her: Currer Bell and Charlotte Brontë. If the famous Currer Bell had expressed herself with unusual boldness in her novels, Charlotte Brontë remained timid, reserved, fearful, frail, unsuited to lead the brilliant but artificial and exhausting life of the society to which Currer Bell had introduced her.

But how could she persuade her father? She was so wretched at having in a way betrayed him that, unable to go on, she decided to confess everything to him. '. . . It was very hard and rough work at the time,' she wrote to Ellen on 11 April 1854, 'but the issue after a few days was that I obtained leave to continue the communication. Mr Nicholls came in January; he was ten days in the neighbourhood. I saw much of him. Still papa was very, very hostile, bitterly unjust. I told Mr Nicholls the great obstacle that lay in his way. He has persevered. The result of this, his last visit, is that papa's consent is gained, that his respect, I believe, is won, for Mr Nicholls has in all things proved himself disinterested and forbearing. . . . In fact, dear Ellen, I am engaged.

'Mr Nicholls, in a few months, will return to the curacy of Haworth. I stipulated that I would not leave papa, and to papa himself I proposed a plan of residence which should maintain his seclusion and convenience uninvaded and in a pecuniary sense bring him gain instead of loss. What seemed at one time impossible is now arranged, and papa begins really to take a pleasure in the prospect. For myself, dear Ellen, while thankful to One who seems to have guided me through much difficulty, much and deep distress and perplexity of mind, I am still very calm, very inexpectant. What I taste of happiness is of the soberest order. I trust to love my husband. I am grateful for his tender love to me. I believe him to be an affectionate, a conscientious, a high-principled man; and if, with all this, I should yield to regrets, that fine talents, congenial tastes and thoughts are not added, it seems to me I should be most presumptuous and thankless. . . .

'It is possible that our marriage may take place in the course of the summer. Mr Nicholls wishes it to be in July. He spoke of you with great kindness, and said he hoped you would be at our wedding. I said I thought of having no other bridesmaid. Did I say rightly? I mean the marriage to be, literally, as quiet as possible. . . .'

The very next day Charlotte invited Miss Wooler also to her wedding. She told her of her joy at the sight of her father's contentment, her sense of relief at the thought that Mr Nicholls would henceforth be the support and comfort of his old age, adding with the serenity of an unselfish soul: 'The destiny which Providence in His goodness and wisdom seems to offer me will not, I am aware, be generally regarded as brilliant; but I trust I see in it some germs of real happiness. . . .'

Returning from a visit to Mrs Gaskell, Charlotte stopped in Leeds to do some shopping for the wedding, and for the conversion of the store room into a study for her husband. Then she set to work and soon the new little room was pleasantly arranged. Mr Nicholls at that time had another severe attack of rheumatism which worried Charlotte; 'If he is doomed to suffer, it seems that so much the more will he need care and help', she confides to Ellen.

Mr Nicholls, like Charlotte, wanted the marriage to take place quietly. It was fixed for 29 June. Charlotte's two friends arrived the day before. When the packing was done and the preparations completed, 'just at bedtime, Mr Brontë announced his intention of stopping at home while the others went to church'. What was to be done? Who was to give the bride away? There were only to be the officiating clergyman, the bride and bridegroom, the bridesmaid and Miss Wooler present. The Prayerbook was referred to; and there it was seen that the Rubric enjoins that the Minister shall receive 'the woman from her father's or *friend's* hands', and that nothing is specified as to the sex of the 'friend'. So Miss Wooler, ever kind in emergency, volunteered to give her old pupil away.

'The news of the wedding had slipt abroad before the little party came out of church, and many old and humble friends were there, seeing her look "like a snowdrop", as they say her dress was white embroidered muslin, with a lace mantle and white bonnet trimmed with green leaves, which perhaps might suggest the resemblance to the pale wintry flower.' (G)

At last, duly married, Mr Nicholls and Charlotte took the train for North Wales, on the way to Ireland. They embarked for Dublin at Holyhead. After a short stay in Dublin they went to the wild coast where the tumult of the waves breaking furiously against the rocks made a deep impression on Charlotte. To her great joy, she saw that her husband, without being a poet, was very sensitive to the grandeur and splendour of the sea. Then they went to Banagher to Mr Nicholls's uncle and aunt who lived in a pleasant, spacious and well-furnished house. Charlotte then wrote to Ellen: '. . . I must say I like my new relations. My dear husband, too, appears in a new light in his own country. More than once I have had deep pleasure in hearing his praises on all sides. Some of the old servants and followers of the family tell me I am a most fortunate person. . . . I pray to be enabled to repay as I ought the affectionate devotion of a truthful, honourable man. . . .' Next they went to Killarney, and then to the south-west coast. Charlotte, thrilled by so much beauty, was even more amazed at being the object of 'a continuous kind protectiveness'. (G) And yet her joy could not be unclouded, for she remained uneasy about her father, almost reproaching herself for her happiness, so that she and her husband decided to return home.

'Henceforward the sacred doors of home are closed upon her married life. We, her loving friends, standing outside, caught occasional glimpses of brightness, and pleasant peaceful murmurs of sound, telling of the gladness within; and we looked at each other, and gently said, "After a hard and long struggle – after many cares and many bitter sorrows – she is tasting happiness now!

'But God's ways are not as our ways!' (G)

Back in Haworth, Charlotte wrote to Ellen on 9 August: 'Dear Nell, – during the last six weeks the colour of my thoughts is a good deal changed; I know more of the realities of life than I once did. . . . Indeed, indeed, Nell, it is a solemn and strange and perilous thing for a woman to become a wife. Man's lot is far, far different. Tell me when you can come. Papa is better, but not well. . . . Have I told you how much better Mr Nicholls is? He looks quite strong and hale; he gained 12 lbs during the four weeks we were in Ireland. . . .'

On 19 and 21 September, letters to Mrs Gaskell: '. . . It makes me content and grateful to hear him [Mr Nicholls] from time to time avow his happiness in the brief plain phrase of sincerity. My own life is more occupied than it used to be: I have not so much time for thinking: I am obliged to be more practical, for my dear Arthur is a very practical as well as a very punctual and methodical man. . . . My life is different from what it used to be. May God make me thankful for it! I have a good, kind, attached husband, and every day my own attachment to him grows stronger.' Mr Nicholls, whom Charlotte in the distant past had reproached for his narrow-mindedness, was horrified by the unreserved nature of the correspondence between Charlotte and Ellen. He thought that it was always possible for a letter to fall by mischance into the hands of strangers and he feared the consequences. He made Ellen promise to destroy the letters which his wife wrote to her. What gratitude we owe to Ellen for refusing to obey that injunction. 'Arthur', she writes to Ellen in October, 'has just been glancing over this note. He thinks I have written too freely about Amelia [Ellen's sister-in-law]. Men . . . always seem to think us incautious . . . [so] you must burn it when read. Arthur says such letters as mine never ought to be kept, they are as dangerous as lucifer matches . . . "fire them" or "there will be no more", such is his resolve. I can't help laughing, this seems to me so funny. . . .'

The parsonage now experienced astonishing animation, almost unheard of for this place, until lately so full of silence. Mr Nicholls had taken over the heaviest duties of the parish in order to relieve Mr Brontë.

In response to the warm welcome of the Haworth parishioners on Mr Nicholls's return, Charlotte and he invited them to tea and supper in the school class-room. Then they had visitors: Ellen and Miss Wooler and later Sir James Kay-Shuttleworth, who had such respect for Mr Nicholls that he offered him the living of Padiham in Lancashire, a much bigger one than Haworth. Charlotte was very gratified; however she agreed with her husband when he refused it. He could not think of leaving Haworth while Mr Brontë was alive.

Charlotte's inspiration had not dried up with marriage and she found time to begin a new novel. Without disapproving of his wife's fame, Mr Nicholls was a little jealous of it; he wanted Charlotte all to himself. However, he gave in humbly to the demands of her genius which he could not help admiring.

When she read him the first chapters of *Emma*, he said to her very simply: 'The critics will accuse you of repetition.' Mr Nicholls certainly could not replace Emily and Anne but he could listen and understand; Charlotte could trust him and this was a sure comfort to her.

At the beginning of the winter her health seemed to have improved. She was surprised that she rarely had a headache and enjoyed accompanying her husband on his walks. A great walker in spite of his tendency to rheumatism, Mr Nicholls did not fear the wind or rain and found strength and vigour in the wildness of the elements.

One November morning he dragged his wife from her desk and suggested that she come over the moor with him. She told Ellen the story. '. . . We set out not intending to go far. . . . When we had got about half a mile on the moors, Arthur suggested the idea of the waterfall; after the melted snow, he said, it would be fine. I had often wanted to see it in its winter power, so we walked on. It was fine indeed, a perfect torrent raving over the rocks, white and bountiful. It began to rain while we were watching it and we returned home under a streaming sky.' Charlotte did not make this long walk of seven or eight miles in such weather without paying for it. She caught a severe cold, had bad sore throats, grew thinner and weaker.

At the beginning of 1855 she accompanied her husband for a two or three days' visit to Sir James Kay-Shuttleworth's at Gawthorpe Hall. In the course of this stay she went for another walk on damp ground wearing thin-soled shoes, and her chronic cold grew worse.

Soon after her return she had incessant nausea and frequent attacks of faintness and her husband sent for a doctor. All these ills, the doctor declared, were only the symptoms of pregnancy. Patience then; was not hope the best remedy for these temporary troubles? But the frightful sickness grew only worse; the mere sight of food filled the invalid with loathing. 'A wren,' it has been said, 'would have starved on what she ate during these last six weeks.' And it was during this sad period that Tabby's health failed. She died of old age, but one may feel that her days were shortened by the desperate condition in which she saw the last of her children, to whom she had given such a large part of her life.

The other servant, Martha, tended her mistress lovingly, tried to cheer her up, speaking to her of the baby who would bring her joy.

'I dare say I shall be glad some day,' she would say, 'but I am so ill, so weary.'

Then she was forced to stay in bed.[3]

Charlotte's slow and tragic agony was beginning. From her bed she wrote in pencil to Laetitia Wheelwright on 15 February: '... At present I am confined to my bed with illness, and have been so for three weeks. Up to this period, since my marriage, I have had excellent health. My husband and I live at home with my father; of course, I could not leave *him*. ... No kinder, better husband than mine, it seems to me, there can be in the world. ...' Then two short notes to Ellen, undated. She says in the first: '... I am not going to talk about my sufferings, it would be useless and painful. I want to give you an assurance which I know will comfort you – and that is that I find in my husband the tenderest nurse, the kindest support – the best earthly comfort that ever woman had. His patience never fails, and it is tried by bad days and broken nights. ... Our poor old Tabby is *dead* and *buried*. ...'

To write the second she used her last strength: '... I am as thin as a skeleton. I cannot talk – even to my dear, patient, constant Arthur, I can say but few words at once. ...' Mrs Gaskell does not think that she wrote a line after that. 'Long days,' she says, 'and longer nights went by; still the same relentless nausea and faintness; and still borne on in patient trust. About the third week in March there was a change; a low wandering delirium came on and in it she begged constantly for food and even for stimulants. She swallowed eagerly now, but it was too late. Wakening for an instant from this stupor of intelligence, she saw her husband's woe-worn face and caught the sound of some murmured words of prayer that God would spare her. '"Oh," she whispered forth, "I am not going to die, am I? He will not separate us. We have been so happy."' These were her last words.

'Early on Saturday morning, March 31st, the solemn tolling of Haworth church-bell spoke forth the fact of her death to the villagers who had known her from a child, and whose hearts shivered within them as they thought of the two sitting desolate and alone in the old grey house.' (G)

3. See Appendix IV.

Charlotte Brontë's last words, her death, still bring tears. Such a destiny robs us of words. She is at rest but her memory, like a torch which one is proud to keep alight, will continue to bear a message of vigour, nobility and grandeur.

APPENDIX I

A comparison of extracts from *Paradise Lost, Book I*, and *A Romantic Tale*

Milton: *Paradise Lost, Book I*, lines 710–31

Anon, out of the earth a fabric huge
Rose like an exhalation, with the sound
Of dulcet symphonies and voices sweet,
Built like a temple, where pilasters round
Were set, and Doric pillars overlaid
With golden architrave; nor did there want
Cornice or frieze, with bossy sculptures graven:
The roof was fretted gold. . . .
. . . from the arched roof
Pendent by subtle magic, many a row
Of starry lamps and blazing cressets, fed
With naphtha and asphaltus, yielded light
As from a sky.

Charlotte Brontë *A Romantic Tale* (written 1829, aged 13).

The night wind had somewhat cooled the sands of the desert, so that we walked with more ease than before; but soon a mist arose which covered the whole plain. Through it we thought we could discern a dim light. We now likewise heard sounds of music at a great distance. . . . The light grew more distinct till it burst upon us in almost insufferable splendour. Out of the barren desert arose a palace of diamond, the pillars of which were ruby and emerald illuminated with lamps too bright to look upon. The Genius led us into a hall of sapphire in which there were thrones of gold. On the thrones sat the Princes of the Genii.

Paradise Lost, Book I, lines 220–226

Forthwith upright he rears from off the pool
His mighty stature; on each hand the flames,
Driven backwards, slope their pointing spires, and, rolled
In billows, leave in the midst a horrid vale.
Then with expanded wings he steers his flight
Aloft, incumbent on the dusky air,
That felt unusual weight;

A Romantic Tale

On he [the Genius of the Storm] strode over the black clouds which rolled beneath his feet and regardless of the fierce lightning which flashed around him.

(*The Professor*, etc., ed. P. Bentley)

Mina Laury (written 1838 aet. 22)

Miss Laury belonged to the Duke of Zamorna. She was indisputably his property, as much as the Lodge of Rivaulx or the stately wood of Hawkscliffe, and in that light she considered herself. . . . She had ever shown an habitual, rooted, solemn devotedness to his interest which seemed to leave her hardly a thought for anything else in the world beside. She had but one idea – Zamorna! Zamorna! . . . All this Hartford knew, and he knew, too, that she valued himself in proportion as she believed him to be loyal to his sovereign. Her friendship for him turned on this hinge: 'We have been fellow-labourers and fellow sufferers together in the same good cause.'

'. . . Suffice it to say that Lord Hartford, against reason and without hope, had finally delivered himself wholly up to the guidance of his vehement passions [for Mina]. . . .

'My lord, do you not know whose I am?' she replied in a hollow and very suppressed tone. 'Do you know with what a sound those proposals fall on my ear – how impious and blasphemous they seem to be? Do you at all conceive how utterly impossible it is that I should ever love you? . . . I thought you a true-hearted faithful man: I find that you are a traitor.'

'And do you despise me?' asked Hartford. 'No, my lord.'

She paused and looked down. Again she looked up. Her eyes had changed, their aspect beaming with a wild, bright inspiration, truly, divinely Irish.

'Hartford,' she said, 'had I met you long since, before I left Ellibank . . . and dishonoured my father, I would have loved you . . . but I cannot do so now – never. I saw my present master when he had scarcely attained manhood. Do you think, Hartford, I will tell you what feelings I had for him? No tongue could express them; they were so fervid, so flowing in their colour that they effaced everything else. I lost the power of properly appreciating the value of the world's opinion, of discerning the difference between right and wrong. I have never in my life contradicted Zamorna, never delayed obedience to his commands. I could not. He was something more to me than a human being. He superseded all things – all affections, all interests, all fears or hopes or principles. . . . How I should sicken if I were torn from him and thrown to you! Do not ask it; I would die first. No woman that ever loved my master could consent to leave him. There is nothing like him elsewhere.

'Every one knows what I am, but where is the woman in Africa who would have acted more wisely than I did if under the same circumstances she had been subject to the same temptations?' . . .

'Now, Hartford, we must part,' interrupted Miss Laury. . . . 'You have cut me to the heart. Goodbye.' . . . She rose. . . . She went out.

Mr O'Neill said, 'The Duke wished me to inform you, madam, that he would probably be here abour four or five o'clock in the afternoon.'

'Today?' said Miss Laury in an action of surprise.

'Yes, madam.' . . . Always active, always employed, it was not her custom to waste many hours in dreaming. She rose, closed her desk and left the quiet library for busier scenes. . . .

The opening of the front door, a bitter rush of the night wind, and then the sudden close and the step advancing forward were the signals of his [the Duke of Zamorna's] arrival.

Miss Laury . . . just met her master as he entered. His cold lip pressed to her forehead and his colder hand clasping hers brought the sensation which it was her custom of weeks and months to wait for, and to consider, when attained, as the ample recompense for all delay, all toil, all suffering.

'I am frozen, Mina,' said he. 'I came on horseback for the last few miles, and the night is like Canada.' Chafing his icy hand to animation between her own warm, supple palms, she answered by the speechless but expressive look of joy, satisfaction, idolatry, which filled and overflowed her eyes.

'What can I do for you, my lord?' were her first words as he stood by the fire rubbing his hands cheerily over the blaze. He laughed.

'Put your hands round my neck, Mina, and kiss my cheek as warm and blooming as your own.'

If Mina Laury had been Mina Wellesley she would have done so, and it gave her a pang to resist the impulse that urged her to take him at his word, but she put it by and only diffidently drew near the armchair into which he had now thrown himself and began to smooth and separate the curls which matted on his temples. . . . 'Give me your hand, my girl. You are not as old as I am.'

'Yes, my lord Duke, I was born on the same day, an hour after your Grace.'

'So I have heard, but it must be a mistake. You don't look twenty, and I am twenty-five. My beautiful Western – what eyes! Look at me, Mina, straight, and don't blush. . . .

'My acquaintance of ten years cannot meet my eyes unshrinkingly. Have you lost that ring I once gave you, Mina?'

'What ring, my lord? You have given me many.'

'That which I said had the essence of your whole heart and mind engraven in the stone as a motto.'

'Fidelity?' asked Miss Laury, and she held out her hand with a graven emerald on the forefinger.

'Right' was the reply; 'It is your motto still?' And with one of his hungry, jealous glances, he seemed trying to read her conscience. . . .

'Come here, my girl,' he said, drawing a chair close to his side. Mina never delayed, never hesitated, through bashfulness or any other feeling, to comply with his orders.

'Now' he continued, leaning his head towards her and placing his hand on her shoulder, 'are you happy, Mina? Do you want anything?'

'Nothing, my lord!'

She spoke truly; all that was capable of yielding her happiness on this side of Eternity was at that moment within her reach. . . .

'My Fidelity!' pursued that musical voice. 'If thou hast any favour to ask, now is the time. I'm all concession, as sweet as honey, as yielding as a lady's glove. Come, Esther, what is thy petition? And thy request, even to the half of my kingdom, it shall be granted.'

'Nothing' again murmured Miss Laury. 'Oh, my lord, nothing. What can I want?'

'Nothing?' he repeated. 'What? No reward for ten years of faith and love and devotion; no reward for the companionship in six months exile; no recompense to the little hand that has so often smoothed my pillow in sickness, to the sweet lips that have many a time in cool and dewy health been pressed to a brow of fever. . . . For all this, and much more, must there be no reward?'

'I have had it,' said Mina. 'I have it now.'

'But' continued the Duke, 'what if I have devised something worthy of your acceptance? Look up now and listen to me.'

She did look up, but she speedily looked down again. Her master's eye was insupportable. It burnt absolutely with infernal fire. . . . She trembled. 'I say, love,' pursued the individual, drawing her a little closer to him, 'I will give you as a reward a husband, don't start now! – and that husband shall be a nobleman, and that nobleman is called Lord Hartford!' He opened his arms and Miss Laury sprang erect like a loosened bow.

'Your Grace is anticipated,' she said. 'That offer has been made me before. Lord Hartford did it himself three days ago.'

'And what did you say, Madam? Speak the truth now; subterfuge won't avail you.'

'What did I say, Zamorna? I don't know; it little signifies; you have rewarded me, my lord Duke! But I cannot bear this – I feel sick.' With a deep, short sob, she turned white and fell close by the Duke, her head against his foot.

This was the first time in her life that Mina Laury had fainted, but strong health availed nothing against the deadly struggle which convulsed every feeling of her nature when she heard her master's announcement. She believed him to be perfectly sincere. She thought he was tired of her and she could not stand it. . . .

He took a wax taper from the table and held it over Miss Laury. She was white as marble and still as stone. . . . While he yet gazed she began to recover. . . . Not a gleam of anger! Not a whisper of reproach! Her lips and eyes spoke together no other language than the simple words, 'I cannot leave you!'

She rose feebly and with effort. The Duke stretched out a hand to assist her. He held to her lips the scarcely tasted wine-glass.

'Mina,' he said, 'are you collected enough to hear me?'

'Yes, my lord,' 'Then listen. I would much sooner give half – aye, the whole of my estate to Lord Hartford, than yourself! What I said just now was only to try you.'

Miss Laury raised her eyes, sighed like one awaking from some hideous dream, but she could not speak.

'Would I,' continued the Duke, 'would I resign the possession of my first love to any hands but my own? . . . I know you adore me now, Mina, for you could not feign that agitation. . . .'

He had told her that she was his first love; and now she felt tempted to believe that she was likewise his only love. Strong-minded beyond her sex, active, energetic and accomplished in all other points of view, here she was as weak as a child. She lost her identity; her very life was swallowed up in that of another.

APPENDIX 3

A summary of *Gondal's Queen* (taken from Fannie Ratchford's reconstruction)

The Queen of Gondal A.G.A. (Augusta Geraldine Almeda) was born one bright winter morning.

Cold, clear, and blue, Lake Werna's water
  Reflects that winter's sky.
  The moon has set, but Venus shines
A silent silvery star.

It was a sign. Of irresistible beauty, intelligence and charm, she had all the men at her feet. Her cruel selfishness brought tragedy to those lovers: Alexander, Lord of Elba, who for her sake had abandoned his wife, died in a duel with his rival, Prince Julius Brenzaida, on the shores of Lake Elnor.

Down in a hollow sunk in shade
Where dark heath waved in secret gloom
A weary bleeding form was laid
Waiting the death that was to come. . . .

None but one beheld him dying
Parting with the parting day;
Winds of evening, sadly sighing,
Bore his soul from earth away. . . .

Lord Alfred S. of Aspin Castle died by his own hand because the Queen had rejected him to marry Prince Julius with whom she had always been in love. Aware of the ravages she has caused, the Queen is troubled.

I know that I have done thee wrong –
Have wronged both thee and Heaven –
And I may mourn my lifetime long
Yet may not be forgiven.

Yet thou a future peace shalt win
Because thy soul is clear;
And I who had the heart to sin
Will find a heart to bear.

Changing her attitude she soon sees herself as the plaything of Fate. Is she responsible for her cruelty?

I gazed upon the cloudless moon
And loved her all the night
Till morning came and ardent noon,
Then I forgot her light –

No – not forgot – eternally
Remains its memory dear;
But could the day seem dark to me
Because the night was fair? . . .

Why did the morning rise to break
So great, so pure a spell,
And scorch with fire the tranquil cheek
Where your cool radiance fell?

O Stars and Dreams and Gentle Night
O Night and Stars return!
And hide me from the hostile light
That does not warm but burn –

Lord Alfred S. of Aspin Castle had, by a previous marriage, a daughter as beautiful as an angel, with fair hair and blue eyes, called Angelica. She consoled herself for her father's desertion when he became the Queen's lover by giving her tender pity to Amadeus, a young man whose sombre, tragic appearance recalls Heathcliff of Wuthering Heights.

I, the image of light and gladness,
Saw and pitied that mournful boy,
And I swore to take his gloomy sadness,
And give to him my beamy joy. . . .

Guardian angel he lacks no longer!
Evil fortune he need not fear:
Fate is strong, but love is stronger;
And more unsleeping than angel's care.

Angelica and Amadeus fell in love. But Augusta Geraldine Almeda, the terrible Queen, cast her eyes on Amadeus and he was lost. Amadeus was sent into exile and outlawed, as was Angelica.

Fernando de Samara of Areon Hall in Gaaldine, after unwillingly betraying for love of the Queen, his betrothed whom he had left in Gaaldine, committed suicide in the dungeons to which his fatal love had led him. After months of repenting his folly and sin, troubled about what will be his fate beyond the grave, he cries:

And say not that my early tomb
Will give me to a darker doom:
Shall these long agonising years
Be punished by eternal tears?

No; *that* I feel can never be;
A God of *hate* could hardly bear
To watch through all eternity
His own creation's dread despair! . . .

If I have sinned, long long ago
That sin was purified by woe:
I've suffered on by night and day;
I've trod a dark and frightful way.

Well thou hast paid me back my love!
But if there be a God above
Whose arm is strong, whose word is true,
This hell shall wring thy spirit too!

We must now follow the Queen and the increasingly complicated drama of intrigue and dramatic events in which she is involved.

As a reward for his conquests in the Island of Gaaldine Prince Julius, husband of the Queen, had become King of Almedore. Spurred on by his wife and by his own ambition, he wished to reign alone over both islands, recoiling before no disloyal action, no crime, to attain his ends. Insensitive to the shedding of blood, to devastation, to utter poverty, the price of his triumphs in battle, he became intoxicated with his glorious success, never satisfied.

Tyrants weave with their own hands the net that will entrap them: the patriots allied themselves with outlaws to form a plot against Prince Julius Brenzaida, King of Almedore, Emperor of Gondal.

Angelica, seeing in this a sign of Fate, put herself at the head of the conspirators in order to take a terrible revenge against the Queen in the person of Julius. Amadeus, chosen by destiny, struck the fatal blow, but fell in his turn, victim of the Emperor's guard.

Terrible was the shock to the heart of the Queen, who all through her tumultuous life had never ceased to be consumed by passion for Julius.

One disaster leads to another. Henceforth a rootless plant, she will be at the mercy of conflicting winds. With the death of the Emperor, the Empire crumbles. She flees with her daughter, little Alexandrina. In the child's features she finds, in a softened form, those of Julius. But in the sudden grip of reawakening ambition the maternal feeling vanishes; she must break the ties, however gentle, to go forth bold and free, to conquer again.

The Queen entrusts the child to the protection of the moor but the mother in her is filled with fear for it is no longer the radiant summer. Then

I might have left thee, darling one,
And thought thy God was guarding thee!

Now it is grim winter.

And coldly spreads thy couch of snow
And harshly sounds thy lullaby. . . .

Farewell, unblessed, unfriended child,
I cannot bear to watch thee die!

She wishes to go but cannot.

The night is darkening round me,
The wild winds coldly blow;
But a tyrant spell has bound me
And I cannot, cannot go.

Augusta Geraldine Almeda recaptures her throne. She is crowned in the Cathedral of Regina. *In spite of appearances, this fickle creature does not forget Julius, and fifteen years later declares her undying love.*

Cold in the earth, and the deep snow piled above thee
Far, far removed, cold in the dreary grave!
Have I forgot, my only Love, to love thee,
Severed at last by Time's all-wearing wave?

She is incapable of remorse, of lasting repentance, but sin carries punishment within itself; she is haunted more and more by her memories, and nothing in her eventful life can rid her of them.

Augusta feels the need to wander alone over the moors of Elmor, escorted only by a pair of lovers who pay little attention to her.

Angelica, walking alone by the shores of the lake, found the Queen asleep in the warm rays of the sun. She drew her dagger and was about to strike the woman who had cast disgrace on the life of Amadeus and on her own, when the Queen heaved a sigh, revealing such deep distress that, in her hatred, Angelica did not wish to release her from her sufferings by putting an end to her life. She was not long in repenting this decision and promised her hand to Douglas if he agreed to dispatch her deadliest enemy to hell.

After a furious struggle the Queen died, leaving Douglas alone with his trophy: avenged, but betraying her promise, Angelica had fled.

So ended Augusta Geraldine Almeda, Queen of Gondal, victim of the gifts of Venus, the star which had presided over her birth.

The Three Periods of the History of Gondal

Emily and Anne in their notes distinguish three periods in the History of Gondal:

The first wars which lasted from the foundation of the kingdom of Gondal to the discovery of the island of Gaaldine and to its partition among the princes of Gondal;

The wars of conquest, from the marriage of Julius with the Queen to the death of the latter;

The civil wars between Republicans and Royalists.

These periods correspond directly with the history of Glasstown in which Emily and Anne had collaborated, and then with the history of Angria by Branwell and Charlotte.

Only four of Emily's poems deal with the conflict between the Republicans and Royalists. The manuscript of the first of these four poems, dated 2 October 1844, has as title: 'D.G.C. to J.A.', without any further detail about the two speakers.

Come, the wind may never again
Blow as now it blows for us;
And the stars may never again shine as now they shine;
Long before October returns,
Seas of blood will have parted us;
And you must crush the love in your heart, and I the love in mine.

For face to face will our kindred stand,
And as they are so shall we be;
Forgetting how the same sweet earth has borne and nourished all –
One must fight for the people's power,
And one for the rights of Royalty;
And each be ready to give his life to work the other's fall.

Emily's poems often had merely initials as titles, and to the despair of those who have deciphered the manuscripts, she used the same initials for different characters or varied abbreviations for the same people.

In September 1846, Anne Brontë finished the companion poem to the one above. It was entitled 'I dreamed last night and in that dream', signed 'E.Z.', and dated the 12th. The following stanza is its climax:

Back foolish tears! the man I slew
Was not the boy I cherished so
And that young arm that clasped the friend
Was not the same that stabbed the foe.
By time and adverse thoughts estranged,
And wrongs and vengeance, both were changed.

Emily's second poem, untitled, and dated 2 June 1845, is, thinks Miss Ratchford, another credo of an inhabitant of Gondal during this struggle between Republicans and Royalists:

How beautiful the earth is still.

The third, of August 1845, has as its title: 'Written on the dungeon wall – N.C.' (Northern College).

I know that tonight the wind is sighing,
The soft August wind, over forest and moor;
While I in a grave-like chill am lying
On the damp black flags of my dungeon floor.

Anne repeats this theme and this situation in a series of dialogues between a Royalist and his sweetheart 'Zerona L.': 'Weep not too much, my darling.'

Finally, Emily's fourth and last poem connected with these events, is dated 9 October 1845, and has a hundred and fifty-two lines. 'Julian M. and A. G. Rochelle' is a high poetic achievement. It celebrates the power of the imagination.

'A messenger of Hope comes every night to me,
And offers, for short life, eternal liberty.

'He comes with western winds, with evening's wandering airs,
With that clear dusk of heaven that brings the thickest stars;
Winds take a pensive tone, and stars a tender fire,
And visions rise and change which kill me with desire. . . .

'But first a hush of peace, a soundless calm descends;
The struggle of distress and fierce impatience ends;
Mute music soothes my breast – unuttered harmony
That I could never dream till earth was lost to me.

'Then dawns the Invisible, the Unseen its truth reveals;
My outward sense is gone, my inward essence feels –
Its wings are almost free, its home, its harbour found;
Measuring the gulf it stoops and dares the final bound!

'Oh, dreadful is the check – intense the agony,
When the ear begins to hear and the eye begins to see;
When the pulse begins to throb, the brain to think again,
The soul to feel the flesh and the flesh to feel the chain!'

This has also been published under the title of 'The Prisoner'.

APPENDIX 4

Mr Brontë's opposition to Charlotte's marriage

When Mary Taylor, a relentless enemy of misused parental authority, learned of Mr Brontë's determined opposition to Charlotte's marriage with Mr Nicholls, she was extremely indignant.

On 19 April 1856, a year after Charlotte's death, she wrote to Ellen from New Zealand, '. . . I can never think without gloomy anger of Charlotte's sacrifices to the selfish old man.'

No doubt 'the old man' had become selfish, but is it not natural to think that Charlotte's precarious health worried him more than he could perhaps say? He had lost his wife and five of his children; she was the only one left to him; he must have been apprehensive about her marrying.

John Lock and Canon W. T. Dixon, in their book, *A Man of Sorrow* (p. 452), recount that, shortly before Charlotte's death, when the doctor had declared that there was no hope, Mr Brontë spoke in the following terms to his servant: 'I told you, Martha, that there was no sense in Charlotte marrying at all, for she was not strong enough for marriage.' (p. 310.)

INDEX

Ackroyd, Tabitha, 44–5, 65, 67, 93–4, 95, 107, 207, 250
Advantages of Poverty in Religious Concerns, The, 25
Agnes Grey, 31, 157 n. 2, 166, 187, 226
Ambleside, 108, 226
Arabian Nights, The, 37
Arnold, Matthew, 160
Athenaeum, The, 165, 166, 214
Atkinson, Mr, 227
Atlas, The, 214
D'Aubigné, Agrippa, 230
Aylott & Jones, 163–5

Ballads of Ossian, by MacPherson, 36
Balzac, Honoré de, 222
Banagher, 17, 248
Bell, Acton, *see* Brontë, Anne
Bell, Currer, *see* Brontë, Charlotte
Bell, Ellis, *see* Brontë, Emily
Bell, Mary, 17
Benson, A. C., 100
Blackwood's Magazine, 37, 45, 86, 165, 184
Bonnell, Henry, H., 18
Book of Nature, The, 35
Bookman, The, 30
Boswell, James, 68
Bradford, 23, 95, 112
Branwell, Charlotte, 24 n. 2
Branwell, Elizabeth, appearance and character, 31; and domestic training of the Brontë girls, 31–2, 68; and education, 31, 45, 68; and Charlotte, 104, 106, 115, 123; and proposal to start a school, 113–14; and financial help given, 115; and Branwell, 123; death, 123
Branwell, Joseph, 24 n. 2
Branwell, Maria, *see* Brontë, Maria
Britannia, 165
Brontë, Anne, and *Juvenilia,* 19, 50–1, 54, 68–9, 75, 79, 156–7, 163; birth, 26; character, 47, 80, 100, 172, 198; and Emily, 50–1, 69, 156–7, 194; and Elizabeth Branwell, 65, 123; at Dewsbury, 89, 90–1; delicacy, 89, 94, 172, 195, 198; and Charlotte, 90, 113, 195, 198–201; as governess, 100, 107, 113, 120, 124, 142; and William Weightman, 110; and Branwell, 124, 151–2, 153; and *Poems,* 163; and *Agnes Grey,* 166, 168, 176, 183; and *The Tenant of Wildfell Hall,* 180; and visit to Smith & Elder, 187–9; and visit to Scarborough, 199–201; death, 201
Brontë, Branwell, and *Juvenilia,* 19, 50, 51–6, 68–9, 71, 75–6, 93, 184–5; birth, 26; and relationship with father, 37, 81, 167, 190; ability, 37, 65, 95; early life, 46–7, 48, 184–5; and Charlotte, 48, 56, 61, 69, 75, 92–3, 111, 185; appearance, 48, 111; character, 48, 81–2, 108, 142; poetry, 55; and Emily, 69; as painter, 81, 83, 86, 95; in London, 86; ambitions, 81, 86–7, 108; as tutor, 107–8, 124, 142; dissipation, 108, 111, 150, 167, 190; and Hartley Coleridge, 108; and William Weightman, 109, 122–3; as railway clerk, 111; and Elizabeth Branwell, 123; and Mrs Robinson, 150–3, 167; and *Jane Eyre,* 184–5; death, 190–1
Brontë, Charlotte, and Mrs Gaskell, 15, 209, 224–5, 231, 242–3; and Kay-Shuttleworths, 15, 218–20, 224–5, 249–50; and *Juvenilia,* 18–19, 36, 48–9, 50–6, 68–9, 70–1, 72–7, 78–9, 92–3,

Brontë, Charlotte—*cont.* 170; birth, 26; and Elizabeth Branwell, 32, 45, 104, 114, 115, 123; domesticity, 32, 57, 100, 107, 171; and literature, 35–7, 67–8, 69–70; and relationship with father, 39, 104, 135–6, 142, 154, 169–70, 172, 177–8, 196, 205, 232, 238–9, 246–7; and *Jane Eyre,* 41–2, 44, 45, 78, 169, 170–1, 175–6, 177–9, 233; and Cowan Bridge School, 41–4; education, 41–6, 57–61, 62, 81; and Catholicism, 46, 121; and Branwell, 48, 50, 56, 61, 75–6, 92–3, 111, 128–9, 142, 145, 153–4, 167, 172, 174–5, 185–6, 190–1; ambition, 57, 87; at Roe Head, 57–61, 83–5; and Miss Wooler, 57, 91, 94, 232, 247, 249; and meeting with Ellen Nussey, 57–9; and Mary Taylor, 57, 60–1, 62, 79–80, 116, 143–4; as story-teller, 60; and *Shirley,* 60, 205–7, 208, 209, 213, 216–17, 240; and life at Haworth, 62, 64–6, 97; and the Rydings, 63; and Norton Conyers, 63, 103; and Ellen Nussey, 62–8, 79–80, 144–5, 174–6, 198–203, 209, 214–15, 227, 228, 232–3, 249; character, 80, 82, 91–2, 148; and Emily, 83–4, 89, 115, 136, 155; letter to Southey, 87–9; at Dewsbury Moor, 89–93, 96; and Anne, 90, 94, 113, 172, 187–9, 193, 195, 196, 199–202; and Tabby, 93–4, 171, 207; and Henry Nussey, 104–7; as governess to Sidgwicks, 100–3; and holiday with Ellen Nussey, 104–7; and Wordsworth, 108; and William Weightman, 109–11, 122; as governess to Whites, 112–13; and proposed school, 113–14, 123, 135, 140, 141; and Brussels, 115–18; and Martha Taylor, 118, 122; at Mme Heger's, 118–22, 126–34; and M. Heger, 119, 122, 129, 130, 132, 137–40, 141, 142–4, 146–50; and Mme Heger, 129–31, 132–3; and *Villette,* 131, 169, 228, 232, 233–5, 240; ill-health, 144, 191, 205, 209, 228, 232–3, 250; and *Poems,* 162–6; and *The Professor,* 166, 168–70, 174, 181, 204, 228; and Rev. Nicholls, 167, 236–8, 243–7; and *Jane Eyre,* 170, 181, 235; and Mr Williams, 178–80, 181–2, 239; and G. H. Lewes, 179, 180–1, 208–9, 218, 221–2; and Thackeray, 181–2, 211–12, 221–3, 229; on *Wuthering Heights,* 184–5; and visit to Smith & Elder, 187–9; and Mr Taylor, 206, 228–9, 236; financial earnings, 207–8; and Harriet Martineau, 210, 213–14, 226–7, 240–1; visits to London, 211–14, 221–3, 229–31, 239–40; and George Smith, 210–11, 221, 223, 236; visit to Edinburgh, 223–4; and trip to Scarborough, 232–3; marriage, 247; married life, 247–50; and *Emma,* 249–51; pregnancy, 250–1; death, 15, 17, 251

Brontë, Elizabeth, 26, 43–4

Brontë, Emily, and *Juvenilia,* 19, 50, 68–9, 75, 79, 185; birth, 26; and *Ossian,* 36; and moors, 47, 83–4; character, 47, 80, 82, 120, 186; and Branwell, 69, 154, 184–5; and Anne, 69, 84; and Charlotte, 83–4, 89–90, 114–15, 184–5, 193–6; at Roe Head, 83; as poet, 84, 90–5, 114–15; as governess, 84, 89–90; and Tabby, 94; domesticity, 94–5; and journey to Brussels, 117; at Mme Heger's, 118–22; appearance, 121; and return to Haworth, 124; and *Poems,* 162–3, 166; and *Wuthering Heights,* 183–5; illness and death, 193–5

Brontë, Rev. Patrick, and Mrs

Gaskell, 15, 33–5; birth, 21; education, 21–2; livings, 22; published works, 23; marriage, 24; and Charlotte, 24, 97, 104, 135–6, 169–70, 177–8, 199–202, 215, 219–20, 235, 237–9, 245–6; and birth of children, 27; move to Haworth, 29; death of wife, 29–30; character, 32–5, 93; faith, 34; and children's education, 35, 37–8, 45, 68, 81; and Branwell, 37, 81, 95, 167, 190, 191; and death of Elizabeth and Maria, 43; appearance, 64; curates, 109, 135, 166; and proposal to start a school, 113; journey to Brussels, 117–18; failing eyesight, 135, 169–70; ill-health, 66, 166, 192, 219, 235, 244; and Mr Nicholls, 166, 237–9, 243–4, 246–7; and *Jane Eyre*, 178; and Emily, 194, 196; and Anne, 198, 199; and *Villette*, 234
Brontë, Maria (née Branwell), 23–6, 29
Brontë, Maria, 26, 38–9, 43–4
Brontës at Cowan Bridge, The, 41
Brontës' Life and Letters, etc., The, 17
Brontës' Web of Childhood, The, 18, 36, 53, 148
Brookfield, Mr, 223
Brookroyd, 89, 198, 202, 223
Brown, John, 93, 106, 151
Brown, Mrs John, 217
Brown, William, 93
Brunty, Hugh, 21
Brunty, Patrick, *see* Brontë, Patrick
Brussels, 15, 114–16, 117, 123, 126–34
Bryce, Mr, 105
Bunyan, John, 35
Burder, Mary, 22, 30
Busfeild, Mrs, 136, 140
Byron, Lord, 67, 70, 71

Cambridge, 21–2
Campbell, Thomas, 67
Carlyle, Mr and Mrs, 223
Chambers, Messrs, 163
Chapelle, M., 127
Charlotte Brontë and her Circle, 17
Chatterton, Thomas, 117
Childe Harold, 36
Children's Friend, The, 41
Colburn's New Monthly Magazine, 165
Coleridge, Hartley, 108
Coleridge, Samuel Taylor, 108
Complete Poems of Emily Jane Brontë, The, 156
Corkhill, Miss, 136
Cottage in the Wood, The, 23
Cottage Poems, 23
Cowan Bridge, 37, 41–4
Cranford, 166
Critic, The, 165, 166

Daily News, The, 165, 240
de Quincey, Thomas, 166
Dearden, William, 33
Deerbrook, 210
Dewsbury Moor, 22, 89–91, 116
Dickens, Charles, 204
Dixon, Miss, 127
Dobell, Sydney, 225–6
Driver, Mr, 45
Drumballyroney, 21
Drury, Caroline, 109
du Maurier, Daphne, 19
Dublin University Magazine, The, 165, 166

Easton, 106, 202
Edinburgh Review, The, 165, 218
Eliot, George, 222
Emma, 212, 249
Examiner, The, 214

Fennell, Jane, 24 n. 2, 46
Fennell, Mr, 23, 24 n. 2, 46
Fielding, Henry, 37
Filey, 202, 232

Firth, Elizabeth, *see* Mrs Franks
Forçade, Eugène, 193, 207
Franks, Mrs, 26, 30, 34, 61 n. 1

Garrs, Nancy, 30
Gaskell, Julia, 231
Gaskell, Mrs, and *The Life of Charlotte Brontë,* 15–16, 18, 35–6, 41, 133–4, 150–1; and Kay-Shuttleworths, 15, 218–19; and Ellen Nussey, 15; and George Smith, 15; and Miss Wooler, 15; visit to Brussels, 15, 118–19; and Mr Nicholls, 15; and Patrick Brontë, 15, 35–6; and *Juvenilia,* 18; and Branwell, 19, 150–1, 153; and Rev. Carus Wilson, 41; and Charlotte, 88, 126, 213–14, 231, 242–3, 244–5; and Mme Heger, 130, 133, 150; and M. Heger, 133, 150; and Mrs Jenkins, 122; visit to Haworth, 244–5
Gaskell, Rev., 231, 245
Gawthorpe Hall, 218, 250
Goldsmith, Rev. J., 54
Goldsmith, Oliver, 37, 67, 117
Grant, Mr, 245
Grenfell, Lydia, 99
Grimshaw, Mr, 26
Grundy, Mr, 111, 123, 152
Gulliver's Travels, 35

Halifax, 84, 111, 120
Halifax Examiner, 33
Halifax Guardian, 42
Harrogate, 102
Hartley, Margaret, 95
Hartshead, 22–3, 26
Hatfield, C. W., 148, 156
Hathersage, 144–5
Haworth, 27–9, 216–18
Haworth Museum, 18
Haworth Parsonage, 38, 244
Heatons, the, 68
Heger, Constantin, 119–22, 124–5, 126, 127–30, 133, 135–42, 142–49, 150
Heger, Mme, 118, 120–1, 126–30, 135, 150
Heger, Dr Paul, 137, 149
Henriade, La, 62
Henry, Earl of Moreland, 45
Hodgson, Mr, 105
Hogg, James, 86
Hood's Magazine, 165
Hudson, Mr and Mrs, 106
Hume, 67

Infernal World of Branwell Brontë, The, 19 n. 5
Intelligence Extraordinary, 46
Ireland, 17, 21, 22, 46, 236, 247
Ivanhoe, 36

Jane Eyre, 91, 169, 174–82, 197, 206, 207; and Cowan Bridge, 41–4; and the *Juvenilia,* 19, 74, 77
Jenkins, Mrs, 115, 116, 117, 122
Jerrold's Magazine, 165
John Bull, 45
Johnson, Dr Samuel, 37, 68, 117
Juvenilia, 18–19, 50–6, 68–9, 70–1, 72–81, 91–2, 108, 129–30, 156–60; *An Adventure in Ireland,* 18, 71, 75, 170; *The Green Dwarf,* 36; *Gondal's Queen,* 51, 52, 79, 156–61; *Young Men,* 51–2, 54–5, 74; *Our Fellows,* 51, 52; *Islanders,* 51, 52–3; *The Young Men's Magazine,* 52; *A Romantic Tale,* 54, 55; *The Characters of Great Men of the Present Age,* 55; *The Spell,* 55, 72, 78, 81, 170; *Albion and Marina,* 56, 170; *Ernest Alembert,* 71; *The Bridal,* 72; *The Foundling,* 72; *Arthuriana,* 72; *The Secret,* 72, 73; *Richard Lionheart and Blondel,* 72; *High Life in Verdopolis,* 72; *My Angria and the Angrians,* 74, 79; *A Peep into a Picture Book,* 74, 76; *A Leaf from*

an Unopened Volume, 74; *The Scrapbook*, 74; *Mina Laury*, 75, 77, 78, 170; *Caroline Vernon*, 108; *Gondal Chronicles*, 156, 157; *History of the First Wars*, 156; *Angustus Almeda's Life*, 156; *The Emperor Julius's Life*, 156, 157; *Poems of Gondal*, 156, 160; *The Prisoner*, 159

Kay-Shuttleworth, Sir James and Lady, 15, 18, 218, 220, 224–5, 249, 250
Keighley, 27, 41, 68, 110, 136, 157
Kendal, 108
Kenilworth, 69
Kingsley, Charles, 15–16
Kingston, Elizabeth Jane, 123
Kipping House, 26
Kirby, Mr and Mrs, 95
Kockleburg, 115, 118, 122

Law Hill, 89
Leeds, 81, 104, 105, 106, 198, 200, 247
Leeds Intelligencer, 45
Leeds Mercury, 45, 205
Letters on the Nature and Development of Man, 227
Lewes, G. H., 218, 221–2
Leyland, Joseph Bentley, 81, 152–3, 172
Life of Charlotte Brontë, The 15, 33, 41, 72, 114, 123, 153, 225, 243, 245
Lille, 116
Literary Gazette, The, 165
Liverpool, 104, 151, 152, 216
Lock, John, and Dixon, W. T., 118 n. 1
Longley, Dr, 241
Luddenden Foot, 111, 152
Luddites, 27, 34

Macbeth, 214
McClory, Eleanor, 21, 22
Mackay, Angus M., 41, 137
Maid of Killarney, The, 23
Man of Sorrow, A, 118 n. 1
Manchester, 139, 169, 170, 231, 243
Martineau, Harriet, 210, 213, 226–7, 240–1
Martyn, Henry, 22, 99
Mary Barton, 243
Milbanke, Annabella, 70
Milton, John, 35, 55, 67, 81
Miscellaneous and Unpublished Writings of Charlotte and Patrick Branwell Brontë, 18
Morgan, Rev. William, 22–3, 24

National Portrait Gallery, 83, 224
Newby, Mr, 168, 186–7, 188
Nicholls, Rev. Arthur Bell, and Ellen Nussey, 15; and Mrs Gaskell, 15, 18; and Charlotte, 17, 166–7, 236–9, 241–7; remarriage, 17; and Patrick Brontë, 17, 237–8, 243, 246–7, 248, 249; early life, 236; character, 236–7; and marriage to Charlotte, 247; married life, 247–51
North American Review, 193
Norton Conyers, 63, 103
Nussey, Ellen, and Mrs Gaskell, 15, 153; visits to Haworth, 39, 64–7, 174, 198, 228, 232, 249; meeting with Charlotte, 57–60; and Mary Taylor, 57, 97, 122; and *Reminiscences of Charlotte Brontë*, 58; Charlotte's visits, 65, 145, 164, 176, 209, 223, 227, 232; character, 79; and holiday with Charlotte, 104–6; and Anne, 200–2; Charlotte on, 214–15
Nussey, Henry, 97, 107, 113

Oxenhope, 245

Palladium, 226
Pamela, 37, 45, 72

Paradise Lost, 35, 55, 81
Parent, Claire Zoé, 130
Pascal, Blaise, 141
Patchett, Miss, 84
Peel, Sir Robert, 61
Penzance, 23, 24, 25, 31, 36
Pilgrim's Progress, 35, 67
Poems, 31, 162–6, 192
Ponden Hall, 68
Pope, Alexander, 67
Postlewaite, 107
Proctor, Mrs, 223
Professor, The, 19, 76, 166–7, 169–70, 204, 228

Quarterly Review, The 197

Rachel, 230
Ratchford, Fannie Elizabeth, 18, 20, 36, 49, 51, 53, 74, 148, 156, 162
Rawdon, 112
Reminiscences of Charlotte Brontë, 58
Revue des Deux Mondes, 192, 209
Richardson, Samuel, 37, 72
Richmond, G., 224
Rigby, Miss, 197
Ritchie, Lady, 222
Roe Head, 39, 57–61, 71, 83–5, 89–93, 120
Robinson, Mr, 124, 144, 145, 151
Robinson, Mrs, 151–3
Robinsons, the, 113, 120, 142
Royal Academy, 86
Rural Minstrel, The, 23
Ruth, 243
Rydings, 63, 89

Scarborough, 199–201, 233
Scatcherd, Miss, 43
Schmidt, Mr, 145
School for Scandal, 67
Scott, Sir Edward, 153
Scott, Sir Walter, 36, 67–8, 69
Selby, 106
Shakespeare, William, 35–6, 67
Sharpe's Magazine, 15
Sheridan, Richard Brinsley, 37, 67
Shirley, 15, 42, 109, 122, 205, 206–7, 208, 209, 213
Shorter, Clement, 17–18, 34, 39, 41, 61, 130, 137–8, 153, 156
Sidgwicks, the, 63, 75, 100–3
Sinclair, May, 16, 161
Smith, C. C. Moore, 30
Smith & Elder, 28, 187, 192, 204, 228
Smith, George, 205, 211–14, 221, 226, 229, 230, 239
Smith, Mrs, 211, 221, 230, 239
Southey, Robert, 68, 87–8
Sowerby Bridge, 111
Spectator, The, 192, 214
Stonegappe, 100, 104, 112, 114
Sugden, Sarah, 109
Swarcliffe, 102, 103
Swift, Jonathan, 35
Symington, J. H., 18

Tait's Edinburgh Magazine, 165
Tales of a Grandfather, 36
Tales of Hoffmann, The, 122
Taylor, Martha, 97, 118, 122, 128, 206
Taylor, Mary, and Charlotte at Roe Head, 57, 60–1; and relationship with Charlotte, 79–80, 90, 91, 115–16, 117–18, 122–3, 144, 187; character, 80, 144; visit to Haworth, 97; in Brussels, 114, 117–18, 122–3; in Germany, 128; emigration to New Zealand, 143–4
Taylor, Mr, 206, 211, 228, 236
Teale, Dr, 198, 200
Temple, Miss, 43
Tenant of Wildfell Hall, The, 29, 186–7
Thackeray, William M., 204, 211, 212, 221–3, 230, 231
Thomson, James, 67
Thornton, 26, 30, 31
Thorp Green Hall, 113, 142, 151, 152

Thoughts Suggested to the Superintendent, 42
Three Brontës, The, 16 n. 1
Tighe, Mr, 21
Times, The, 137, 148, 153, 165, 213, 214

Upperwood House, 112, 113, 114

Verlaine, Paul, 78
Vie des soeurs Brontë, La, 78 n. 1
Villette, 15, 42, 169, 207, 228, 229, 233, 236, 237, 239, 240; and *Juvenilia,* 19, 235; and Brussels, 126, 131–2; and Hegers, 149, 234–5
Vincent, Mr, 110–11
Voltaire, 62

Weightman, William, 109–10
Wesley, Charles, 22, 26
Wesley, John, 21, 22, 26
Wethersfield, 22, 30, 117
Wheelwright, Dr, 211
Wheelwright, Laetitia, 122, 211, 214, 224
Wheelwright, Mrs, 138
Whipp, Fanny, 106
Whites, the, 122–13, 115, 116, 136
Wilberforce, William, 22
Williams, Mr, 188–9, 204, 205, 211, 222
Wilson, Rev. Carus, 37–8, 41–2
Wilson, John, 86
Wilson, Mr, 169
Windermere, 224
Winkworth, Catherine, 225
Wise, Thomas J., 17–18, 71
Wooler, Miss, and Roe Head, 57, 62, 83; and Charlotte, 62, 91, 94, 116, 168, 232, 247, 249; at Dewsbury Moor, 89, 116; and Anne, 94
Wordsworth, William, 67, 87, 104

York, 157
Youthful Memoirs, 41